# MIDNIGHT CRY

# MIDNIGHT CRY A SHOOTING ON SAND MOUNTAIN

Lesa Carnes Shaul

NewSouth Books
an imprint of
The University of Georgia Press
Athens

**NSB**

© 2024 by the University of Georgia Press
Athens, Georgia 30602
www.ugapress.org
All rights reserved
Designed by Mary McKeon
Set in Adobe Caslon Pro
Printed and bound by Sheridan

The paper in this book meets the guidelines for
permanence and durability of the Committee on
Production Guidelines for Book Longevity of the
Council on Library Resources.

Most NewSouth/University of Georgia Press titles are
available from popular e-book vendors.

Printed in the United States of America
28  27  26  25  24  C  5  4  3  2  1

Library of Congress Control Number: 2024937297
ISBN: 9781588385338 (hardback)
ISBN: 9781588385314 (epub)
ISBN: 9781588385321 (PDF)

*For my parents, Tom and Gail Carnes, who always believed in me,
even when I didn't
and
Ann Scott Kilpatrick, who loved despite, which is the true way*

I hear the sound of a mighty rushing wind,
And it's closer now than it's ever been.
I can almost hear the trumpet as Gabriel sounds the chord,
At the midnight cry we'll be going home.
—"Midnight Cry"

Some call it bootlegging. Some call it racketeering. I call it a business.
—Al Capone

# CONTENTS

# PREFACE

My childhood was made of stories.

Some of them were tragic, like the story my parents told me about the March 1944 tornado that devastated the Pine Grove community in rural north Alabama, leveling the two-room schoolhouse and killing twelve-year-old Jimmy Mitchell, my father's cousin. According to family lore, Jimmy had escaped from the schoolhouse with the other children but suddenly turned and ran back into the building. The tornado struck; the walls collapsed. Jimmy died on the way to the hospital. Since the phone lines, primitive as they were on Sand Mountain in 1944, were all taken down by the storm, Jimmy's parents, Lawrence and Clara Nell Mitchell, frantically drove to two different hospitals, miles apart, looking for their son. My father, one of the students at the school, was struck by a piece of flying debris and suffered an eight-inch gash down his right leg, which a local doctor closed with only four loose stitches. When my father took me swimming, I could see the silvery, stretched remains of that scar down his thigh.

Some of them were heroic, like when my maternal grandmother, a teacher at Pine Grove School at the time of that same tornado, piled injured children into her car and drove across the rubble of the brick schoolhouse to take them to the Sand Mountain Infirmary in nearby Albertville. My mother, who attended Boaz Elementary rather than Pine Grove School (for she was, after all, a city girl), kept all of the newspaper clippings from area papers, which hailed Lillian Miller as a hero. "It was through the presence of mind of Mrs. Miller," read an article in the March 9, 1944, issue of the *Southern Democrat* in Oneonta, Alabama, "that the pupils were not in the building that was blown away. She saw the tornado approaching in time to get the children out of the building and into the open." But Jimmy Mitchell's death haunted her for the rest of her life.

Some of the stories were comically absurd, like the one my father told me about the Future Farmers of America members at Douglas High School playing a prank on their faculty sponsor. The boys managed to lead a cow to the second floor of the main building to the sponsor's regular classroom, the poor creature stumbling and staggering up the unfamiliar stairs. When he saw the cow outside his classroom, the FFA sponsor ordered one of the boys to take off his shirt, which he used to cover the cow's eyes, enabling him to lead the cow back down the stairs and into a nearby pasture. Then the sponsor removed the makeshift blindfold, returned it to the shirtless prankster, ordered him to put it back on, and went back to his teaching duties.

The story that fascinated me the most, however, was about a sixteen-year-old boy who, one calm May night in 1951, shot the Marshall County sheriff, two deputies, and the chief of police from nearby Boaz, killing three of the four men. I do not remember exactly when I first heard this story, but I do remember that when I was in middle school, the account of what I came to think of as "the Kilpatrick shooting" recurred to me with increasing frequency. I knew only the rough outlines of the story, filled in over the years with more detail. I learned that the young boy's name was James Kilpatrick, and that his father, Aubrey Kilpatrick, had been a bootlegger, and the lawmen had shot this bootlegger in front of his home. Since my parents were teetotalers, I was surprised at the sympathy they expressed for the elder Kilpatrick's death; rather than denouncing Aubrey Kilpatrick's illegal (and, to them, immoral) activities, they focused on the stories of his kindness and generosity toward those hit by hard times in the Double Bridges community outside Boaz. My father told me that Aubrey had provided a pony and a bag of feed for a little boy whose father had died. Although he was not a churchgoing man, when Aubrey found out that a local minister had to walk three miles to get to his church, he gave him a mule to ride. Whatever folks thought about Aubrey Kilpatrick's bootlegging, they appreciated his benevolence toward his neighbors.

I misunderstood for years the reason why Aubrey Kilpatrick had been shot by the lawmen. I assumed that the cause was related to his illegal alcohol trafficking since every version of the story I had heard described Kilpatrick as "Aubrey the bootlegger," like that was his medieval guild name. In the various permutations told and retold by relatives, Sheriff Ezekiel "Zeke" Boyles "had it out" for Kilpatrick and was determined to stop this hillbilly bootlegger from breaking the law in his county. I heard Boyles described as hotheaded and possibly corrupt, although the most damning criticism I heard about him was that he was "from off" (i.e., from off Sand Mountain), although where Boyles lived was less than twenty miles from where the Kilpatrick farm stood. Boyles, two of his deputies, and the Boaz chief of police had gone to the Kilpatrick farm on a Thursday close to midnight to serve a warrant to Aubrey, not for bootlegging, but for charges of assaulting two of his tenant farmers. No one knew who fired the first shot in what was doubtless a tense and dangerous standoff, but when the smoke cleared, Aubrey Kilpatrick lay dead a few feet shy of his front stoop.

His oldest son, James, emerged from the house, saw his father on the ground, went back inside, grabbed a .30-caliber carbine, exited a side door, and picked off the lawmen one by one. The sheriff and the police chief were killed outright; both deputies were gravely wounded but managed to escape. The deputy who had been shot in the head and neck and somehow driven the car off the property and back to Boaz City Hall later died in a Gadsden hospital, but his passenger, the other gunshot deputy, lived to tell the tale—four times, in fact, as the star witness at the trials that followed. After a series of mistrials, convictions, appeals, and plea agreements, young James was eventually sent to prison for killing the chief deputy, and he served a relatively brief sentence divided between two Alabama prisons. The Kilpatrick family—the husband and father dead, the eldest son imprisoned, the widow struggling to raise the seven children still living at home—remained in their community, for years the objects of both compassion and contempt.

That narrative was only the skeleton of all the perspectives and memories and half-remembered half-truths that I raptly absorbed from my childhood through my teenage years, so I limned those bones with the flesh created by my storybook-and-movie-fed imagination. I reconstructed Aubrey Kilpatrick as a modern-day Robin Hood, defying an oppressive system that sought to limit the freedoms of honest country folk. His son James I romantically envisioned as a carbine-toting Hamlet hell-bent on avenging his father's murder. I tried to imagine what it must have been like for James, only sixteen, to see his father shot just a few feet from the front door of the family's small house, the anguish and sorrow and fury that must have flooded through him as he grabbed that .30 carbine and began shooting at the men who had come onto his family's property close to midnight and, in what so many newspaper accounts described as "a hail of bullets," gunned down the father he both feared and idolized. At sixteen, I myself was more concerned with making the perfect mixtape for my boyfriend, saving up enough chore money to buy a new pair of Guess jeans, and teasing my bangs to the ideal height. For a few years I forgot about what everyone I knew referred to as "the Kilpatrick shooting," immersing myself in the ephemera of high school and college.

In 1995, when I was a graduate student in English at the University of

Georgia, the campus was abuzz with the news that Dennis Covington, whose book *Salvation on Sand Mountain: Snake Handling and Redemption in Southern Appalachia* had just been announced as a finalist for the National Book Award, would be visiting Athens. One of my professors suggested that I be the one to give Covington a campus tour and ferry him to and from his hotel in Athens the evening of his talk. My fellow graduate students, most of them from places significantly larger and more sophisticated than Sand Mountain, often teased me about being from the north Alabama hills, recycling Jeff Foxworthy jokes about kissin' cousins, feudin' kinfolks, and incestuously pruned family trees. One time I returned from class to the basement office I shared with three other teaching assistants to find an article taped to the door describing a series of mysterious cattle mutilations on Sand Mountain that had state investigators baffled and the locals claiming that aliens had done it. So I put on my best bonnet and hitched up my wagon to show Mr. Covington around town.

(I'm kidding, of course, about the bonnet and wagon.)

After Covington's campus talk, I drove him back to his hotel, and we sat in the lobby chatting for an hour or so. I told him about my family, about growing up on a chicken farm outside Boaz, about hearing rumors of snake handlers off in the piney woods of Marshall and Jackson Counties (but never actually knowing any personally). He then asked, "What story did you hear growing up that has stuck with you the most?" From the shallow grave of memory rose the specter of the Kilpatrick shooting. I talked and talked until Covington's eyelids began to flutter from exhaustion. Feeling like Coleridge's compulsively chatty Mariner, I finally released my captive listener, and as he left to take the elevator to his room, Covington said, "That story obviously has a hold on you. You ought to write about it."

And indeed I wrote, but not about the Kilpatrick shooting. I finished my dissertation on Robert Penn Warren's poetry, earned my PhD, and entered a maze of years filled with teaching, academic writing, and settling into the routines of career and motherhood. In 2009 my parents, remembering my fascination with the Kilpatrick shooting, called to tell me that James Kilpatrick had died. In 2011 my father gave me a copy of a book that had been written about James Kilpatrick, a ghostwritten "memoir" crafted by Dana Maria Hill, a longtime friend of the Kilpatrick family who had shaped James's story into a compelling tale of revenge and redemption. *Blazing Guns, Wild Horses, and the Grace of God: The James Kilpatrick Story* presented Kilpatrick's first-person account of his hardscrabble childhood on Sand Mountain, leading up to the events that took place the night of May 17,

1951, and culminating in the life of service and faith he led after getting out of prison.

And here's the part that—I don't know if "haunts" is the right word—makes Current Me smile wryly at the missed opportunities and foolishness of Past Me. In 1984, when I was sixteen and self-absorbed in the spectacularly solipsistic way that only teenagers can refine, a kind and quiet man, about fifty years old, the same age as my father, worked for a couple of weeks in our kitchen. My parents and I had moved from our remote chicken farm to the center of Albertville, onto a lovely tree-canopied street that the residents proudly referred to as "Million-Dollar Avenue." We weren't millionaires, but my mother, who had grown up poor, felt like we had finally arrived. Built in 1927, the house we moved into needed some renovation and updating, so my father hired a cabinetmaker from Boaz whose work and character were highly praised throughout the area. I'm sure I darted through the kitchen for snacks as the cabinetmaker worked, and I probably deigned to say hello on a few occasions.

Only after the renovations were finished and the cabinet builder was no longer working in our kitchen did my father say, "You know who that man was, don't you? That was James Kilpatrick, the one who was involved in that shooting years and years ago when he was your age." If I had been a different type of teenager, maybe I would have spent more time talking to him, perhaps working up my courage to ask him about the shooting that irrevocably changed the course of his life. Maybe the hard-won empathy I eventually developed through experience and maturity would have been jump-started by getting to know this man, by asking him what it had been like to go through such loss and guilt and pain, if I had taken Atticus Finch's advice to his daughter Scout: that to understand this story I had to climb inside James Kilpatrick's skin and walk around in it. But I was an American teen near of the end of the twentieth century. I had my MTV. I was safe, complacent, and smug.

Through the years, I have carried this story with me, every once in a while taking it out and holding it up to the light to see what would glimmer in the different facets. I think I'm finally able to do it justice.

Northeast Alabama

# MIDNIGHT CRY

# CHAPTER 1

# The Bootlegger

In the late 1940s and early 1950s, a time often depicted in popular culture as a golden age of innocence and postwar prosperity, Aubrey Kilpatrick was the middleman in the moonshine supply chain in northeastern Alabama. When he was not farming or working with horses, he often drove his 1933 Ford up into the Tennessee mountains, loaded the hidden compartment in his trunk with jugs of what his son James later referred to as "the finest white lightning in the South," and brought the contraband liquor back to his farm outside Boaz. There, an assembly line of Kilpatricks, from the adults to the children old enough to walk, got the moonshine ready for distribution and sale. The matriarch, Elizabeth, scalded glass bottles in giant pots of boiling water, while the younger Kilpatricks placed cardboard funnels in the necks of the cooling bottles lined up along makeshift board-and-sawhorse work surfaces in the yard. According to local lore, Elizabeth Kilpatrick made what her eldest son described as "the best peach syrup on the mountain," a blend of sweetened peach puree and moonshine. Being the oldest son and heir apparent to the family business, James Kilpatrick saddled up his fastest pony and made home deliveries around the community.

Bootlegging in a dry county was a thriving and profitable supplement to the meager income generated by farming on Sand Mountain, both during the Depression and in the years that followed. While a few entrepreneurs in the more remote hills of north Alabama operated stills and made their own hooch, there were no wealthy moonshine kingpins in Marshall County. Instead, most of the bootleggers ran operations like Aubrey Kilpatrick's— they procured, bottled, and distributed. Home deliveries of various sorts were commonplace across America in the first half of the twentieth century. Dairy products, ice, and dry goods were loaded onto "peddlers' wagons" and delivered to residences both in town and out in the country, and in some rural communities, traveling vegetable trucks set up transient "curb markets" at crossroads and in parking lots.

On Sand Mountain, people could also count on local bootleggers to bring unlabeled bottles of moonshine in paper sacks to either the front or back door, depending on one's preference or religious affiliation. Once the Alabama Beverage Control Board began regulating the sale of liquor and malt and brewed beverages in 1937, the added benefit of untaxed exchange made unlicensed, freelance wholesalers like Aubrey Kilpatrick quite popular, although not necessarily rich. Mixed with honey, moonshine could soothe an infant's teething pain or a child's cough. Tempered by sweet syrup or Coca-Cola, the potent liquor could enliven adult gatherings at the private, members-only "clubs" established to skirt the restrictive alcohol laws in dry counties like Marshall. Drunk straight from the bottle, perhaps furtively behind a barn or out in the woods, white lightning could dull the ache of disappointing crops, failing marriages, or recurring nightmares involving combat in World War II. Sand Mountain was a seller's market, and James Kilpatrick's pony with its bulging, clinking saddlebags was a welcome sight around the Double Bridges community.

By all accounts, including those of his own children, Aubrey Kilpatrick was a hard man. Hard times made hard people. Born in 1912, Kilpatrick turned twenty just as the Great Depression was gnawing its way across the nation, leaving no region untouched, with the despair captured in newspaper and newsreel images of flannel-suited Wall Street businessmen flinging themselves from skyscraper windows and dirt-encrusted farmers fleeing the ravages of the Dust Bowl. In the Deep South, the economic collapse experienced by the rest of the nation was exacerbated by the low wages and low crop prices that had been plaguing the region long before the stock market crash of 1929. As Kenneth J. Bindas points out in *Remembering the Great Depression in the Rural South*, most southerners who did have jobs worked as sharecroppers, tenant farmers, or factory workers, never making enough money to save but enough to pay for their home and food for their families. However, even those with very little knew they were lucky and tried to scrape together a small meal for anyone who asked. As one farmer interviewed by Bindas reminisced, "Those were the good old days, but those good old days were pretty rough times."

In the South, few experienced a sudden and dramatic change in fortune when the Depression hit; rather, fortune simply seemed even more elusive, a farther mirage. The election of Franklin Delano Roosevelt and the creation of New Deal programs such as the Works Progress Administration, the Civilian Conservation Corps, and, most important for north Alabama, the Tennessee Valley Authority offered hope and motivation to thousands of struggling Americans. Yet many southerners, especially the belligerently proud hill folk on Sand Mountain, saw the programs as government interference and unwanted charity. While some southerners criticized local and state governments for their limited responses to worsening conditions, others (usually the wealthy landowners) applauded the continued emphasis on individual initiative and the absence of government involvement. Even if that initiative took the form of moonshining and bootlegging, most rural Alabamians were willing to put their moral and legal objections to alcohol aside to maintain a sense of personal freedom and independence. Up on Sand Mountain, there was a little more money to be made from dealing in white lightning than in reluctant soil, but the times demanded any source of income possible, especially when the soil exacted such a backbreaking price. Thomas Jefferson may have extolled the virtues of agrarian life, claiming, "Those who labor in the earth are the chosen people of God, if ever he had a chosen people," but few in the rural South during the Depression could afford such idealism. They had mouths to feed, backs to clothe, roofs to mend. Owning a patch of land may have made farmers nearer to God, but the bankers hovered much closer.

Like his ancestors, many of whom were farmers who had emigrated from Ireland in the nineteenth century, Aubrey Kilpatrick was accustomed to a life of tilling the earth. Aubrey was known by his friends and neighbors as "Aurbie," a metathesis of consonants common in Sand Mountain speech due to dialect transportation from Ireland to America in the eighteenth century. By the early 1930s, the son of Joe and Ola Kilpatrick had either inherited or bought enough land in Marshall and DeKalb Counties to be considered a young man of some means. To paraphrase Jane Austen, it is a truth universally acknowledged that a single man in possession of a good-sized plot of farmland must be in want of a wife. On December 16, 1932, Aubrey Evelyn Kilpatrick married Nellie Elizabeth Pankey, a dark-haired, nineteen-year-old girl from the Sardis community that straddled the Marshall and Etowah county line. The newlyweds settled into a small cabin on Aubrey's land, working side by side to build a life and a family together.

Unlike the stereotype of the coarse, grubby farmer clad in overalls and a straw hat, Aubrey Kilpatrick, while not quite a dandy, was considered a sharp dresser, meticulously groomed with a neat moustache and wire-rimmed spectacles. He was handsome in a severe, almost Teutonic fashion, and his posture bespoke a man accustomed to sitting ramrod straight in a saddle. Despite his sartorial style and disciplined mien, Aubrey was at heart a brawler, as quick with his fists as he was with his favorite gun, a nickel-plated Smith & Wesson .44 revolver. Known throughout the area as an expert saddle-horse trainer, Aubrey traveled around the state attending horse shows and rodeos, and he often visited the farms of horse breeders to offer his skills in training and riding. But Aubrey was not the benevolent horse whisperer who gentled a recalcitrant animal into obedience. According to Sherril Thomas, a close friend of the Kilpatrick family, "Aurbie didn't train horses. He broke 'em." This cruel streak included his fellow man as well as animals. In one story told by family members and recounted in Dana Hill's *Blazing Guns, Wild Horses, and the Grace of God*, Aubrey owned one particular horse that defied all attempts to be trained, a "high-spirited and crazy" mare that only her master could ride. Saturday afternoons in Boaz were "town days," when farm families often shopped at local businesses, ate at favorite restaurants, or visited with relatives who lived within the city limits. As a prelude to the rowdier town nights that followed the influx of day-trippers and the bustle of the afternoon activities, men often gathered in the town square and common areas to swap tales, play cards, throw dice, and occasionally take a surreptitious nip from a flask or bottle.

One Saturday, Aubrey rode his favorite mare into town, right into the middle of a group of men who had been gambling and drinking. Such a display was typical for Aubrey Kilpatrick—he relished the image of himself as a Wild West outlaw, tougher and meaner and better with guns and horses than any other man in the area. A slurring, stumbling challenger, emboldened by drink, demanded to ride the horse despite its restless canter, flattened ears, and rolling eyes. At first Aubrey refused. Then, perhaps considering the potential for comedic spectacle or simply wanting to shut the fool up, Aubrey turned the reins over to the man and watched him clumsily hoist himself onto the horse's back. As expected, the indignant mare bucked and reared, causing the man to slip sideways in the saddle, and broke into a run with her perpendicular rider hanging on and hollering for help. The horse thundered past a power pole, which the unfortunate man's head hit with a resounding thud, killing him instantly. No charges were filed against Aubrey for the man's death—all agreed that the man had been the victim of his own foolishness and drunkenness—but the incident merely added to the dangerous persona Aubrey consciously cultivated. Tales of Aubrey Kilpatrick and his "killer horse" thrummed throughout town, and mothers swept children out of yards and into houses for safety whenever the bootlegger and his murderous steed galloped by.

Despite his hardness, his cruelty, and his penchant for violence, Aubrey was devoted to his family, especially his oldest son, James. By 1951, eight children had been born to Aubrey and Elizabeth Kilpatrick, five boys and three girls. Aubrey taught the older boys to ride, rope, and tame horses, and by the time James was six years old, he was already an accomplished horseman. Residents of Boaz old enough to remember the intact Kilpatrick family recall seeing them riding their horses into town on Saturdays, often joined by neighbors and their children on horseback, with Aubrey treating each child to a candy bar and a Coca-Cola. On Saturday nights, the entire family piled into a pickup truck and attended a weekly horse show in the nearby town of Crossville. When touring rodeos came to Birmingham, Aubrey often took only James, a special excursion shared between a father and his firstborn son. These rodeos dazzled James, who, like many horse-loving children growing up in rural areas, dreamed of riding and roping his way to fame. Westerns were the most popular film genre during this era, with moviegoers across the nation thrilled by the adventures of cowboys riding the range, outsmarting villains, and wooing pretty prairie lasses. Whenever a precious quarter could be secured for the picture show, James went to the Saturday matinees at the Rialto Theater in Boaz, imagining himself as a young sidekick to Roy Rogers, with his own favorite horse galloping alongside Trigger. At one rodeo event in Birmingham, western superstars Gene Autry and Johnny Mack Brown were the featured celebrities, and, according to a story James loved to tell years later, Brown watched James work with the horses and allegedly asked Aubrey and Elizabeth if he could take their son to California with him. James later reminisced, "Now, I don't know if he was serious or just kidding, but my mother would absolutely not agree to it. I missed my chance at breaking and training horses for the rich and famous. Sometimes I wondered what my life would have been like if she had agreed to let me go. Imagine a small country boy like me breaking horses for a western hero."

The lessons Aubrey taught his children, his sons in particular, were part and parcel of growing up out in the country. Besides training and riding horses, the boys learned from their father how to drive trucks, cars, and tractors; shoot a variety of guns, both for hunting and defending the homestead; and deliver a load of moonshine. And they worked, from sunup to sundown. Like all farm families, the Kilpatricks lived by the unrelenting seasonal rhythms of planting and harvesting, but the children nonetheless found time for the kind of unfettered, unsupervised play rarely experienced by kids today. They fished, hunted squirrels and possums, and swam in the nearby creek. The farm's demands superseded educational progress; few adolescents in farming communities made it past seventh or eighth grade.

In the Kilpatrick household, domestic duties went beyond just working the crops—Aubrey expected his sons, especially James, to recruit itinerant workers and haul livestock. When James was only twelve, Aubrey often sent him on a twenty-mile trek to collect farmworkers from Gadsden, the slight, rangy boy deftly operating the one-ton farm truck from Marshall to Etowah County. The fact that he had no driver's license was of little concern. Sometimes, in the spirit of multitasking, James carried along bottles of clear liquid as incentives for the workers to make the trip up to Sand Mountain. Some of the bottles contained water; others contained a more bracing tonic. James would ask the prospective day laborers if they wanted "just water" or "the good water." Other potential employers shook their heads in wonder as workers shuffled away from their offers and headed toward the pickup truck driven by the boy with the "good water." Off James would go, men crowded into the truck bed, with some standing on the running boards.

Not every demand from their father was met with the Kilpatrick children's absolute submission. Preferring to ride horses or take off into the woods for a quick hunting expedition, James and his younger brother Billy sometimes chafed at their father's impromptu requests for liquor deliveries, drunken joyrides, or forays to rough up a rival bootlegger. A firm believer in sampling his own wares for quality-control purposes, Aubrey counted on James to act as a designated driver while he and his friends rode around and refreshed themselves with moonshine. Saying no was not an option, so James and Billy came up with creative (albeit passive-aggressive) modes of revenge for being called upon at a moment's notice to do their father's bidding. A favorite tactic of the two older brothers was to spike the moonshine with castor oil, a commonly used laxative and all-purpose panacea for everything from heartburn to stalled childbirth. One hapless victim of this prank, a customer from Gadsden who had taken a taxi out to the Kilpatrick farm to purchase some of the "good water," became so ill after consuming the purgative cocktail that he stayed in the Kilpatricks' cornfield for hours, unable to make the taxi ride home. Such shenanigans did not deter future customers from buying Aubrey Kilpatrick's moonshine, and the thrashing that Aubrey gave to James and Billy for tampering with the liquor did little to squelch their howls of laughter as they remembered the poor man fertilizing the cornfield.

Just as every cloud has a silver lining, it also contains a turbulent darkness that threatens to erupt into a storm. Aubrey had a quick temper and quick hands, both of which sent his children scurrying for cover. He did not spare the rod, and the punishments that he meted out for intentional misbehaviors and unintentional errors would be deemed child abuse by today's standards. The Kilpatrick children weren't so much hardened as they were annealed, their resilience formed by alternating patterns of tough love and even tougher reprimand. Conflating fear with respect, Aubrey prided himself on dominating any creature that crossed his path. He could break horses; he could break people, too. Some detractors referred to him as a "ring-tailed rounder," while more frank denigrators called him "a pure-d son-of-a-bitch." In the *Birmingham News* article published the day after his death, Aubrey was described as "a widely known saddle horse trainer . . . known for his fiery temper and his willingness to fight on short notice." In that time and place, men like Aubrey Kilpatrick were either the law or on the wrong side of it. Somehow, Aubrey had managed for years to walk the line between both. He had been the target of suspicion and even official visits by agents from the Alabama Beverage Control Board, yet he had eluded arrest each time a search took place on his farm. An article in Guntersville's *Advertiser-Gleam*, published a week after his death, stated that Aubrey had "kept officers from searching his place for whiskey." How he kept these officers at bay is unknown—perhaps he had a rudimentary grasp of his constitutional rights as a private citizen, or maybe he was wily enough to hide any evidence before the officers arrived. He might have even been able to convince the agents that it was in their best interest to get in their cars and drive away, offering either a bribe or payment in other, more liquid forms. Corruption was not out of the question, of course, since enforcement of both national and state prohibition laws was notoriously difficult. In one instance, a warrant was sworn out against Aubrey for interference with an officer, but the warrant was never served. Regardless of the persuasive tactics involved, Aubrey remained in business.

For weeks before their final showdown, Zeke Boyles and Aubrey Kilpatrick had engaged in a few instances of chest thumping and territory marking. At times Aubrey seemed almost to provoke the sheriff, cruising slowly down Gunter Avenue in Guntersville, virtually daring the local police to stop him and search his car. In early spring of 1951, the Guntersville police pulled Aubrey's car over outside town and detained him for carrying an unlicensed pistol. At the hearing Aubrey told the judge he had just purchased the gun and was on the way home with it when he was stopped. The judge dropped the case but warned Aubrey that he needed to obtain a permit from the sheriff to transport the gun. Sheriff Boyles, surely enjoying this small victory, refused to give Aubrey the permit but magnanimously allowed him to carry the gun home. "We've had several complaints that you are too handy with a gun," the sheriff told Aubrey. "Be careful that you don't start any trouble with this one."

Whether or not the gun involved in this incident was Aubrey's favorite .44 is unknown. The night that Zeke Boyles and the other officers drove up to the Kilpatrick home, Aubrey emerged with two guns: the Smith & Wesson .44 and a .32 pistol, which was later found wrapped in a sack in his pocket, no bullets discharged. Only the .44 was fired, five times into the windshield and body of Zeke Boyles's car. Like his favorite western gunslingers, Aubrey Kilpatrick died with his gun in his hand. But it was not a clean death, and he gasped his last breath shortly after his oldest son, the one he had taught to ride and shoot and drive, had exacted bloody revenge against the men who had killed his father. The death certificate issued by the state of Alabama reveals one side of the account that would later become integral to the prosecution of James Kilpatrick: "Aurbie E. Kilpatrick" had been "shot while resisting service of warrant." Signed by Howard "Moose" Hardin, the Marshall County coroner who immediately became the interim sheriff upon Boyles's death, the certificate delivered a damning verdict against a dead man: "justifiable homicide."

Bootlegging and guns may have been the peripheral factors that led to the shootout, but the event that led the sheriff's black Pontiac to the Kilpatricks' front door close to midnight on May 17, 1951, was the escalation of a feud between Aubrey and a family of sharecroppers on his land. The consequences of this conflict left four men dead, four wives widowed, fourteen children fatherless, and a county divided. Call it fate, call it simply the inevitable convergence of two strong-willed men with differing agendas, but Aubrey Kilpatrick and Sheriff Zeke Boyles were on a collision course as ineluctable as the *Titanic* steaming its way across the North Atlantic toward the iceberg.

# CHAPTER 2

# The Sheriff

At over 380,000 words, the 1901 Constitution of the State of Alabama is twelve times longer than the average state constitution and forty-four times longer than the U.S. Constitution. Rooted in a predominantly agricultural economy and white supremacy, it is the longest and most amended constitution still operative anywhere in the world. Since its creation in 1901, 951 amendments have been tacked on to the original document, micromanaging every minute facet of Alabama life, from the structure of its legislature to taxation to funding the sheriff's posse in Morgan County. Fiercely protected by originalists and arduously fought by progressivists, the Alabama constitution has been the subject of heated debate and national censure in the 120 years since its inception. Historian Wayne Flynt, one of the most consistent and vocal opponents of the 1901 constitution, asserts in *Alabama in the Twentieth Century* that "most if not all the state's formidable problems had their origins in the 1901 document." Pulling no punches, Flynt argues that the continuing governance of such a document "is testimony to the continuing power of the economic and political elites that put it in place, the racial insensitivity of many whites, and lack of concern about the state's negative national and international reputation."

Nearly every original section and subsequent amendment work to diffuse governmental authority throughout the state while keeping firm control in the hands of powerful landowners and catering to out-of-state corporate interests. Who can vote, who can run for office, how long an elected officeholder can stay in power, and the degree to which counties can exert home rule in tax ordinances are all scripted in excruciating detail throughout the 1901 constitution, even weighing in on matters such as bingo parlors, mosquito control, prostitution, and the disposal of dead animals. Where law enforcement was concerned, Section 138 of the Alabama constitution dictated that "a sheriff shall be elected in each county by the qualified electors thereof, who shall hold office for a term of four years, unless sooner removed, and he shall be ineligible to such office as his own successor." In 1938, following a proposal by the 1936–37 state legislature, Amendment 35 was ratified: "A sheriff shall be elected in each county by the qualified electors thereof who shall hold office for a term of four years unless sooner removed, and he shall be eligible to such office as his own successor." While the term limit was the same, the alteration to the self-succession clause opened the door for sheriffs across the state to establish a significant degree of power spanning a decade or more. The timing could not have been better for Ezekiel Montgomery Boyles of Marshall County.

Named for the doctor who delivered him in his parents' home on Georgia Mountain in 1905, Ezekiel Boyles, known by everyone as "Zeke," grew up on Brindlee Mountain, one of a scattering of sandstone formations at the tail of the Appalachian Plateau. As on Sand Mountain, farming on Brindlee Mountain was an often-Sisyphean undertaking, and after marrying Eva Etchison on Christmas Eve of 1924, Boyles decided to move closer to town. After working in a local hardware store and driving a Weinberger grocery truck, he began his sixteen-year career in law enforcement by working as a night watchman in Guntersville, eventually earning a position as deputy under Marshall County sheriff Robert Moody and chief deputy under Sheriff Dono Taylor. In 1938 Boyles ran as the Democratic candidate for sheriff of Marshall County. While Boyles was a well-known figure around Guntersville and the Warrenton community just outside town, up on Sand Mountain he was a less familiar name, and he directed many of his campaign ads toward voters in Albertville and Boaz. Promising the restoration of law and order throughout the county, Boyles emphasized his commitment to all the county's citizens; in one campaign ad that appeared in the April 27, 1938, *Guntersville Advertiser and Democrat,* Boyles stated: "Having made every effort possible to personally contact each voter, but due to the short period of time was unable to do so. I take this method to ask for your VOTE and INFLUENCE on May 3rd." After narrowly winning the election in June 1938, Boyles was sworn in as sheriff of Marshall County on Monday, January 16, 1939.

Serving as sheriff of a north Alabama county in the late 1930s presented its own unique challenges. Even after the Twenty-First Amendment repealed national Prohibition in 1933, many Alabamians continued to support local prohibition and repeal initiatives. Though statewide sales resumed in 1937, because of local option laws, some counties remained dry well beyond the end of national Prohibition. Like most counties in north Alabama, Marshall County took a hardline stance on "the Devil's brew," and enforcing this post-Prohibition prohibition meant that the county sheriff had his work cut out for him. Both on and off Sand Mountain, moonshiners and bootleggers had a long-established customer base throughout the county, with fast boats ferrying illegal liquor across the newly formed Guntersville Lake and fast cars transporting crates of "scant pints" to thirsty buyers on remote mountain farms.

Only a week after being sworn in, the new sheriff shut down "two big stills with four men operating them," "starting things off at a lively speed," as the *Guntersville Advertiser and Democrat* cheerfully noted. In its weekly crime report, the *Advertiser* often praised Sheriff Boyles's efforts to keep Marshall County dry. In February 1939, less than a month after his induction as sheriff, Boyles raided seven stills, confiscating "a pair of mules, wagon, and thirty gallons of liquor," leading the *Advertiser* to proclaim, "Sheriff Boyles has been in office only a few weeks, and if his activities are kept up liquor will soon be a scarce article in Marshall County." Nor did the pace of alcohol-related arrests abate as spring blossomed. In March 1939, despite the demands of "serving papers and making preparations for the Spring term of Circuit court," Sheriff Boyles and his deputies raided "a few wildcat stills in different sections of the county." These forays yielded over fifty gallons of liquor and resulted in the destruction of a "160-gallon still." With a certain degree of smugness, the *Guntersville Advertiser and Democrat* crowed once again that such efforts, with the assistance of state and federal agents, "will soon make 'moonshining' and violation of the prohibition laws in general a very unprofitable and unsatisfactory business in Marshall County."

Not all of Sheriff Boyles's cases involved hunting down moonshiners and bootleggers. In June 1939, only five months into his first term as sheriff, Boyles investigated a crime that shocked the tiny town of Grant, located a few miles northeast of Guntersville and southeast of Huntsville. On the night of June 6, two men, Edward McDonald and Hubert Chandler, robbed a store owned and run by Irvin Whitaker. After clearing the till and murdering Whitaker, McDonald and Chandler torched the store in hopes of covering their crime. Chandler was severely burned when he applied a lighted match to the store's gasoline-soaked supply room. While McDonald went on the lam, Chandler was apprehended at a Huntsville hospital where he was undergoing treatment for his burns; he then died after his transfer to a hospital in Guntersville. Sheriff Boyles was not fully convinced that Chandler's death was caused by the burns and ordered an autopsy to prove that someone acting on behalf of McDonald or even McDonald himself had not gotten to Chandler and poisoned him to guarantee his silence.

According to the June 21, 1939, *Guntersville Advertiser and Democrat*, "Organs from Chandler's body were sent to Auburn for examination following his death," and "Sheriff Boyles was officially notified Tuesday that no poison was found in the stomach of Hubert Chandler." Only four years old at the time, the State Toxicology Lab at Alabama Polytechnic Institute in Auburn featured two of the nation's leading forensic investigators: Director Hubert W. Nixon and Assistant Director Carl J. Rehling. Twelve years later, Rehling was the one who performed the autopsies on Boyles, Washington Bennett, Leonard Floyd, and Aubrey Kilpatrick.

Such sensational crimes were rare in Marshall County during Sheriff Boyles's first term. Most of the time, his investigations and arrests involved the ubiquitous illegal liquor trade. Newspaper stories featuring Boyles's apprehension of sneaky backwoods wildcatters and intercounty bootleggers depicted a sheriff on a mission to uphold the law and protect his constituency. Sometimes Boyles dismantled stills and poured out the moonshine; other times he confiscated cars, corn, and sugar. Two brazen moonshiners built a still and plied their trade less than a mile from the sheriff's office at the Marshall County Courthouse in Guntersville. Boyles and his deputies simply walked to the area known as "Polecat Hollow," arrested the men, and escorted them on foot back to the county jail.

On occasion Sheriff Boyles traveled out of state to collect or extradite prisoners, but for the most part he stayed close to home. In December 1939 Boyles and his family moved into a handsome new house in town. The sheriff's wife, Eva Hutchinson Boyles, was frequently mentioned in the local paper for her civic and social activities, including the Women's Missionary Union at the First Baptist Church of Guntersville. Their daughters, Doris and Marion, were also frequently mentioned for their church work around town, and Marion even garnered a newspaper mention after an appendectomy ("She is doing nicely"). In one particular instance Boyles was able to combine his love of family with his duty to law enforcement; in December 1940, according to the *Guntersville Advertiser and Democrat*, the sheriff and his family drove from Guntersville to Los Angeles to retrieve Carmen Burt, a man charged with burglarizing a warehouse in Boaz, to bring him back to stand trial in Marshall County. The journey by car must have taken several days, undoubtedly filled with memory-making stops along the way. One can only imagine the return trip, however, with a captured, manacled fugitive wedged into the back seat, perhaps flanked by the Boyles sisters.

In 1942 Boyles ran for reelection and won again. As the country launched its fight against the Axis powers, the sheriff of Marshall County continued his own war against liquor traffickers on and off Sand Mountain. To demonstrate his triumphs, Boyles would often hold public spectacles that featured him pouring hundreds of gallons of confiscated liquor worth thousands of dollars into the gutter in front of the county jail. These events drew scores of spectators, some perhaps wistfully watching the contraband moonshine trickle into the city's sewers. Despite the seriousness with which Boyles took his duties, especially where alcohol prohibition was concerned, the popular sheriff often engaged in lighthearted town productions ranging from slapstick to just plain silly. As a fundraiser, the Women's Society of Christian Service at the First Methodist Church sponsored a "Womanless Wedding" at the Palace Theater in Guntersville. Part unintentional echo of the all-male casts in early seventeenth-century Shakespearean productions, part rural drag show, this lively farce featured several prominent civic leaders of Guntersville dressed as women in a burlesque comedy about a celebrity wedding. (City alderman Robert Bishop played "Greta Garbor" [sic], and A. L. "Tiny" Burdette, head of security at the Guntersville TVA Dam, took on the role of "Marlene Deuthrich" [sic].) Sheriff Boyles starred as the voluptuous former Ziegfeld girl and film star Billie Dove, a performance that surely brought down the house.

Another community revel that Boyles participated in was a "scrub bull trial" in Marshall County. Such "trials" were neither new nor specific to Alabama or even the South. In the *Mother Jones* article "Inside the Bizarre Cow Trials of the 1920s," Cynthia Graber and Nicola Twilley describe an unusual trend that began in the early twentieth century and developed into a nationwide fad until World War II. According to Graber and Twilley, "Scientists had recently developed a deeper understanding of genetics and inherited traits; at the same time, the very first eugenics policies were being enacted in the United States. And, as the population grew, the public wanted cheaper meat and milk. As a result, in the 1920s, the USDA encouraged rural communities around the United States to put *bulls* on the witness stand— to hold a legal trial, complete with lawyers and witnesses and a watching public—to determine whether the bull was fit to breed." As part of its "Better Sires: Better Stock" program, launched in 1919, the USDA even published a pamphlet that outlined how "to hold a legal trial of a non-purebred bull, in order to publicly condemn it as unfit to reproduce. The pamphlet calls for a cast of characters to include a judge, a jury, attorneys, and witnesses for the prosecution and the defense, as well as a sheriff, who should 'wear a large metal star and carry a gun.'"

The July 9, 1942, issue of the *Guntersville Gleam* announced, with mock gravity, a scrub bull trial over which Sheriff E. M. Boyles would preside as the arresting officer of this criminally inferior bull. The owner of the "scrubbiest bull" would win a twenty-five-dollar defense bond, and the proceedings, unprecedented in Marshall County (although an annual occurrence in rural areas in Texas, Oklahoma, and Illinois for nearly twenty years), were expected to draw "a large audience." These scrub bull trials lost their popularity during World War II, particularly in late 1942 and early 1943, when many American newspapers began publishing reports that two million European Jews had already been murdered. The idea of promoting "eugenic selection" to create "superior breeds" seemed uncomfortably close to the emerging news accounts of human beings being culled, transported, and slaughtered like cattle. But in the heady ignorance of 1942, in a small town in north Alabama, the scrub bull trial emceed by Sheriff Boyles was an amusing exercise in livestock breeding and community pride, some midsummer silliness to stave off the anxiety of local boys packing up and heading to fight in Europe and the Pacific.

By September 1945 the war was over, and across America the soldiers who survived came home to continue their former lives or begin new ones. The September 12, 1945, edition of the *Guntersville Advertiser and Democrat* celebrated the homecoming: "Already a trickle of returning soldiers is appearing in our communities as a result of the war's end. Very soon now our young men will be again taking their rightful place in our social and economic affairs. And not the least grateful are the young ladies." Some area businesses targeted the newly discharged soldiers for modern amenities and services; one ad for Southern Bell and Telegraph Company in the September 21, 1945, *Albertville Herald* announced, "When the boys come back to the farm / They'll want telephone service, together with other modern conveniences. War has taught them—and their families—to rely on telephone service." Yet despite the postwar push for modernity, most of the young servicemen who left Marshall County returned from the war prepared to do what their fathers and their fathers' fathers before them had done: raise crops, cattle, hogs, and chickens.

The best-known and most propagated images of post–World War II America depict smiling young veterans purchasing suburban homes in places like Levittown, taking the train into the city for work, mowing neat green squares of lawn, and attending neighborhood barbecues and potlucks. In rural areas, however, most soldiers who returned went back to family farms to eke out a living while others sought new careers in town, perhaps foreseeing the decline in small-scale farming that would gather momentum in the 1950s. After serving in the U.S. Coast Guard for three years, both stateside and overseas, Washington Bennett came home to Guntersville to rejoin his wife, Jane, and his two children, Sarah and William. At age thirty-seven, Bennett had already begun a career in law enforcement in Marshall County as a deputy for the sheriff's department, following a family tradition of lawmen that went back to his grandfather, who had been a Marshall County sheriff in the late 1800s. Bennett and Zeke Boyles had both been deputies under Sheriff Quintus Donovan "Dono" Taylor from the late 1930s till the early 1940s, and both were pallbearers at Taylor's funeral after the former sheriff was killed in a head-on collision between the car he was driving and a Crescent bus on the highway that ran between Guntersville and Huntsville. Bennett had been close to Sheriff Taylor, accompanying him and his wife to watch Bennett's alma mater, Georgia Tech, play football against Kentucky in Atlanta. Just prior to Taylor's death, Bennett had volunteered for service in the Coast Guard, leaving Guntersville, his job, and his family for three years. Perhaps feeling that the time had come for him to make the leap from chief deputy to sheriff, in January 1946 Bennett announced his candidacy for sheriff of Marshall County. He would not be Zeke Boyles's only challenger during that contentious campaign.

Alabama politics, like the state's weather, can be capricious and unpredictable. Whether at the state or local level, an officeholder who once earned the praise of constituents may become the target of intense scrutiny and criticism. By 1946, it seemed as if Zeke Boyles's popularity and public approval were waning. Even the Guntersville newspaper, usually a Greek chorus of encomia for the sheriff, seemed almost weary of reporting yet another destroyed still and more gallons of moonshine poured into the gutter. Zeke Boyles had perfected his role of leading actor in performative prohibition, but the audience was getting restless. The war was over, and people wanted to celebrate, especially in Guntersville, where the lake was rapidly becoming a tourist hotspot. In the 1940s, tens of thousands of boating enthusiasts descended on the small town to enjoy the Dixie Motor Races. Hailed as the new "Playground of the South," Guntersville grew to accommodate the influx of tourists, rapidly building restaurants, filling stations, and motels.

In January 1946, as the deadline approached for applying to run for public office, the *Guntersville Advertiser and Democrat* reported that E. M. "Zeke" Boyles, Charlie M. Grant, Washington M. Bennett, and Joe B. Gorman had officially declared their intent to run for sheriff. After the May primary, two contenders emerged: Zeke Boyles and Charlie Grant. Destined to be a bridesmaid but never the bride, Bennett good-naturedly endorsed Boyles, his former boss. But perhaps feeling that something smelled rotten in Polecat Hollow, Grant's supporters launched a public smear campaign against their man's opponent. It didn't help that in late May, right before the election, a man described in the Guntersville newspapers as "a relative of Sheriff Boyles" was arrested in a raid involving "stills, some whiskey and home brew." After stating that "State ABC [Alcoholic Beverage Control] men and the sheriff's force made all the raids except the one in which a relative of the sheriff was involved," the *Guntersville Gleam* article about the arrests dated Friday, May 24, 1946, coyly commented, with no pretense of objectivity: "We heard two reports about that." One of the reports alleged that Boyles and his deputies did not know about the raid; another claimed that the sheriff knew about the raid but recused himself from taking part in it. The name and exact relationship to the sheriff of this "relative" were not mentioned in any of the newspaper coverage, but the gossip around town kept coming back to one person: Zeke Boyles's son-in-law.

This revelation was like chum in the water, and the sharks who supported Charlie Grant smelled blood. All the subtle digs and thinly veiled insinuations of the earlier, fairly civil and polite campaign ads turned downright ugly by the end of May. Since the *Guntersville Gleam* was published only once a week, seven days' worth of rumors and accusations exploded messily in the May 31 edition, right on the front page. Along with photographs featuring the candidates for the June 4 election, three large political ads appeared. On the left side of the front page, a boxed ad asked readers, "What are the Facts." In smaller print, the question continued: "ABOUT THE RAID ON THE STILL WHERE TWO MEN WERE CAPTURED, ONE OF WHOM WAS THE SHERIFF'S SON-IN-LAW?" The gloves were off, and the mud-filled hands were ready to sling. The rest of the ad read as follows:

> The sheriff has stated that he directed this raid from his office. It is a fact that he was not in his office at the time of this raid. We have heard from reliable sources that he was at Friendship [Church] on Brindlee Mountain at an all day singing at the time of this raid.
>
> It is also a fact that Mr. Boyles made the statement that he would not have had this to happen for five thousand dollars.
>
> There is no record of a divorce suit by the sheriff's son-in-law or daughter.
>
> THESE ARE FACTS. THEY CAN BE VERIFIED.

Paid for by "friends of Charlie Grant," the ad all but directly accused Boyles of, at best, being ignorant of his son-in-law's illegal activities or, at worst, turning a blind eye.

In the center of the front page, an ad paid for by Boyles assured voters, as he had in previous campaigns, that if he were elected, he would continue to give his constituency "the best of service." But to the right of the Boyles ad, another box contained a direct and personal attack on, if not Boyles's character, at least his temperament: "THINK How in the Hell has Zeke Boyles got so mean in the past 30 days?" Page 3 of this same edition showed just how mean Boyles could get, especially when publicly called out and provoked. He first established his faithful church attendance (a must in the Bible Belt), stating that he was a "member of the First Baptist Church, Guntersville, Alabama" and that he had "taught a Sunday School class for twelve years" and "failed to attend Sunday School only seven Sundays and this was due to sickness or urgent business." The ad then touted Boyles's reputation for being especially tough on illegal alcohol trafficking:

> His record will stand up with any former Sheriff as to the number of raids made and stills seized. He has never failed to use his office and his deputies to investigate any complaint or report of anyone violating the prohibition law.

Then the piece went in for the kill:

> PROOF OF THIS IS THE FACT THAT HE DIRECTED FROM HIS OFFICE AND WAS THE CAUSE OF A RAID BEING MADE THAT NETTED ONE STILL AND TWO MEN, ONE OF THE MEN BEING THE FORMER HUSBAND OF HIS DAUGHTER.

The ad went on to assert that Boyles had "delivered over four hundred telegrams and cablegrams to the Fathers, Mothers and Wives of service men in Marshall County without receiving one penny for it," urging readers to check with the local Western Union office for verification.

But the ad wasn't finished defending Boyles against his detractors—the final paragraph inflicted a damning coup de grâce: "Compare this record of E. M. Boyles as a Citizen and Sheriff of Marshall County for the past seven years with that of CHARLIE M. GRANT, WHO HAS OPERATED A POOL ROOM IN THE CITY OF GUNTERSVILLE for the past seven years and then make your own decision as to which one you want as your Sheriff for the next four years." In the context of mid-twentieth-century rural north Alabama, "pool room" was coded language, signaling a veritable den of iniquity laden with overtones of gambling, sin, and vice. What good Christian in Marshall County would want a billiards joint racketeer in charge of law and order instead of a Sunday school teacher who compassionately (and free of charge) delivered death notifications to the anxious family members of U.S. servicemen?

Not to be outdone, both Charlie Grant and his supporters launched two final ads on the last page of the May 31 *Guntersville Gleam*. In the paid political advertisement placed by Grant himself, he assured voters that he would not "betray this fine spirit by resorting to underhand methods or mud slinging." Since Grant had no doubt been apprised of the front-page campaign ad, seemingly in support of his candidacy, that asked what had made Zeke Boyles so mean over the past month, he adamantly denied placing the ad, stating that "as a Christian gentleman" he would never sanction "such an ad," presumably an oblique reference to the use of the word "Hell" on the front page of the town's newspaper. The companion ad, paid for by "Friends of Charlie M. Grant of Guntersville, Ala.," "ACCEPTED ZEKE BOYLES' CHALLENGE OF A COMPARISON BETWEEN MR. GRANT'S AND MR. BOYLES' RECORD AS A CITIZEN AND BUSINESS MAN IN GUNTERSVILLE." In an almost point-by-point rebuttal, the ad chided Boyles for mentioning "his church affiliation along with his politics"; it also implied that Boyles's stance on moonshining was not as rigorous as the frequent raids might suggest, since "the number of men arrested for this offense are few." As for the military telegrams and cablegrams, the ad's sponsors charged that "Mr. Boyles was paid for some of the trips he made to deliver such messages." Finally, the ad insinuated that the cronyism, corruption, and preferential treatment during Boyles's term as sheriff would end with Grant's "house cleaning in the sheriff's office and the jail." It wasn't quite the Petticoat Affair or the Teapot Dome scandal, but it was enough. Charlie Grant was elected sheriff of Marshall County in June 1946, defeating Boyles by a margin of 1,245 votes.

Whatever private beef Zeke Boyles may have had with Charlie Grant, publicly the former sheriff accepted his defeat graciously and published a notification immediately after the election in the *Guntersville Gleam* urging everyone in the county "to get behind Charlie and help him make you a good Sheriff." Boyles even sheepishly added, "when I get back from Bucks Pocket, I will be for him 100%." Buck's Pocket, a natural canyon (or "pocket") of the Appalachian Mountain chain along South Sauty Creek near Guntersville, was known not only for its rugged natural beauty and stunning vistas but also as a secluded location where vanquished politicians could go to lick their wounds. The origin story of Buck's Pocket as such a retreat appeared in a June 10, 1986, *Gadsden Times* article, which traced the lore to Governor James "Big Jim" Folsom's defeat in the 1942 gubernatorial election; after his unsuccessful campaign, Folsom urged "other losing candidates to meet at Buck's Pocket to mourn their loss and plan their future political strategy": "Ever since, the legend goes, defeated politicians are supposed to travel to Buck's Pocket the day after elections, climb atop Point Rock and shout to the world that they lost." Whether or not Zeke Boyles actually went to Buck's Pocket is not found in public record, but he did seem to settle into civilian life with relative ease and a certain degree of prosperity. The *Guntersville Gleam* reported a lighthearted exchange between the two former adversaries—even though Zeke Boyles's term ended at midnight on Monday, January 20, 1947, the ousted sheriff was still answering calls after his expiration date; the article quoted Boyles as joking with Grant, "Charlie, I started to phone you at 12:15 this morning and tell you there was a hurry call over at the county line, but I decided to let you get one more night's sleep before your troubles begin." Grant replied (with a grin, the article noted), "If you had called me . . . I'd have come down to the jail and rolled you out and made you go with me."

Charlie Grant's tenure as sheriff of Marshall County seemed at the beginning to be much like his predecessor's, with a few exceptions. A series of poisonings claimed several dogs and a cat in Guntersville, including Grant's own police dog, prompting the sheriff to offer a fifty-dollar reward ("from his own money," the *Advertiser-Gleam* noted) for any leads. A brawl between carnival workers and Arab townspeople in the spring of 1947 led to a shooting, whereupon Sheriff Grant promptly closed the carnival down, fearing that the ready availability of firearms among both parties to the conflict would escalate the situation into a full-blown riot. Aside from these bizarre occurrences, most of Sheriff Grant's law keeping involved rooting out stills, destroying the equipment, and disposing of the contraband liquor. One *Guntersville Gleam* article excitedly described a confiscated still as having a "1500 gallon gas tank, the kind that is put under ground at service stations." The usual dismantling tool of choice, an ax, was too small for this job, and "the officers had to set off 3 sticks of dynamite under it." As with Boyles's public displays of being hard on illegal alcohol production and trafficking, Grant kept up the tradition of Saturday "pourings" in front of the county courthouse in Guntersville. With headlines like "A Whiskey Pouring Is Scheduled Saturday" and "A Liquor Pouring at the Jail Saturday," the Guntersville newspaper guaranteed visible, theatrical proof that the county sheriff was working around the clock to wet the ground and not the throats of the local constituency. Only the liquor that was being held as evidence in unsettled cases remained bottled, but Grant certainly had more than enough distilled spirits, moonshine, and homebrew to dump into the county jail yard, averaging between thirty and sixty gallons per spectacle.

While these staged "pourings" were ritualistically familiar to the townspeople of Guntersville, perhaps what turned if not public opinion but private sentiment against Charlie Grant's zeal for prohibitive measures was his highly publicized crusade against alcohol sales in Marshall County. "WAKE UP, DRY VOTERS!" trumpeted one political advertisement sponsored by Grant in October 1948. Since the passage of the Alabama Beverage Control Act of 1937, Marshall County had consistently voted "dry," or against the manufacture and sale of alcohol. As James Benson Sellers explains in *The Prohibition Movement in Alabama, 1702–1943*, this act "provided that the probate judge of any county, upon written petition of twenty-five percent of the qualified voters of the county at the last general election, should be required to order an election not less than thirty nor more than forty-five days from the date of filing the said petition." The simply worded ballot asked one question: "Do you favor the legal sale and distribution of alcoholic beverages within this county?"; the voters simply had to indicate "yes" or "no." Enough of Marshall County apparently felt like it was high time to revisit the matter in 1948, and a special referendum was scheduled for October.

No other issue could polarize the citizenry of Marshall County like liquor. Some argued that going "wet" was inevitable, a sign of the changing attitudes in postwar Alabama and a recognition of the revenue that could be generated by the controlled sale of alcohol. Why should the folks in Huntsville over in Madison County get fine new schools and paved roads from the pockets of those in Marshall County who were willing to cross the county line to purchase liquor, wine, and beer? A significant majority of Marshall Countians, however, were firmly and adamantly opposed to liquor sales. Churches (predominantly Baptist and Methodist) sponsored "movie nights" at which reel-to-reel films cataloging the evils of drink were screened, followed by rousing temperance lectures and prayer meetings. B. F. Sims, a Guntersville lay preacher, published in the *Advertiser-Gleam* a grim diatribe warning that "whenever beverage alcohol walks in peace and happiness walks out." Echoing an argument made by temperance societies for decades, Sims cautions that "whenever liquor finds lodging in the home it prints an ugly picture—prints frowns on Daddy's face and wrinkles on Mother's brow." Having alcohol in the home would lead to marital discord and divorce, because "when Mr. Boose [*sic*] steps in those ties are broken." A neighborly cocktail could also wreak destruction: "Oh ye bighearted bottle sucker, who gives your neighbor drink, there's woe pronounced against you."

While Sheriff Charlie Grant's political advertisement lacked the hellfire and brimstone of the religious "dry" voters, it nonetheless conveyed the notion that complacency could bring about the ruination of the county. Worried that the antiliquor contingent would stay home from the polls, assuming that what had been would always be, Grant contended (somewhat illogically) that "going wet" would "not only legalize whiskey" but also "bootlegging": "If [the "wet" law] should pass, the liquor would be supposed to be sold only in the state stores, but actually it would be sold in all kinds of places all over the country. And there wouldn't be much the officers could do about it. . . . If the dry law were to be voted out, the lid would be off." Grant needn't have worried. From Boaz to Bucksnort, from Albertville to Arab, and from Grant to Grassy, voters in the 1948 special election came out in force to keep their county dry, maintaining the status quo by a four-to-one margin. But the closest vote came from the county seat itself—in an augury of things to come, Guntersville only narrowly supported the majority, with just 127 votes between the wets and the drys. In one Guntersville polling district, the result was 129 for wet, 132 for dry. One contrarian in the tiny community of Thompson who did not drink or even feel particularly strongly about prohibition voted wet against 106 dry votes, perhaps, as the *Advertiser-Gleam* speculated, just wanting "to be different."

Usually it's difficult to point to one event or isolate one factor that shifts the tide of public opinion in any election. Sometimes a scandal shakes the voters' faith; sometimes private grumbling about an elected official's performance grows into openly expressed dissatisfaction. Most of the people old enough to vote in the late 1940s or care about their sheriff's effectiveness are no longer alive, and, short of criminal indictments, few records or polls exist that give a full picture of how Marshall County residents felt about the job their sheriff was doing. Newspaper articles and editorial pieces could reveal the degree to which constituents approved or disapproved of a sheriff—sometimes inferences can be made by what is not said rather than what is. A common adage among politicians observes that one doesn't really launch a campaign because, in essence, he or she is always running for office, even while in office. In April 1949, nine months before incumbents or new candidates were required to file their intent to seek office in Marshall County, Guntersville's *Advertiser-Gleam* reported a granular account of the sheriff's activities for the previous six months. At the top of the list, befitting the zeitgeist, were arrests made for distilling (9), stills destroyed (43), "gallons of mash destroyed" (6,300), "gallons of homebrew destroyed" (63), and, as a thumbed nose to the bordering counties with their ABC-controlled legal sales, "State Store whiskey destroyed" (428 pints). Other of the sheriff's accomplishments included arrests for "public drunkness" [sic], "unlawful killing a dog," "disturbing religious worship," "seduction," and "carnel [sic] knowledge." For every criminal scenario possible in Marshall County, Sheriff Grant seemed to be the watchman at the gate, exacting justice against murderers, bigamists, speeders, and truants with equal vigilance.

Aside from going undercover to break up rooster fights in Albertville, investigating incidents of domestic violence ("The man had hit his wife a lick up the side of the head"), and running "a tribe of swarthy complexioned people" out of town (the newspaper headline reads, "Indians (or Gypsies) Have Moved On"), most of Sheriff Grant's single term in office appears remarkably tame, without a hint of scandal. Yet the same tide that swept Grant into office in 1946 seemed to have ebbed by 1949. Despite Zeke Boyles's accusation that his challenger was "operat[ing] a pool room in the city of Guntersville" during the 1946 campaign, if individuals or establishments engaged in drinking and gambling in Marshall County, Grant did not hesitate to go after them. Perhaps that was part of Charlie Grant's lack of popular appeal. He appeared to be a true believer, at least in his public persona. As the fifteenth-century monk and poet John Lydgate opined, "You can please some of the people all of the time, you can please all of the people some of the time, but you can't please all of the people all of the time." Mixing politics and law enforcement means that a sheriff can't be too good, or the corrupt machinery of established power factions will grind him into the dust, or too bad, or the indignation of the virtuous will drive him out of office and possibly into prison. Whatever it was, Zeke Boyles had that ineffable something that inspired people's confidence and garnered widespread public support. By 1950, Boyles and Grant were set for another election showdown.

Being out of law enforcement during the four years of Charlie Grant's term must have felt strange to Zeke Boyles. After all, he had begun his official career in 1931 at age twenty-five as a deputy under Sheriff Robert Moody; then he had served as chief deputy under Sheriff Donovan "Dono" Taylor from 1935 until 1939. At age forty-one, Boyles had spent sixteen years wearing a badge, keeping the peace, apprehending criminals, raiding stills, and enjoying the prestige of being the top lawman in the county. But Zeke Boyles was not one to let grass grow under his feet, and he turned the energy and drive that had made him such a formidable politician and sheriff toward running a successful furniture and appliance business in Guntersville. In 1945 Boyles had gone into partnership with Levie and Bains of Albertville, purchasing an implement building next to a mule barn owned by Claud Crain. The idea of a furniture store next to a mule barn seems odd, but the arrangement apparently worked well for Boyles and William T. "Billy" Bains. Offering an array of goods ranging from Frigidaire refrigerators and stoves to sofas and living room furniture to bedroom suites, Guntersville Electric Company thrived in the lake town's rapidly growing business district. In one particularly ambitious promotion, the store offered a free toy stove to "the first 600 little girls age 6 to 10 years who call at the Guntersville Electric Co." in December 1947. Weekly drawings gave patrons who had grown tired of lumpy bedding the chance to win a Restonic Triple Cushion Interspring Mattress, with ads promising "Absolutely Nothing to Buy! No Essays or Themes to Write!" (The latter enticement no doubt appealed to rural customers in Marshall County, where illiteracy rates reached close to 25 percent of the population in the 1940s.) The store also sponsored a city league softball team and a Christmas toy drive for children whose families had fallen on hard times close to the holidays. With his ready smile and general bonhomie, Boyles emerged as a prosperous and civic-minded businessman, remaining firmly entrenched in the public affairs of the town he had made his home.

Despite the store's success, Boyles was still lured by the siren song of his first calling. In April 1950 a notice in the *Advertiser-Gleam* announced the candidates for sheriff in that year's election—the list included the incumbent Charlie Grant, Mack Moss, L. P. Dickson, and, not surprisingly, Zeke Boyles. In anticipation of his candidacy, Boyles had sold his part-ownership of the Guntersville Electric Company in a gesture to convince the voters of Marshall County that he would devote all his time and energy to his elected office. After a primary election on May 2, 1950, the two names on the ballot for sheriff were familiar ones: Charlie Grant and Zeke Boyles. Boyles received 4,074 votes, 524 short of a clear majority over the field, while Grant won 1,842 votes. The campaign ads that appeared in local newspapers during the 1950 sheriff's election cycle lacked the vitriol and personal attacks of the previous election. No one asked what the hell had made Zeke Boyles so mean, at least not publicly, and no one accused Charlie Grant of running any pool halls in Guntersville. Aside from insinuations of political jockeying, both candidates' political advertisements merely encouraged voters to "check the records" of each man's time in office and, above all, to go to the polls. On May 30, 1950, Boyles handily won his third term as sheriff, defeating Grant by a margin of 1,587 votes. Boyles was back.

A photograph of the thrice-elected sheriff flanked by his two right-hand men appeared in the *Advertiser-Gleam* in January 1951. In the center stood Sheriff Zeke Boyles, grinning his trademark confident grin; to his left was Chief Deputy Washington Bennett, tall and bespectacled, looking more like an anxious accountant than a gun-toting county lawman. To Boyles's right was Deputy James Lang, wearing a faintly bemused expression on his broad, plain face, his tie slightly askew. In less than six months, Boyles and Bennett would be dead, and Lang so severely wounded that he would never work in law enforcement again.

# CHAPTER 3

# The Place

Bootlegging wasn't what got Aubrey Kilpatrick killed, at least not directly. When most Americans think of bootleggers, they imagine Jay Gatsby's illicit "drug stores," jazz clubs and speakeasies, and souped-up coupes with hidden trunk compartments zooming along dark Appalachian mountain roads fleeing from revenuers. But the history of alcohol regulation in America, especially in Alabama, is far more complex than the passage of the Eighteenth Amendment to the Constitution in 1919 and its subsequent repeal by the Twenty-First Amendment in 1933. As Daniel Okrent marvels in his book *Last Call: The Rise and Fall of Prohibition*, "How did a freedom-loving people decide to give up a private right that had been freely exercised by millions upon millions since the first European colonists arrived in the New World?" Various national temperance movements, which gained strength and voice in the nineteenth century, pitted their agenda against a nation that Okrent describes as "awash in drink almost from the start." In the early years of the republic, the notion of "temperance" was more of a personal preference, a self-imposed governor on the tendencies toward excess in both food and drink. In his autobiography, Benjamin Franklin listed "Temperance" among his list of aspirational virtues (the very first in his "to-do" rankings), pithily stating, "Eat not to fullness; drink not to elevation." As much as many Americans would like to believe the colonial past to be the paragon of moral restraint and personal sacrifice preceding a subsequent, slow-moving train wreck toward decline and degeneracy, the new nation consumed far more alcohol than modern Americans do today. As Okrent wryly points out, "[F]iguring per capita, multiply the amount Americans drink today by three and you'll have an idea of what much of the nineteenth century was like."

Upon its conferral of statehood in 1819, Alabama became part of a national conversation about alcohol, entrenched both in de facto morality and de jure legality. Established in 1798 and annexed in 1804, the territory of Mississippi was an organized, unincorporated territory of the United States, with the western half becoming the state of Mississippi in 1817 and the eastern half redesignated as the Alabama Territory until it was admitted to the Union two years later. As James Benson Sellers notes in *The Prohibition Movement in Alabama, 1702–1943*, "One of the most interesting of the regulations made by the Mississippi Territorial Assembly was an act passed in 1812 which provided that 'any person elected to serve in the House of Representatives of this territory, who shall, either directly or indirectly, give or agree to give an elector, money, meat, or drink, or other reward, in order to be elected, or for having been elected for any county, shall be expelled.'" Other than the issue of political "treating," the records from the provisional assembly make no other mention of the manufacture, distribution, and taxation of alcoholic beverages and reveal no alterations to existing liquor laws. Such was to be expected, for the early settlers—whether Spanish, French, English, or, eventually, American—had no qualms about the "morality" of drinking. As Franklin espoused, "temperance" was more an issue of behavioral restraint, moderation being the goal in all matters public and private. Excess in either direction was seen as extreme and undesirable; along the spectrum between "sot" and "teetotaler," a comfortably buzzed middle ground was considered the ideal for both social and personal interactions. Yet the problems created by alcohol consumption had always been a cause for concern in America, expressed in coded or often explicitly overt language linked to race and class. In the South, as Sellers indicates, early nineteenth-century lawmakers worried that "certain men and certain groups of men were not to be safely trusted with a strong drink" and pushed for laws that would "limit the sale of intoxicants to soldiers, to slaves, and especially to Indians." By the time Alabama became a state on December 14, 1819, the national foundations for temperance and prohibition movements were already in place, and the unique demographics of the state required an à la carte legislative approach rather than an all-inclusive set of laws concerning alcohol.

While movies, television shows, and other media often depict Alabama as a singular, monolithic entity, the history, settlement patterns, geography, demographics, and cultures of the twenty-second state admitted to the Union reveal a diversity as varied and storied as the nation itself. The Gulf Coast region of Alabama is not the same as the Black Belt, nor is the Wiregrass region the same as the Shoals. Sand Mountain, a sandstone plateau in northeastern Alabama, has its own unique history, shaped by the topography and geology that distinguish this region from the rest of the state. As part of the southern tip of the Appalachian Mountain chain, Sand Mountain for thousands of years was home to various Indigenous tribes; in historical times, Cherokee and Creek villages occupied the area on and around Sand Mountain. Sequoyah, the creator of the Cherokee syllabary, spent his most creative and innovative years in what is now DeKalb County, one of the five Alabama counties whose boundaries are either entirely or partly on the plateau.

Yet even as Sequoyah ingeniously formulated a system for his people to capture in writing their history and culture and to express their desires and protests regarding the future of their ancestral lands, white settlers were rapidly filling up the hills and valleys of north Alabama, pushing out the Native tribes and undergirding the federal removal of Cherokees and Creeks from 1820 to 1850. One of the central counties on Sand Mountain, Marshall County, was created by the Alabama legislature in 1836 and named for U.S. Supreme Court chief justice John Marshall, whose court was instrumental in the enforcement of the Indian Removal Act of 1830. Jackson County, established in 1819, was named for Andrew Jackson, the architect and engineer of the death march known as the Trail of Tears; Blount County, established the earliest of the Sand Mountain counties (in 1818, before Alabama had even been granted statehood), took its name from Governor Willie Blount of Tennessee, who sent Andrew Jackson and his troops to Alabama during the Creek War of 1813–14; DeKalb County, established along with Marshall County in 1836 as part of the land taken from the Cherokees in the unfairly wrought Treaty of Echota, paid homage (in a rather random and generic way) to Johann von Robais, Baron de Kalb, a Bavarian-born Revolutionary War hero, who, by all indications, never set foot in the territory that became Alabama. Of the five Sand Mountain counties, only one county—Etowah, from the Muskogee word *italwa*, meaning "town"—recognizes its native roots in its name.

As the usurped land across north Alabama was declared open for settlement by the United States government, frontiersmen, farmers, and fortune seekers began to move into the area. Most of the types of settlers drawn to north Alabama had different backgrounds and intentions from those who laid claim to other parts of the state. The earliest European settlements in what is now Alabama were in the coastal south, specifically near Mobile, founded by the French in 1702. During the "Alabama Fever" land rush that began during the territorial period in 1817, the population of the new state exploded from just under 10,000 registered (i.e., white) inhabitants in 1810 to over 300,000 by 1830. In the Black Belt region of the state, the fertile swath that stretches across Alabama like a low-slung sash, planters from Virginia, the Carolinas, and Georgia came seeking the fresh, fecund soil where they could plant the cash crop of cotton year after year. Historian Wayne Flynt explains in *Alabama in the Twentieth Century* that many of these settlers were well educated, and many had been government and civic leaders in their native states. They were well-heeled slave owners and became the cotton-growing plantation owners of the Black Belt. They also arrogated and wielded inordinate power in state political affairs for the next century, even though they were a distinct minority population-wise.

Geology begets history. Without access to the Gulf of Mexico and the attendant transportation and trade opportunities, Mobile would have never been noticed by French explorers, much less have grown into the powerful port city it became and remains to this day. Without the Black Belt's preternaturally rich soil and artesian aquifers, the region never would have developed a slave-dependent economy that transformed the land after the Civil War and the Emancipation from the most valuable acreage in America into some of the most economically challenged counties in the state (and, therefore, also in America). Humans want to live where they can thrive, and these desirable settlement locations typically involve plentiful food sources, readily available water, and abundant arable land. Sand Mountain, despite its remarkable natural beauty, was not an area conducive to growing, well, much of anything, at least not as far as the major cash crops of the nineteenth century were concerned.

As noted earlier, "Sand Mountain" is actually a sandstone plateau, a geologic formation where the soils tend to be shallow. Sandstone soils are acidic and low in nutrients. Geological data from the Alabama A&M and Auburn University Extension Service reveals that of all the soils found in Alabama, those found on Sand Mountain are the most ecologically sensitive soils. Anything put on or in these soils, such as septic tanks or animal manures, is subject to leaching toward bedrock and directly into the groundwater sources. The hog and poultry industries that turned this region profitable in the mid- to late twentieth century were only a glimmer down time's telescope when the first farmers began to settle on Sand Mountain in the nineteenth century. These settlers, mostly poor farmers who migrated to northeastern Alabama from the hill country of Tennessee, Georgia, and North Carolina, did not ride the fluffy white wave of cotton production as did other parts of the state. Instead, most of the settlers devoted their efforts to subsistence farming, relying mainly on corn, tomatoes, and potatoes to feed their families. While a few brave souls on Sand Mountain grew cotton, the soil was so rapidly and utterly depleted by this nutrient-devouring plant that many farmers turned from cotton farming to soybeans, which did not exhaust the soil to the same degree. Cotton may have been king in other parts of the South and Alabama, but it did not rule on Sand Mountain.

The people who came to live on Sand Mountain were not solely shaped by their environment; they brought with them their customs, practices, beliefs, and folkways from their native countries, predominantly the rural areas of England, Ireland, and Scotland. Fiercely proud and independent, these immigrants embodied centuries of traditions rooted in opposition to colonization, resistance to aristocratic authority and government control, and fidelity to kith and kin. They also brought with them a contentious legacy of tolerance versus temperance when it came to alcohol. On one hand, the making and imbibing of beer, wine, and distilled spirits was deeply rooted in Appalachian culture, which encompassed an amalgam of English, Irish, and Scottish folkways. On the other hand, especially among Protestants (which comprise most churchgoing southerners), the remnants of early European temperance movements played a central role in influencing attitudes toward drink and drinking. As with most of the nation, stances on alcohol in the South often ran along religious lines, with predominantly coastal-dwelling Catholics in favor and mostly interior-dwelling Protestants against. Even among Protestant denominations, the temperance spectrum shaded more heavily toward Baptists and Methodists. Across the South, Episcopalians are sometimes referred to as "whiskey-palians," and alcohol-related jokes poking fun at other denominations (i.e., Baptists refusing to wave at Methodists in the liquor store parking lot) are a tired but reliable staple of regional humor. Yet relegating the pro- versus anti-alcohol divide in Alabama to religion alone does not take into account complex issues of race and class. On Sand Mountain, perhaps due to the scarcity of a culturally inflective racial "Other" in the mid-twentieth century, social class was the determinant for policies and regulations concerning the sale and consumption of alcohol.

Class and racial prejudices are so often inextricably intertwined, like a malignant tumor crisscrossed by vital blood vessels, that attempting to separate one from the other results in the fatal termination of meaningful analysis. This kind of intersectionality rears its hybrid head in Alabama's long and complicated history with alcohol—where (if anywhere) it should be sold, who gets to drink it, and whether moralism should supersede economic benefits. From the state's foundational beginnings, the provisional legislators of the Alabama Territory wanted to make sure that "slaves, and especially . . . Indians" did not get their hands on "intoxicants," but in the late eighteenth and nineteenth centuries, state leaders and powerbrokers decided that another, perhaps even more subversive population needed to have temperance imposed upon them: poor whites. The unspoken addition of the word "trash" hangs over the phrase, like a suppressed but nonetheless odorous burp. In his 1989 book *Poor but Proud: Alabama's Poor Whites*, Auburn University historian Wayne Flynt sought to define this marginalized group that lacked clear margins. While Flynt's primary goal was not to generate pathos or imbue poor whites with the kind of tragic dignity evoked in Walker Evans and James Agee's *Let Us Now Praise Famous Men* (1941), *Poor but Proud* does address the class-based Great Chain of Being (white) that held sway in Alabama from its inception. Coinciding with the wave of "whiteness studies" explorations that emerged in the late 1980s and preoccupied academia and popular culture through the 1990s, Flynt's book advances the basic premise that prejudicial attitudes and discriminatory laws in Alabama were not entirely racially based but hinged also upon class, or rather, racialized class distinctions.

In the class-based hierarchy of Alabama whites, Flynt points out, the planter class (which he calls the "Big Mules," both in this book and in his seminal 2004 work, *Alabama in the Twentieth Century*) occupied the highest ranks in terms of wealth, power, landownership, and political influence, with affluent merchant- and professional-class whites just below the planters, followed by middle-class whites, and so on. Engaging in a bit of linguistic hair-splitting, Flynt points out that "to the extent that 'poor white trash' had any meaning at all, it described a small residue of people who may be distinguished not only from middle- and upper-class whites but from impoverished poor whites as well." The title of Flynt's book indicates a defiant defense of the nontrashy whites as being "poor but proud," the white equivalent of the noble savage. In 2016, contemporaneous with Donald Trump's presidential campaign and a national reckoning with the discontentment of poor white Americans (J. D. Vance's best-selling 2016 book *Hillbilly Elegy: A Memoir of Family and Culture in Crisis* was one manifestation of this heightened interest in the white underclass), Louisiana State University historian Nancy Isenberg published *White Trash: The 400-Year Untold History of Class in America*. Both Flynt and Isenberg penetratingly examine the prevalence and political manipulation of class identity in America, with Flynt focusing exclusively on Alabama, and Isenberg revealing how southern stereotypes gained traction outside the South.

Race plays an integral role in the power dynamics of class, especially in the South, and the delineating factors that separated the upper and middle classes of whites in Alabama ranged from the intangible and ideological (overt, conspicuous racism among "poor white trash" versus the insidiously veiled racism among the "better" sorts of folks) to the tangible and material (the "virtuous" poor whites kept themselves and their rented property clean and tidy, while "poor white trash" lived in filth and squalor). To allude to characters from Alabama novelist Harper Lee's *To Kill a Mockingbird*, representing the "poor white" league in Alabama were Team Cunningham and Team Ewell, the latter of which must always be the villain and the ultimate loser.

Invariably, one of the tangible and material indicators of being "poor white trash" was drunkenness. Flynt mentions the prevalence of the alcohol-soaked "poor white trash" stereotype: "Refusing to pursue whatever meager opportunities came their way, they were satisfied with a subsistence existence consisting of a bit of corn and whiskey." Conversely, the "poor but proud" whites "believed themselves more religious than the upper class to whom they assigned distinctive sins of affluence: horse racing, gambling, cheating, unethical business practices, materialism, excessive drinking, and idleness." In the southern white pecking order, drunkenness became the dog whistle for "trash," and writers from the antebellum planter class gleaned much comedic fodder in detailing the exploits of social cellar-dwelling poor whites. Flynt cites Alabama writer Daniel R. Hundley, who arranged the chapters of his 1860 book *Social Relations in Our Southern States* according to a descending order of social class: "The Southern Gentleman," "The Middle Class," "The Southern Yeoman," "The Southern Bully," "Poor White Trash," and "The Negro Slaves." All that "poor white trash" seemed to care for, according to Hundley, was "to live from hand to mouth; to get drunk, provided they can do so without having to trudge too far after their liquor."

Middle-class whites in Alabama were undoubtedly conscious of the bidirectional sniffs of disapproval: the amoral wealthy were condemned for the decadence of alcohol consumption, and the "shiftless and idle" poor whites drew consternation for moonshining and bootlegging along with fighting while under the influence. Indeed, the emergence of temperance movements in Alabama was fueled largely by the efforts of middle-class whites, who saw themselves as the gatekeepers of morality, strategically positioned between the profligate rich and the debased poor. According to James Benson Sellers in *The Prohibition Movement in Alabama*,

[S]ome of the opposition [to temperance sentiment] grew out of the nature of the people and their long-established habits and traditions. Most gentlemen of the Old South were accustomed to use intoxicants. They prided themselves on knowing when to quit, but they regarded whiskey as a food and considered ardent spirits an important concomitant of hospitality.

Following this logic, wealthy white men could "hold their liquor," but poor white men, men of color, and women of any color were liable to become unruly, unstable, and dangerous under the influence of alcohol—paternalism at its finest.

Among Alabamians at the turn of the twentieth century, opinions about alcohol consumption and sales continued to split along class lines. The diverse populations of Alabama's largest cities—Birmingham, Montgomery, and Mobile—produced several vocal and influential temperance groups, but for the most part, urban voters tended to vote wet more readily than their rural counterparts. As with the modern opposition to pornography, the push for prohibition created some strange bedfellows. Evangelical Protestants found themselves aligned with bootleggers in the fight against legal alcohol sales, albeit for different reasons. From the pulpit to the piney-woods stills, opponents of government-sanctioned alcohol control made their opinions quite clear. In some dry counties, preachers threatened to read before their congregations the names of those who petitioned to put the wet/dry issue to a vote. Bootleggers in rural communities promoted their wares as "unstamped liquor," indicating that any revenue generated from sales would go straight into the seller's pocket and not government coffers. Thus emerged the curious paradox that kept prohibition alive in the South for so long: a deep anti-authoritarian streak ran parallel to the region's traditionally strong religiosity and cultural conservatism.

Despite Alabama beating the federal government out of the gate where prohibition was concerned—Alabama took it upon itself to enact statewide prohibition in 1907, twelve years before Congress passed the Eighteenth Amendment to the U.S. Constitution—not all Alabamians agreed with this legislation, especially in the southern part of the state. In a 2013 article titled "'Boardwalk Empire' of the South: Prohibition Brought Violence, Corruption to Mobile," Brendan Kirby explains that the port city "was practically in open revolt" against both state and federal laws, and "Bank of Mobile president N. J. McDermott wired legislators representing Mobile County that 'unless anti-prohibitionists win, please give notice that

Mobile is prepared to secede from the State of Alabama.'" The northern counties, however, consistently and righteously stayed dry, particularly the counties that were on and around Sand Mountain. While many residents of Sand Mountain towns did not "agree with drinkin'" and had no interest in purchasing or imbibing, they nonetheless resented the imposition of government controls on what they saw as individual choice. Some in Marshall County did not want their home county to "go wet," fearing that "less desirable" factions might wreak havoc if given unfettered access to alcohol, but many otherwise law-abiding citizens saw no contradiction in belonging to private clubs that served alcohol or traveling to a wet county to purchase alcohol to be consumed in the privacy of their own homes. Marshall County stayed dry until 1984, when Guntersville took advantage of new legislation that allowed municipalities with a population of seven thousand or more to hold a referendum on alcohol sales. The new law went into effect in May 1984, and in July of that year, Guntersville voters approved the legalization of alcohol by a stunning two-to-one margin. But in 1951, Marshall County was still bone-dry, at least on paper, and bootlegging was a profitable enterprise in a dry county.

The place was almost too small for two big men like Aubrey Kilpatrick and Sheriff Ezekiel "Zeke" Boyles. Shaped like a rhinoceros head in profile, Marshall County, Alabama, is a tiny county, the third smallest in a state that ranks thirtieth in size among all states in the United States. According to the 1950 census, Marshall County had a population of 45,090, only slightly more than the number of fans who attended the 1948 Iron Bowl at Legion Field in Birmingham. But within the 623 square miles that comprised this small county existed two different and often competing ways of life. Even the county's governance was divided. Although Guntersville was the established seat of Marshall County, officials in the more populous town of Albertville successfully argued in 1935 that getting down Sand Mountain into Guntersville to conduct business at the county courthouse, especially during the winter when the roads were virtually impassable, posed a hardship for hilltop dwellers, and a second courthouse was built in Albertville. From the beginning of the twentieth century, most of Marshall County's sheriffs had come from Guntersville and its adjacent communities, a fact that made the law-abiding on Sand Mountain feel underrepresented and the lawless bold.

While Guntersville had its own small enclaves on Brindlee Mountain and Georgia Mountain, Sand Mountain stood almost as an island unto itself. As one lifelong resident of the small Sand Mountain community of Horton commented, "Folks on Sand Mountain stayed on the mountain, pretty much. Anything off the mountain might as well have been the moon." Fierce rivalries sprang up, not only among high school sports teams on and off Sand Mountain, but also among civic leaders and business owners. Teenagers from Guntersville taunted their Albertville and Boaz counterparts with shouts of "mountain goats!" while Sand Mountain teens responded with "river rats!" Each faction even formed and propagated stereotypes about the other. Many in Guntersville believed their town more progressive and sophisticated than those up on the mountain, while residents in Albertville and Boaz sniffed disapprovingly at the decadence they imagined must be rampant in a resort town. Despite pockets of overt or covert dissent, however, two forces held sway over the entire county: the sheriff and the antiliquor laws. Aubrey Kilpatrick had run afoul of them both. Bootlegging wasn't what got Aubrey Kilpatrick killed, at least not directly, but it put him in the crosshairs—both figuratively and literally—of Marshall County law enforcement.

# CHAPTER 4

# The Fuse and the Fusillade

The men in the car were nervous, jittery. They knew Aubrey Kilpatrick's reputation. They knew he had a house full of guns and was more than willing to use them. They also had one of Aubrey Kilpatrick's children in the car with them. Maybe the lawmen had no intention of using Billy Kilpatrick as a bargaining chip or collateral or even a human shield, but there they were, close to midnight, approaching the Kilpatrick homestead, which would undoubtedly arouse suspicion, given the elder Kilpatrick's illegal side business.

Even as roomy as the 1950 Pontiac Chieftain was, on this warm May night the car was packed with anxious, sweating bodies. At the wheel was Deputy James Lang; riding shotgun was Chief Deputy Washington Bennett. Behind Lang, in the back seat, sat Sheriff Zeke Boyles, and to his right sat Boaz police chief Leonard Floyd. This particular Pontiac sedan was a popular choice for law enforcement in the early 1950s, although most police forces chose the four-door model to facilitate the transport of prisoners. This car, which belonged to Zeke Boyles, was a two-door sedan with a solid black exterior rather than the customized black-and-white paint job preferred by police departments across the country. The car had neither roof-mounted flashing lights nor any markings to indicate its official use. As the Pontiac turned off Alabama State Highway 168 onto the Kilpatricks' long, curving driveway, James Lang noticed a car sitting slightly off the road with its lights off. Inside the car were fifteen-year-old Billy Kilpatrick and Fred Howard Burns, the son of a neighboring farmer who had more or less moved in with the Kilpatrick family. The boys had been out possum hunting and were returning home after dark, around 10:45 p.m. The lawmen questioned the boys and, upon discovering that Billy was one of Aubrey Kilpatrick's children, demanded that the two teenagers get into the car with them.

The purpose of picking up the boys is unclear—surely Boyles and the others knew that the confrontation with Aubrey was bound to turn ugly, so why put these two boys in harm's way? Perhaps the officers felt that having a Kilpatrick child in the car with them could deescalate any potential conflict, or maybe the men feared that the two boys—armed for the alleged hunting expedition and, like many rural youngsters of the time, already proficient in handling firearms—were positioned at the end of the driveway as lookouts. Either way, Billy and Fred were told to get into the car, with Billy seated in the back and Fred on his lap. The boys' hunting dog rode in the back floorboard, and the packed car left the Kilpatrick farm and returned to Boaz. Again, the motive for this action is unknown. Were the officers planning to question the boys, possibly hoping to frighten them into confessing plans for an ambush or revealing whether Aubrey had anticipated a visit from Boyles because of the events that had transpired earlier in the day? No record exists concerning the information revealed in the short drive from the Kilpatrick farm to the Boaz police station (neither Lang nor the boys recounted these details in their testimonies), but apparently whatever the lawmen found out was enough to cause them to leave Boaz and return to the Kilpatrick property. Before driving up to the Kilpatrick house, the men stopped at a nearby house, at Fred Burns's request, to release the dog.

What happened next splits into two competing narratives. How can one singular, cohesive account emerge when the ones left to do the telling were two traumatized survivors on opposite sides of the law? Trauma, like love, warps the mind a little. Memory is not objective. The human mind is not a video camera or a wax cylinder or even a fairly tidy file cabinet. Even time, that most inexorable factor of human existence, becomes distorted when the brain is flooded with norepinephrine and cortisol, two neurochemicals released when individuals experience sudden, heightened stress. Add shocking violence, physical pain, and intense grief to the mix, and what trauma victims perceive may differ radically, even if the fellow sufferers are active participants in the unifying traumatic event. The subjective tinctures of emotional investment, value systems, and communal identity color memories generated under the least threatening of circumstances; memories formed under duress more often resemble reflections found in a carnival funhouse mirror than exact replications of experience.

Based on the collective testimony of James Lang, pieced together from the three trials in which he served as the prosecution's star witness, here's what the surviving deputy remembered about the events that occurred just before and after midnight on Thursday, May 17, and Friday, May 18, 1951:

As the Pontiac rolled to a stop several yards from the right corner of the Kilpatrick house, Lang could see through a front window that Aubrey

Kilpatrick was sitting at a table, removing his boots, with his wife, Elizabeth, standing across from him. Once he became aware of the car's presence, Aubrey picked up a pistol—his trademark nickel-plated Smith & Wesson .44—and stepped out the front door to confront the men in the car. Lang testified that Kilpatrick said to the men, "Don't get out of that car, or I'll kill you," a warning that apparently went unheeded since one of the officers opened a car door and proceeded to get out. Aubrey then "fired the first two shots. These went into the car." Then Lang asserted that Washington Bennett, the deputy in the front passenger's seat, stepped out of the car and fired one shot over the roof of the car, striking Aubrey center mass. Sheriff Boyles then exited and walked to the front of the vehicle, "where he was shot."

This order of events was crucial to the prosecution's case—if Aubrey shot first, then the subsequent gunfire from the officers was returned in self-defense. None of Aubrey Kilpatrick's bullets hit any of the passengers in the car. The shots that killed Sheriff Boyles and Chief Floyd instead came from Aubrey Kilpatrick's oldest son, James, whom Lang recalled as "approaching from a small embankment to the chimney on the side of the house"; from there, according to Lang, the younger Kilpatrick fired several shots from what appeared to be a rifle. After edging toward the spot where his father lay in front of the house, James then returned to the cover afforded by the chimney "and began shooting again." During Lang's various testimonies he reported that he had heard shots coming from both sides of the house, which implicated tenant farmers Tom Upton and Fred Goble in the shootout. One by one the officers fell after they emerged from the car. Lang, shot through the chest, staggered away from the Kilpatricks' yard and up the driveway toward a nearby house, hoping to rouse its occupants (assuming they had not been awakened already by the bursts of gunfire) and get help. Rescue came, however, in the form of his fellow deputy, as Washington Bennett, also critically wounded but miraculously able to pilot the bullet-riddled Pontiac, pulled alongside Lang and yelled for him to get into the car. Once they arrived at Boaz City Hall, a relatively short drive that must have seemed interminable to the two dying men, an ambulance took Lang and Bennett to Holy Name of Jesus Hospital in Gadsden. Lang survived. Bennett did not.

James Kilpatrick's account of that night is far more layered and complex, chiefly because he was able to share his story in two different time frames: his trial testimonies, which occurred in 1951, 1952, and 1953, and a later first-person narrative pieced together by Boaz author Dana Maria Hill, written and published after Kilpatrick's death in 2009. In *Blazing Guns, Wild Horses, and the Grace of God* (2011), Hill serves as James Kilpatrick's amanuensis, shaping into highly readable prose his retelling of details from his childhood, the events leading up to and occurring on the night of the shooting, his trials and imprisonment, and his release from prison after serving four years of a ten-year sentence. Most of the book, however, belongs to the "redemption arc," which recounts Kilpatrick's postprison life as a husband and father, with special emphasis placed upon his life-altering religious conversion and subsequent years of devout Christian faith and service.

If, as American writer Robert Penn Warren claims in his poem "Wind and Gibbon," "History is not Truth. / The truth is in the telling," then James Kilpatrick's various tellings represent his identity constructs at two different points in his life. During his trial testimonies, James emerges as the dutiful, loyal son, so shocked at the sight of his father's bleeding body in front of the family home that he saw no choice but to take up arms to avenge his father's murder and defend his mother and younger siblings. In *Blazing Guns*, published two years after his death, the narrative reconstruction paints James's life in broad, archetypal strokes: the battle between good and evil, the liberating power of love, the journey from sin to redemption. William Faulkner writes in *Light in August*, "Memory believes before knowing remembers. Believes longer than recollects, longer than knowing even wonders." How James Kilpatrick remembered the events of May 17 and 18, 1951, says as much about how he saw himself—both as a boy and, later, as a man—as his retellings reveal the collective values of his family, his community, and the culture that shaped and defined him.

What lit the fuse that burned through the day and into the night of May 17, 1951? Aubrey Kilpatrick was no stranger to trouble; he had had more than one run-in with the law, sometimes avoiding jail, sometimes not. He had clashed with local law enforcement and state alcohol revenuers over his illegal whiskey sales, and, at times, the liquor he drank rather than sold fueled stomp-and-gouge brawls that landed him in the drunk tank, his anxious wife, children in tow, showing up to bail him out. Call it fate, call it an ominous alignment of the stars, call it the inevitable showdown between two stubborn, territorial men, but whatever the cause, what began as a typical day in the lives of everyone connected to Aubrey Kilpatrick and Zeke Boyles slowly and relentlessly ticked toward tragedy.

The day before, Aubrey and his brother-in-law, Troy Williams, had traveled south to deliver a truckload of ground cornmeal to Florida. It was an arduous trip that took the better part of a day, the pickup truck laden with five- and ten-pound bags of meal and trundling along the two-lane highways that bisected the state, but the market was good, and Aubrey had a wife and eight children to feed, clothe, and provide for. After conducting their business and taking a quick nap in the cab of the truck, Aubrey and Troy drove back to north Alabama, legitimately earned folding money tucked away in their wallets. Aubrey's absence caused little disruption in his family's lives, chiefly because he had raised his sons to manage the farm's numerous tasks. James, Billy, and Harold—ages sixteen, fifteen, and fourteen, respectively—would be up at dawn the next morning, as they were every day at sunrise, to tend to the animals and the fields. James routinely arose without prompting or complaint to feed the horses and bottle moonshine for delivery.

On that particular day, Aubrey had two important reasons compelling him to return home as quickly as possible. First, May 17 was Harold's fourteenth birthday, and while none of the Kilpatrick children ever had what one would consider lavish birthday parties, a special dinner followed by homemade cake would bring the family together in celebration. Second, Aubrey harbored growing suspicions that one of the sharecropping families he had taken on simply weren't pulling their weight. Truman and Burnice Whitehead had seemed like solid folks, hard workers who had fallen on hard times and needed a way to make a living, but it was their twenty-one-year-old son who caused Aubrey considerable consternation. William Whitehead ran with a rough crowd, often bringing his rowdy friends to the small cabin where he and his family lived on the Kilpatrick property. There, far too often for Aubrey's liking, the young men would drink, roughhouse, play cards, and shoot dice, their raucous shouts carrying across the field to the main house. Aubrey was not opposed to such activities in principle, but when the merrymaking cut into work time (and therefore his livelihood), he resorted to shotgun diplomacy to remind his tenants of their obligations and his expectations.

The Whiteheads were not the only workers on the Kilpatrick farm. While not a landowner on a grand scale, Aubrey possessed over two hundred acres, enough land to require help beyond what his three teenaged sons could provide. Itinerant workers and day laborers could assist with seasonal peaks, but, as with many farms large and small across the South, the Kilpatrick farm hosted several on-site working families who occupied shotgun shacks anywhere from a few hundred yards to a mile from the main house. Sharecropping and tenant farming comprised the dominant economic model of Alabama agriculture from the late nineteenth to the mid-twentieth centuries, although both designations, as historian Kenneth E. Phillips points out, are usually grouped together under "tenancy" and difficult to define discretely because the system to which they belonged was nebulously complex. Although generally referred to as "tenants," the two most common forms of these laborers were sharecroppers and cash renters, a subtle but significant stratification. To sharecrop, basically all one had to do was show up with the willingness and ability to work and strike an agreement with the landowner for a portion of the projected crop, usually one-third to one-half of either the harvest or the profits. Cash renting, as the name implies, involved a more formal contract between landowners and farmers, thus giving cash renters a higher degree of economic and social status within a community. Tenant farming reached its peak during the Great Depression, with over 65 percent of all farmers working within the tenancy framework (of which 39 percent were sharecroppers).

Ironically, the New Deal program that was designed to protect and sustain American agriculture during the Great Depression sounded the death knell for widespread farm tenancy. The Agricultural Adjustment Act of 1933 established the Agricultural Adjustment Administration, whose policies sought to subsidize producers of basic commodities for cutting their output. The intentions of the AAA were temporally laudable but perhaps shortsighted, at least for landless farmers: the subsidies and production limits helped restore and stabilize crop prices to pre-Depression levels, but fewer acres meant a diminished need for tenants to work the land. World War II saw the mass exodus of small-scale farmers from the fields, some going off to war, some taking jobs in wartime production factories. The popular World War I song "How Ya Gonna Keep 'Em Down on the Farm (After They've Seen Paree)?" proved to be just as prophetic for veterans of the Second World War. By 1950, tenant farming had decreased to about 37 percent of all Alabama farmers, with sharecroppers making up only 27 percent of all tenants. The industrialization of southern towns and the mechanization of southern agriculture had rendered tenant farming virtually obsolete, but the old ways died hard on Sand Mountain.

Being a cash renter or a sharecropper in Alabama in 1921, 1931, or even 1941 wasn't the archaic aberration it later became. By 1951, however, being a landless farmworker intimated a quixotic resistance to the changes that were transforming the Deep South. Some, even without their own land, stuck to farming because it was the only occupation they knew, clinging to a romantic agrarian ideal of working the soil for one's livelihood, even if that soil belonged to someone else. For others, however, tenant farming was preferable to the organized, industrialized occupations that were taking the place of farming across the South—better to live close to the land, to sync one's rhythms with nature, than with some mill owner's time clock. Besides the troublesome Whiteheads, Aubrey Kilpatrick had several other trustworthy tenant farmers living in rented homes on his land. Of these tenants, two in particular, Tom Upton and Fred Goble, admired their landlord greatly and had earned his trust through hard work and loyalty. They were almost like family, often spending their free time at the Kilpatrick home, sharing meals and the occasional drink from Aubrey's supply of moonshine.

When Aubrey returned from his Florida trip on the afternoon of May 17, Fred Goble had bad news for him. Late April to early May is the optimal time to plant cotton in northern Alabama, and despite Aubrey's repeated orders for the Whiteheads to get seed in the ground, nothing had been planted. Instead of holding up their end of the agreement, Fred told Aubrey, the Whiteheads had been dicing and gambling out at their cabin. Tired, angry, and maybe more than a little drunk, Aubrey decided to take James and Billy to pay the Whiteheads a visit. When Aubrey knocked on the Whiteheads' door, two young men, William Whitehead and one of his friends, David C. Dean, a foundry worker from Gadsden, emerged from the cabin. Heated words turned into threats, the scene quickly escalating toward violence. When William attempted to throw a punch, Aubrey drew his .44 and pistol-whipped the man to the ground, whereupon David Dean rushed in to join the fray. Aubrey fired twice at him, once over his head and once between his legs. Suddenly, guns were everywhere—some of the men inside the house rushed out with shotguns and rifles, and James pointed a rifle through the open window on the passenger side of the truck. With the risk of mutually assured destruction real and imminent, all the men froze in place, a tableau resembling something out of the westerns the Kilpatrick boys loved to watch for a quarter at the Rialto Theater on Saturdays. No more shots were fired, but verbal volleys ensued, with Burnice Whitehead shouting that they were going to call the law, and Aubrey commanding the family to pack up their belongings and get off his land. If they didn't, he warned, the next shots he fired would hit their mark. Aubrey got into his truck, and he, James, and Billy drove away, headed back to their house.

True to their word, the Whiteheads did call the law. Although the Kilpatrick farm sat just beyond the Boaz city limits and therefore outside the town's police jurisdiction, Chief of Police Leonard Floyd went out to talk to Aubrey. As an officer of the law, Floyd could not condone one man brandishing and firing a weapon at another, even if the latter had the reputation for stirring up trouble. Floyd knew from experience the kinds of disruptions the Whiteheads had caused while sharecropping for other landowners in the area, particularly the younger Whitehead's propensity for drinking, gambling, and consorting with shady characters. Best just to let them move on, Floyd told the still-fuming landlord, good riddance to bad rubbish. At that point, the Whiteheads had not sought a warrant for Aubrey's arrest. While Aubrey was certainly no one's ideal of an upstanding, law-abiding citizen, Floyd knew him to be a man of his word, and the two men agreed that if a warrant were issued later in the day, Aubrey could wait until the next morning to go to the police station and make bond. Suppertime was calling, and the day had been long and eventful, to say the least. Aubrey still had one more task before he could rest: two of the drunken revelers at the Whitehead cabin had driven their car through a neighbor's fence after leaving the gathering. Feeling responsible for the damage caused by his tenants, Aubrey had sent Fred Goble to get wire to repair the ruined section. Floyd left the Kilpatrick farm and went home to join his own family for the evening meal, believing the matter settled and peace restored.

Shortly after Floyd's visit, two sheriff's deputies, Washington Bennett and James Lang, drove out to the Kilpatrick farm to investigate the Whiteheads' complaint. The pair decided to split up—Bennett would talk to Aubrey, and Lang would interview the Whiteheads. Lacking a warrant, the two deputies presented their visit as simply a courtesy call, a chance to hear each side of the story and cool enflamed tempers. Regardless of the day's turmoil, the cattle, horses, and chickens still needed tending, so James and Fred Goble went about the evening chores. Billy remained with Aubrey until Bennett asked the second Kilpatrick son to go to the store for cigarettes, even though Billy was under the legal age to both drive and purchase tobacco. The conversation that transpired between the chief deputy and the bootlegger will never be known since both men would be dead in less than nine hours, but according to James Lang's testimonies, Bennett and Aubrey discussed an agreement like the one Aubrey and Chief Floyd had agreed upon, that if a warrant were served that night, Aubrey would go to the police station the next morning and make bond. As James Kilpatrick testified in his second trial, just before he left the yard to go to the barn, he overheard his father tell Bennett, "I won't go to jail with you because of them sorry tenants," to which Bennett allegedly replied, "I won't blame you."

When Lang returned to the Kilpatrick home to pick up Bennett, Aubrey had gone to the barn to help James and Fred Goble. For all involved, the day's work was done. Lang drove Bennett home to Guntersville then returned to his own home in Albertville. But the atmosphere on the Kilpatrick farm was still unsettled. Aubrey sent Fred Goble and James, armed, to guard the barn nearest the house. Another barn had been burned the year before, although not by the Whiteheads. Still, burning a barn struck at the heart of a farm, and Aubrey was taking no chances with a family of vindictive tenants living less than a mile from his own home. As one last precaution for the day, a tying-up of the volatile threads that still fluttered uneasily, Aubrey drove into town to check if a warrant had been taken out for his arrest. E. C. "Celie" Amberson, the night desk manager and radio dispatcher at the Boaz Police Department, informed Aubrey that no warrant had been issued, therefore no bond could be paid at that time. Satisfied that his agreements with both Chief Floyd and Chief Deputy Bennett would be honored, Aubrey made the three-mile trip back to his house, where his wife and children waited to settle in for the night.

What happened to reignite a situation that seemed to have been defused? Did the Whiteheads, independent of any outside influence, simply stew throughout the evening and conclude that they could no longer countenance Aubrey Kilpatrick's assault on their son? Or did Sheriff Zeke Boyles finally see a way to show the bootlegger who was in charge in Marshall County, a power play in an increasingly dangerous game? Whatever the impetus, after a phone call from the sheriff, William Whitehead and his sixteen-year-old brother went to the Boaz police station at 10:00 p.m. that night to find out what they needed to do to get Aubrey Kilpatrick arrested. The sheriff called Deputy Lang and told him to meet him and Chief Deputy Bennett at the Albertville police station; from there, the three men, traveling in Boyles's 1950 Pontiac Chieftain, arrived at city hall in Boaz, where the two Whitehead sons were waiting. The older Whitehead son, the one Aubrey had pistol-whipped, showed the officers a bruise on his neck and described how the intoxicated and irate landowner had fired his pistol twice during the altercation. Since a warrant must be issued by a justice of the peace, Lang and the two Whiteheads made the short drive to R. L. Turner's home at 10:30 p.m. Although the Turner house was dark and its inhabitants asleep, James Lang was a man on a mission, and he knocked on the front door until someone answered. Clad in pajamas and a robe, Squire Turner completed the warrant at his kitchen table, filling in the requisite information and indicating where Whitehead should sign. Since he could not read or write, William simply marked an x over his name. The warrant, penned in Turner's looping Palmer Method script, read as follows:

Before me, R. L. Turner, a Justice of Peace, personally appeared William Whitehead, who, by me being first duly sworn, deposes and says that there is probably cause for believing, and he does believe, that within twelve months before making this affidavit and in said county A. E. Kilpatrick unlawfully and with malice aforethought did assault William Whitehead with the intent to murder him with a gun, against the peace and dignity of the State of Alabama.

When Lang and the Whiteheads returned to the police station in Boaz, Zeke Boyles took the warrant papers from William and tucked them into the breast pocket of his shirt, where they would remain until the coroner removed them.

Three miles from the Kilpatrick farm, Sheriff Zeke Boyles, Chief Deputy Washington Bennett, and Deputy James Lang got into Boyles's car and were soon joined by Boaz chief of police Leonard Floyd, whom Boyles had summoned to ride along with them. They left city hall and drove up State Route 168, the highway dark and devoid of vehicles that late on a Thursday night. As they crested the hill before turning down the long dirt driveway that led to the Kilpatrick home, Lang saw a 1936 Ford Coupe stopped on the side of the road. In the old car were Billy Kilpatrick and Fred Howard Burns, just arriving home after an evening possum hunt.

"What's your name, son?" asked Zeke Boyles through the open window of the car.

"Billy Kilpatrick, sir."

"You Aubrey Kilpatrick's boy?"

"Yessir," Billy replied.

"Then I guess y'all had better ride on to the house with us," Zeke said, less a request than a command. Leonard Floyd stepped from the car to allow the two boys to crawl into the back seat. With its six apprehensive passengers, the Pontiac rumbled slowly toward the Kilpatrick home, its glossy black exterior catching the occasional glint of moonlight through the trees.

Inside the house a single lamp illuminated the front room. Since the small cabin was only a temporary lodging until the new house was finished, little effort had been made to create anything other than the most functional of spaces. Of the eight Kilpatrick children, six were asleep inside the house,

James was out at the barn with Fred Goble, and Billy was wedged between Zeke Boyles and Leonard Floyd in the back seat of the car that was making its way up the drive. Weary after forty-eight hours of traveling, drinking, and feuding, Aubrey dropped into the rocking chair in the front room to remove his boots. He was sick, he told his wife, his head hurt, he didn't feel well, he was going to bed. Just as he had one boot halfway off, he and Elizabeth heard a car, its engine idling down as it stopped in front of the house. Aubrey slipped his foot back into his partially removed boot, picked up his .44, walked through the open door, and made his way down the steps into the yard. Then all hell broke loose.

# CHAPTER 5

# The Aftermath

Imagine the chaos: darkness, trees, uneven terrain, the wails of a grief-stunned wife and the cries of terrified children, the shouts of angry men carrying guns, riot gear, and tear gas. For some of the witnesses and investigators that night, the crime scene may have appeared in staccato bursts, like the popping strobe of a camera flash. Others may have perceived the scene as emerging slowly in blooming chiaroscuro, like a latent image soaking in developer, as frantic law enforcement officials from six counties descended on the Kilpatrick farm, sweeping the property with their police-issue flashlights.

In moments like these, time becomes fluid. Only pictures capture the stark, still spots of time, and *Gadsden Times* photographer Leon Reeves was one of the first members of the media on the scene. He was a twenty-five-year-old navy veteran who had served on a PT boat during World War II, and he later worked for thirty years as a supervisor at the Fort McClellan Army Chemical School. But on that night, May 17 ticking into the small morning hours of May 18, 1951, Reeves held in his hands the instrument that would record crucial evidence for the subsequent trials in which prosecutors sought to convict James Kilpatrick for murder and manslaughter, and defense attorney George Rogers fought to keep his young client from being sent to the electric chair. An avid photographer from the age of nine, Reeves aimed his camera and shot photograph after photograph. With each flash, he showed the world the blood-stained earth where Aubrey Kilpatrick had died just a few feet from his front door, and the zigzagging tire marks where Deputy Washington Bennett, shot in the neck and bleeding to death, managed to maneuver the hulking Pontiac Chieftain away from the Kilpatrick homestead and coax his critically wounded fellow deputy James Lang into the car so that they could get help and medical attention. The photographs that Leon Reeves took that night did not offer the same procedural evidence that forensic analysis or witness testimonies did, but they revealed to shocked newspaper readers and courtroom attendees the extent of the carnage at the Kilpatrick farm. Reeves testified at two of the five trials in which James Kilpatrick was tried for murder, manslaughter, and assault with intent to murder, calmly and professionally describing the images he had taken. While the horror of what Reeves saw through his camera's eye would have made most men tremble, his hand never shook.

Accompanying Reeves to the scene were two reporters from the *Gadsden Times*, young women from different journalistic backgrounds but who shared the byline for the next morning's story about the shooting. Katy Croft, only twenty, had taken a job with the newspaper immediately after graduating from high school in Gadsden. She had started off as a gofer, answering the newsroom telephone and fetching coffee for the reporters and editors. Eventually, through careful observation, perseverance, and sheer talent, she worked her way into a reporting position, covering the crime and city hall beats. Seventy years after the shooting, she recalled the baptism by fire in reporting she had gained from being a conscientious pupil with patient, experienced mentors. She commented, "I learned more from working my way up in the newsroom than most students learn in journalism school."

At about half past midnight on Friday, May 18, Croft received a phone call at her parents' home in Gadsden where she was living at the time, the night desk dispatcher relaying the information about the shooting that had come in over the police scanner and directing her to go to the scene to cover the story. Croft had grown up in Boaz, so the area was familiar to her, but because she was still living at home and did not own a car, her supportive yet protective parents drove her to the Kilpatrick farm, where she met Reeves and reporter Elizabeth "Mimi" Simms. While Croft had come up through the reporting ranks at the *Gadsden Times*, earning her stripes through on-the-job training, Simms had a bachelor's degree from Alabama Polytechnic Institute (now Auburn University) and a master's degree in journalism from the University of Alabama. Regardless of the different paths the two young women had taken, they both found themselves, notepads and pens in hand, ready to put into words the grim details of the Sand Mountain shootout.

Two of the first officers on the scene were Alabama state highway patrolmen E. B. Robbins and A. L. Sisk Jr. When Deputies Bennett and Lang, both barely alive but conscious, had reached city hall in Boaz, the call had gone out over dispatch about the shooting, summoning law enforcement from everywhere within the bandwidth of the police radio. Upon reaching the Kilpatrick farm, Robbins and Sisk were joined by other highway patrolmen, including Lieutenant Roy Bradford. All of the men knew that arrests must be made without delay, so they apprehended every male over the age of ten that was on the premises. Tom Upton and Fred Goble, both tenants on the Kilpatrick farm, were rounded up and taken into custody, as were three of the Kilpatrick sons: James, age sixteen; Billy, age fifteen; and Harold, age fourteen. By the time Bradford arrived on the scene, James, in immense distress and weeping, had already begun to talk. Bradford knew that if any of the suspects, especially James, were taken to the local jail, their lives would be in danger. Tempers were running high—police officers from Boaz, upon realizing that their respected chief had been killed, cursed at Kilpatrick's widow, Elizabeth, demanding to know what had happened and who had fired the shots. Although escaping into the night must have seemed tempting to James, he did not leave the premises. He was, after all, the man of the house now, and he could not abandon his family in the middle of the worst crisis imaginable. Bradford convinced James to go with him to the Etowah County jail, explaining calmly but urgently that James could trust him, that if the boy attempted to flee he would be gunned down by the emotional and no doubt hair-trigger local law officers. While Bradford felt intense sympathy for the frightened boy, especially since he had a son the same age as James, he still had a duty to perform, and he searched James, handcuffed him, and placed him under arrest.

Taking the five suspects—Goble, Upton, and the three Kilpatrick sons—to the Etowah County jail was a smart move. Already a mob was gathering at the Marshall County jail in Guntersville, clamoring for news and demanding justice. The arresting officers, with the suspects all traveling in a caravan of police vehicles, knew that the accused men and boys would be safest in a jail nearly thirty miles away from the scene of the slayings. When asked by a reporter from the *Huntsville Times* about the transfer, Marshall County coroner Howard "Moose" Hardin commented, "We were afraid feeling might flare up when the people learned what had happened." Lieutenant Bradford rode with James but did not question him. Instead, perhaps intuiting that he could trust this man, James confessed to Bradford that he had taken his .30-caliber carbine outside after realizing his father had been shot: "I shot a few times, then I went around to the west side and emptied my gun. I shot a tall man who was holding my brother. I shot Zeke, too." Bradford simply sat silently, letting James talk.

Nowadays it is hard to imagine any suspect willingly implicating himself by blurting out an admission of guilt to a peace officer in the immediate aftermath of a crime, but most people in 1951 were not as immersed in police procedural dramas as Americans are today, much less a terrified, grieving sixteen-year-old farm boy with an eighth-grade education. Miranda rights had not been established in 1951 (*Miranda v. Arizona*, the Supreme Court case instituting the principle that all criminal suspects must be advised of their rights before interrogation, would not happen until 1966), so no one told James Kilpatrick that he had the right to remain silent, although some of the interrogating officers did caution him that anything he said could, and would, be used against him in a court of law. In those fraught moments, Roy Bradford represented the only official James felt like he could trust. Lieutenant Robbins had questioned James after the transport to Gadsden, and the highway patrolman later testified that the boy had been told by his father earlier in the day on May 17 that Sheriff Zeke Boyles and his deputies were "coming after him [Aubrey Kilpatrick]," insinuating that James should be armed and ready in case of a raid. Without legal representation or guardian ad litem to advise him, James told his story to anyone who would listen, and the various officers and investigators were more than willing to let him talk. W. L. Allen, special investigator for the Alabama State Department of Public Safety, questioned James on the morning of Friday, May 18, at the highway patrol office in Gadsden. James voluntarily admitted that he had taken part in the shooting the night before; he told Allen that "strange men" had driven up to his house, shot his father, and then held his brother Billy as a human shield. James also explained to Allen that the gun he had used was a .30 carbine but that he did not know how many shots he had fired.

Perhaps lulled into a false sense of security by Roy Bradford's patient care and steadfast protection, or perhaps exhausted by the previous night's trauma, or perhaps simply wanting to provide his own account of the shootings, James left no doubt in the investigators' minds that he was the one who had killed Sheriff Boyles and Chief Floyd and wounded Bennett and Lang. James did not yet know that Bennett had succumbed to his injuries at Holy Name of Jesus Hospital in Gadsden, only two miles from where he sat in the Etowah County Jail, and that James Lang was recovering from his gunshot wounds in the same hospital. By the time he was booked into the Etowah County jail, James was spent—on the car ride to the jail he had cried, but by the morning after, his grief and terror had been replaced by steely resolve. Later, during the first trial in which James stood charged with first-degree murder in the slaying of Leonard Floyd, Investigator Allen testified that James "showed no sign of fright early the next morning at the Patrol office in Gadsden." Yet James Kilpatrick did not present this face to the world due to a lack of remorse. He was simply doing what he had been raised to do. He had been expected to be a man from the time he could walk. As the eldest son of a strong-willed, domineering, and sometimes violent father, he knew no other way to be.

∞

Across the country, as Americans rose to begin their day on May 18, 1951, newspaper headlines from Marshall County, Alabama, to Oakland, California, to Fort Worth, Texas, to Pittsburgh, Pennsylvania, and all points in between told the story of the gun battle that had taken place on Sand Mountain the night before. In the era before the proliferation of twenty-four-hour cable and internet news outlets, even before the ubiquity of household televisions, newspapers were the preferred purveyors of information in ways that radio and television had yet to master. In a 1951 *Nieman Report, Washington Post* radio station president John S. Hayes warned newspaper editors, "You must be sure that you give coverage to other events which have occurred that day—events, which to you, in the classic tradition of editing, may not seem as important. Unless you do this, you will find the American public looking upon their newspapers as a secondary medium of information where once you had enjoyed some primacy in that field." A prescient warning indeed, but in 1951, local newspapers were the most detailed and reliable source of information about events ranging from the escalating Korean War to a rail disaster in Bryn Mawr, Pennsylvania, to a preseason "baby" hurricane that threatened the Bahamas. On the morning of May 18, the headlines across the front pages of Alabama newspapers proclaimed two attention-grabbing events: on May 17 the U.S. National Security Council had adopted a new policy that committed the United States to support a unified, democratic Korea but not necessarily one brought about by military action and the overthrow of Kim Il-sung; near midnight on May 17, much closer to home for Alabama readers, four men had died in what the *Huntsville Times* described as "a fusillade of bullets."

Newspapers outside Alabama made much of the rural setting with sensational headlines that made the shooting sound like a modern-day Hatfield and McCoy showdown. The *Delta Democrat-Times* of Greenville, Mississippi, trumpeted, "Three Officers Slain in Hills by Feudists." In the *Sapulpa Daily Herald* in Oklahoma, the headline proclaimed, "Four Die in Blazing Mountain Ambush," while the *Californian* out of Salinas, California, offered the headline, "Three Officers, Bootlegger Killed in Gun Battle in Alabama Hill Country." Another California newspaper, the

*Oakland Tribune*, described the event as a "blazing gun battle" that occurred when "the police walked into an ambush in a remote hill country populated by feuding farmers." In North Carolina, the *High Point Enterprise* supplied the particularly dramatic headline, "Four Die as Bootleggers Shoot It Out with Law," and in Tennessee, the *Knoxville News-Sentinel* carried the headline, "4 Killed in Gunfight After Alabama Bootlegger Defies Lawmen." One of the most melodramatic headlines, featured in the *Daily News-Journal* out of Murfreesboro, Tennessee, announced, "Ambushed Law-Men Killed by Lead-Slinging Gang." (The writer of this article must have been especially taken with the phrase "lead-slinging," as he opened with "Three officers and a Sand Mountain bootlegger were killed last midnight when the ambushed law-men shot it out with lead-slinging hill folk in a remote section populated by feuding farmers.") In the articles themselves, Aubrey Kilpatrick was alternately referred to as a "bootlegger," a "farmer," a "saddle-horse trainer," and, perhaps to emphasize Kilpatrick's dual occupations, "a "farmer-moonshiner." Kilpatrick ("a known bootlegger"), his three older sons, and the tenant farmers Upton and Goble emerged as "outlaws" engaged in a "feud" with other sharecroppers "at his place on a lonely country road in the northeast mountainous corner of the county."

Even in Alabama, the newspaper coverage reflected the rest of the state's willingness to scapegoat the residents of Sand Mountain, a place depicted as lawless, backward, and clannish, filled with feuding hillbillies itching for a fight and living in impoverished squalor. The *Huntsville Times* described the Kilpatrick abode as an "old homestead" and a "ramshackle house, located on the Crossville road near the double bridge, three miles east of Boaz." Similarly, the *Birmingham News* characterized the home as "a rundown dwelling." The narrative that took form from these descriptions, in newspapers local and national, fit into many Americans' conceptions of poor southern whites, especially those in the Appalachian regions. James Agee and Walker Evans's *Let Us Now Praise Famous Men* (1941) and Erskine Caldwell's more lurid novels (*Tobacco Road* [1932] and *God's Little Acre* [1933], in particular) had contributed, for better and for worse, to the stereotypes of rural white southerners as either, to use historian Wayne Flynt's phrase, "poor but proud" or belligerent, xenophobic, and lazy. But the divergent and sometimes paradoxical nature of these stereotypes reveals the internal conflict raging within the South as it struggled to define itself in the twentieth century.

At midcentury, perhaps no state exemplified this struggle more than Alabama. On the cusp of New South progressivism yet still deeply mired in racial and economic inequality, the Yellowhammer State vacillated between cutting-edge technological and industrial advancement and retrograde social policy and a stubborn resistance to change. In 1950 German-born aerospace engineer Wernher von Braun had just moved to Huntsville to begin work on the U.S. army's rocket development team at Redstone Arsenal; during the same period, Theophilus Eugene "Bull" Connor served as commissioner of public safety for the city of Birmingham, and George Wallace began his political ascent by serving in the Alabama State House of Representatives. In the northeastern corner of the state, Sand Mountain remained predominantly white and overwhelmingly rural. Even as demographic and social evolution swept other parts of the state, the counties that were entirely or in part on Sand Mountain seemed almost like the land that time forgot. While most people who lived in this area reveled in relative anonymity and isolation from the tumult of modern life, this tabula rasa effect only heightened the tendency for outsiders—southerners and nonsoutherners alike—to project colorful imaginative constructs upon the region.

One word that recurred throughout the newspaper coverage of the 1951 "midnight gun battle" on Sand Mountain—a word that carried profound denotative and connotative implications in the trials that occurred from 1951 through 1953—was "ambush." Both the *Huntsville Times* and the *Birmingham News*, at that time the dominant news outlets for north and central Alabama, used this word in bold headlines: "Four Are Killed in Boaz Battle: Marshall Sheriff, Three Others Die in Ambush at Farm" (*Huntsville Times*, May 18, 1951); "Bloody Gunfight in Marshall: Three Officers Killed in Ambush at Boaz: Farmer they sought to arrest also dead, three young sons, two men held" (*Birmingham News*, May 18, 1951); "Murder Charges Filed for Ambush Killing of Officers" (*Birmingham News*, May 19, 1951). Out-of-state newspapers echoed the ambush angle as well: "3 Policemen, Bootlegger Die in Battle; Alabama Officers Slain in Ambush" (*Pittsburgh Press*, May 18, 1951); "Four Die in Blazing Mountain Ambush" (*Sapulpa Daily Herald*, May 18, 1951); "Bootlegger Ambush Kills Three Police" (*Corvallis Gazette-Times*, May 18, 1951); "Three Officers and Bootlegger Meet Death as Police Walk into an Ambush in Alabama" (*Neenah [Wisc.] News-Record*, May 18, 1951). This small word, derived from the Old French *embuschier*, meaning "to hide or conceal in a bush," was typically associated with military maneuvers, conjuring images of troops concealed in dense foliage or forests, waiting to launch a surprise attack on enemy combatants. Synonyms include "waylay" and "bushwhack," both of which appeared in numerous newspaper articles written in the immediate aftermath of the shooting.

Why did this one word matter so much? It mattered because it shaped public perception and opinion, which in turn affected the narratives that would determine the outcome of the subsequent trials. Outside the region, headlines that contained the word "ambush" to describe the shooting may have simply served as confirmation bias—those inclined to believe the stereotypes about bellicose, trigger-happy mountain men interpreted this news item as reinforcing their existing beliefs about the characters and goings-on in rural southern Appalachia. After all, in the 1940s and '50s, "hillbilly humor" was all the rage, with the antics of the ornery Snuffy Smith appearing in the comic-strip section (also called "the funny pages" or "Sunday funnies") of newspapers across the country. Although the exact location of Smith's fictional home of "Hootin' Holler" was not specified, the denizens of any mountainous region in the southern United States became fair game for the hillbilly stereotype. Snuffy Smith lived in a shack, made moonshine, and was in constant trouble with the sheriff; he also had the propensity to shoot at interlopers, revenuers, and basically anyone who stirred his ire. Making the leap from Snuffy Smith, the fictional cartoon character, to Aubrey Kilpatrick, the slain "farmer-moonshiner" who lived in a "ramshackle house" in an area "populated by feuding farmers," would not have been a far one for readers outside Alabama. For someone in Massachusetts or California or New York or Wisconsin, the funny pages had come to life, but with real bullets and blood.

When the word "ambush" appeared in Alabama newspapers, however, the stakes were higher than just negative publicity, confirmation bias, and the propagation of unflattering stereotypes. George Rogers, the Birmingham attorney representing James Kilpatrick, Tom Upton, and Fred Goble, quickly realized that any potential jurors would be biased from the outset if they had been bombarded with descriptions of the shooting as an "ambush." Besides the May 17 gun battle on Sand Mountain, the attacks led by Chinese forces on South Korean and American troops were the national news items that most frequently included the word "ambush." In 1951 no lawyer wanted his clients associated, if only tangentially, with communists. On June 7 Rogers filed a motion for a change of venue, arguing first and foremost that it was "impossible" for James Kilpatrick "to have a fair and impartial trial in Marshall County," especially since "the newspapers in said County in bold headlines styled the alleged homicide as an 'ambush' and that all of the publicity given the said alleged homicides by the newspapers circulated and published in Marshall County, Alabama, were very unfavorable to the defendant." Rogers emphasized the impact that media coverage of the shooting could have on potential jurors, citing "[g]arbled and unfavorable statements" and "[l]urid and sensational newspaper accounts and certain garbled statements printed in the newspapers." For Rogers to mount his defense of James Kilpatrick, he had to convince jurors that his client was a loyal son avenging his father's murder and protecting his mother and younger siblings, not a teenage outlaw in a "lead-slinging gang," stealthily lying in wait to pick off a carload of lawmen.

Newspapers at home and abroad were not the only sources of information that worried George Rogers. On the morning of Friday, May 18, throughout Marshall and surrounding counties, word about the shooting leapt from household to household like chain lightning. Since most telephones on Sand Mountain were on the party-line system, an excited exchange between two neighbors might as well have been broadcast over the radio. Children at the breakfast table before school overheard details discussed by their parents. Tom Carnes, a retired real-estate appraiser who grew up in the small farming community of Horton just outside Boaz, was sixteen in May 1951. He was riding the bus to school that Friday morning when a classmate of his at Douglas High School boarded the bus and began recounting the gory particulars: the law had gone out to Aubrey Kilpatrick's place, and after one of them had gunned him down in front of his own house, his son James had shot every last one of them. Eighteen-year-old Wayne Smith was awakened early by his mother in their Albertville home, and she whispered to him what she had heard about the shootout so his younger siblings would not overhear. Working men and early risers gathered for breakfast at the Rainbow Café in Albertville and the College Inn in Boaz and gossiped with waitresses about the previous night's slaughter. According to the *Huntsville Times*, "Knots of men, estimated at more than 100, crowded around the side door of the sheriff's office at the Courthouse here today, trying to learn how the bushwhacking was done, and who fired the shots." A Marshall County farmer was quoted as saying, "You read about those things happening elsewhere, but never this close to home. Everyone knew and liked Zeke. I just can't understand how anybody would pull down on him deliberately."

Those not content with word-of-mouth accounts of the shooting went out to the Kilpatrick farm, with nearly a hundred heedless lookie-loos traipsing over the crime scene before the investigators had completed their examination of where the Pontiac had been parked or the bodies had fallen. Not all the visitors came to snoop—sympathetic friends, relatives, and neighbors of the Kilpatrick family showed up to console the grieving widow, provide food and comfort for the five children still at home, and offer legal advice. In Boaz, friends, family, and members of the community rallied around Police Chief Leonard Floyd's widow and two children; in Guntersville, where Sheriff Zeke Boyles's widow was confined to her bed after a leg amputation, supporters, church friends from in town and up on Brindlee Mountain, and members of the Guntersville Lions Club came to express their condolences, as they did for slain Chief Deputy Washington Bennett, who had died from his wounds just a few hours earlier at Holy Name of Jesus Hospital in Etowah County. In Gadsden, James Lang's family waited anxiously for word about the deputy's condition.

At the suggestion of Boaz businessman and political aspirant Dures Thomas, Elizabeth Kilpatrick hired Birmingham attorney George Rogers to represent James, who had by the Monday after the shooting been transferred from the Etowah County jail to the Marshall County jail in Guntersville. While Rogers had made his legal career in Birmingham, he hailed from the small community of Morris in Jefferson County, just north of the city. He knew how people loved to talk, especially when the story was as sensational as this one, and he also realized that wagging tongues all over Sand Mountain could be just as damaging to his case as the incriminating newspaper articles. His motion for a change of venue emphasized the prominence of the victims and the size of the county in which the killings had taken place: "Marshall County is not a large county and the main topic of conversation has been the guilt or innocence of the defendant. Consciously or subconsciously this has inflamed the minds of said prospective jurors that it would be impossible for them to give a fair trial based on the evidence alone. Hate, vengeance and vindictiveness would enter into the thoughts of prospective jurors subconsciously and affect the verdict." Despite Rogers's passionate objection to the trial being held in Marshall County, Judge J. S. Stone denied the motion. A grand jury had already convened on May 25 and handed down three indictments that found James Kilpatrick, "whose name is otherwise unknown to the Grand Jury than as stated, unlawfully, and with malice aforethought," killed Leonard J. Floyd, E. M. Boyles, and Washington Bennett "by shooting [them] with a gun or pistol, contrary to law and against the peace and dignity of the State of Alabama." The first trial was docketed for the end of July 1951, when James would be tried for the murder of Boaz police chief Leonard Floyd.

Before the legal reckoning began, stretching from May 1951 until October 1953, those left behind had to bury their dead. The funerals of all four men—Aubrey Kilpatrick, Zeke Boyles, Washington Bennett, and Leonard Floyd—happened in quick succession within three days of their deaths. The May

24 *Albertville Herald* reported that "[g]reat crowds attended the last rites for each of the victims of the tragedy." The first interred was Washington Bennett, the chief deputy of Marshall County who had been hailed as a hero for driving himself and his fellow deputy, James Lang, to the police station in Boaz despite his mortal wounds. Named for his maternal grandfather, Washington Taylor May, Washington May Bennett had been forty-two when he was killed; he was survived by his wife, a son, and a daughter. Well educated in a time when not many young men from Sand Mountain went to college, Bennett had graduated in 1933 from Georgia Tech, where he was a member of Beta Theta Pi fraternity and played on the freshman football team. After serving in the Coast Guard during World War II, Bennett came home to his wife, Jane, and his two children, Sarah Lou Bennett and William Evans Bennett. Many World War II veterans joined their local constabularies and police forces upon returning home, and Bennett became chief deputy of Marshall County during Zeke Boyles's third term as sheriff. Bennett was no stranger to Marshall County law enforcement—his grandfather, John S. Bennett, had been sheriff of Marshall County from 1880 to 1884. On May 19, less than forty-eight hours after his desperate flight from the Kilpatrick farm, he was buried in City Cemetery in Guntersville.

While Washington Bennett's interment was a relatively quiet affair, Sheriff Zeke Boyles's funeral was a spectacle befitting a slain warrior. The Guntersville newspaper, the *Advertiser-Gleam*, called it "the biggest funeral ever held in Marshall County," with "thousands" clamoring to view the body at the Boyles home as it lay in an open casket on display Friday and Saturday night. On Sunday, May 20, services were held for Boyles in two locations in Marshall County: the first, more formal memorial service took place at First Baptist Church of Guntersville, where three local ministers delivered lengthy eulogies filled with praise for Boyles's law enforcement career and civic commitment as well as humorous anecdotes about his dealings with petty criminals and wayward miscreants. To accommodate the standing overflow crowd, loudspeakers were set up in the church's basement for those unable to squeeze into the main sanctuary. Sheriffs from DeKalb, Etowah, Madison, Jackson, Blount, Morgan, and Cullman counties participated in the rites as functioning and honorary pallbearers, along with law enforcement officers from area towns. After the formal funeral service concluded, a solemn procession of cars and trucks followed the hearse bearing Boyles's body up to Brindlee Mountain.

The long day of mourning and tribute stretched on, with scarcely any part of Marshall County left untouched by the tragedy. In Boaz, two services, only an hour apart, divided the allegiances of the small town. At the Boaz Church of Christ, hundreds gathered to pay their respects to the Floyd family and file slowly past the casket draped with an American flag. Local veterans carefully folded the flag and presented it to Floyd's widow, Opal Annie, and her two children. Just a few miles away, the Double Bridges community prepared to lay Aubrey Kilpatrick to rest in the cemetery at Union First Congregational Methodist Church. Billy and Harold had been released from custody and joined their mother and siblings, but James was not allowed to attend the funeral. Two deputies brought him, in wrist and ankle shackles, from Guntersville to Boaz to view his father's body and say his goodbyes before the service began, a small kindness in itself. Elizabeth Kilpatrick and her children would be able to move into their new house once the crime scene investigation was declared complete at the old cabin, and many friends and neighbors came to help carry furniture and other items the short distance to the new dwelling, although more than a few came out of morbid curiosity to see what evidence remained of the bloody gun battle. After Memorial Day, a granite stone marked the place where Aubrey Kilpatrick was buried in the Union Church cemetery, bearing not his legal name but the one by which he was known throughout the community: "Aurbie E. Feb. 22, 1912. May 17, 1951." His widow, Nellie Elizabeth Pankey Kilpatrick, would not join him there until September 3, 1990. James returned to his cell at the Marshall County jail in Guntersville to await a bond hearing and the convening of the grand jury. In Albertville, James Lang convalesced at home after his release from Holy Name of Jesus Hospital in Gadsden. He had understandably had enough of law enforcement, opting to resign as deputy and make use of his G.I. Bill funding to attend college. He could not walk away entirely, though, since he was to be the star witness—the "lone survivor," as the newspapers called him—in the forthcoming trials.

For the families involved, another kind of survival began. As supportive and generous as the people of Marshall County had been to the widows and children of the slain men, nothing could allay the inescapable sorrow, the mounting bills, the dwindling finances, and the fears about an uncertain future that each widowed mother felt when her children awoke crying from nightmares ("I dreamed somebody shot my daddy"). The judges, the lawyers, and the juries were all men, and inasmuch as these men would decide James Kilpatrick's fate, two women—one James hadn't met before that year, and one he had known his entire life—would sustain him through that long, hot summer and beyond.

CHAPTER 6

# The Women

The summer of 1951 was one ripe for young love. On radios across America, in city apartments and country farmhouses, in cars cruising the Miracle Mile in Los Angeles and parked on various lovers' lanes in Anywhere, USA, Tony Bennett crooned about the song in his heart "because of you." Rosemary Clooney saucily invited suitors to "come on-a" her house for some presumably illicit candy. Patti Page warbled about dancing with her soon-to-be treacherous darling to the "Tennessee Waltz." The idylls of teenage romance permeated the airwaves and silver screens of a nation only five and a half years removed from a world war and poised on the brink of different, longer lasting wars, both abroad and at home. By the end of 1951, President Truman had dramatically increased the American military presence in Korea, and Paul Robeson and William Patterson had submitted a petition from the Civil Rights Congress (CRC) to the United Nations titled "We Charge Genocide: The Crime of Government Against the Negro People."

But in north Alabama, even as young men were being deployed to northeast Asia and concerned citizens in rural towns formed anticommunist leagues, most of the young people on Sand Mountain were living much as their forebears had lived, tied to the land and molded by the rhythms of agrarian and religious life. The front pages of Marshall County newspapers told of church attendance and gatherings, visits by relatives, and 4-H and Future Farmers of America competitions. The eternal cycles of courtship and marriage were also documented in these newspapers: who brought whom to church in a public display of romantic intentions, engagement announcements, detailed descriptions of young brides' wedding dresses, and who served the punch and cookies at receptions in church fellowship halls. Local newspapers such as Guntersville's *Advertiser-Gleam*, Albertville's *Herald*, and Boaz's *Leader* also published notifications of what movies were playing at area theaters, one of the few entertainment venues in these small

Alabama towns where couples could go on dates aside from the ubiquitous church picnics, tent revival meetings, and school functions. The Rialto Theater in Boaz, the Carol and Princess Theaters in Albertville, and the Marshall and Shady Side Drive-In theaters were popular teen hangouts on Sand Mountain, but in July 1951 an event even more compelling than Olivia de Havilland's romance with Montgomery Clift in *The Heiress* drew townspeople of all ages to the Marshall County Courthouse in Albertville, including fifteen-year-old Orbra Ann Scott, affectionately known as "Orbie Ann" by her family and friends: the trial of seventeen-year-old James Kilpatrick for the murder of Boaz police chief Leonard J. Floyd.

Ann Scott was a delicate, slender girl with what her eventual husband, James Kilpatrick, would call "the most beautiful blue eyes in creation." The only child of Orbie "Orb" and Pauline "Tiny" Scott, Ann was a student at Crossville High School and, like many of her peers, spent her time working at various shops, helping with household chores, and dreaming of meeting a handsome, hardworking boy with whom she would eventually build a home and a family. She had heard about the shooting that had taken place at the Kilpatrick farm in May of that year, but like many people on Sand Mountain, she and her family did not think of young James as a murderer; they considered his actions wholly justified, albeit tragic. Only seventeen years before, Huey Long of Louisiana had declared every man a king, and for many on Sand Mountain, James Kilpatrick was a prince defending the family castle from intrusive government interlopers.

The end of July 1951 was not historically hot in northeastern Alabama, but it was July in Alabama, a time of year that led local wags to comment that the humidity was so high that the only way one would know it had rained was if the sidewalks turned dark. In an era when few buildings had central air-conditioning, the atmosphere inside the Marshall County Courthouse in Albertville was undoubtedly stifling and oppressive. The courtroom in which the proceedings took place was designed to seat approximately two hundred spectators, but as the trial began, this capacity was far exceeded as sweaty, church-fan-waving locals practically sat in each other's laps and craned their necks to see over the people seated in front of them. The *Advertiser-Gleam* speculated that "the crowd was one of the biggest that ever came to a Marshall County trial" and "would have filled a room several times as big as the Albertville courtroom." Once the bench seats were jam-packed, other spectators lined and leaned against the courtroom walls throughout each day's testimonies. Attendees from near and far stood and sat in the halls and stairways, hoping to catch glimpses of the accused and various witnesses. The *Albertville Herald* noted that "several hundred people" milled about on the courthouse lawn, some spreading blankets out on the grass and unpacking baskets and paper sacks of food brought from home. Enterprising local vendors sold cold drinks and sandwiches to the people gathered around the courthouse; when some boys tried to scale the brick wall to better hear the testimonies, two of the courthouse windows had to be nailed shut, which no doubt made the temperature inside the courtroom virtually unbearable. It was almost as if the circus had come to town, and Marshall County's teenagers flocked to the venue like Hank Williams was giving a free concert.

At that time, Ann Scott did not know James Kilpatrick. She attended high school in Crossville, which was roughly twelve miles from Boaz, while James had stopped going to school after the eighth grade. Leaving school was not uncommon among children raised in farming communities, and boys often ended their formal education upon reaching puberty, when their strength and endurance made them invaluable field hands. Being the oldest of eight children, James bore the lion's share of the work on the Kilpatrick farm, particularly when his father was on moonshine runs up to Tennessee. James was a bright and personable boy, a merry prankster who made friends by offering children in the Double Bridges community rides to and from school in a wagon pulled by a large goat. But he was not, in the modern parlance, academically inclined, so he did not mourn his departure from readin', writin', and 'rithmetic when he was fourteen. Ann, on the other hand, was a shy and studious girl who went on to graduate from high school in 1953. She was a member of Crossville High School's Library Club for four years and sang in the glee club during her senior year; the quote that accompanies her senior picture in the 1953 *C'Vala* reads, "Great thoughts come from the heart."

Her heart was not what led Ann Scott to the Marshall County Courthouse in July 1951. As she reminisced nearly seventy years after James's first trial, "My friends and I, we were just a bunch of nosy teenagers. We wanted to go see what everybody was talking about." Surely the buzz about the shootout and the local boy standing trial for murder was enough to enthrall almost everyone in the community, but the person who first captured Ann's attention was the thirty-seven-year-old mother of eight with the haunted and haunting expression on her face who sat in the courtroom and moved among the crowds outside after the day's proceedings were over. Elizabeth Pankey Kilpatrick had the world on her shoulders: newly widowed with a son accused of killing three officers and seriously wounding a fourth, two other sons caught up in the sweep of arrests that followed the shooting, a young daughter who found herself assuming adult caregiving duties at the tender age of twelve, and four children under the age of ten still suffering the trauma of the violence that took place at their home back in May.

Barely afloat in a sea of troubles, Elizabeth was nonetheless a constant and conspicuous figure at the courthouse in Albertville for each day of that first trial and all the trials that followed. Not only was she a grieving widow and mother of the accused shooter, but she was also a witness to the event and gave testimony on James's behalf, never wavering in her assertion that one of the officers had fired first and that she had not seen James during the exchange of gunfire that followed her husband's fatal gunshot wound. With eight children ranging in age from seventeen years to eighteen months, Elizabeth loved James with the ferocity reserved for firstborn children. He was her laughing boy, her funny pal who drew people to him with his humor and warmth, her most ardent defender and protector, especially when his father was away on business or at home but deep in the bottle. James may have been standing as a man in a court of law, but he was, in his mother's eyes, still a chubby toddler sitting astride a pony and learning to ride almost as soon as he could walk.

On one of the days Ann Scott was able to sit among the throng of spectators in the courtroom, she could not tear her eyes away from the tall, dark-haired woman who seldom smiled, often wept, and carried herself with a tragic dignity born of immense sorrow and suffering. Since James was not called upon to testify in the first trial, Ann's only glimpse of him was of his back as he sat at a table at the front of the courtroom with his defense attorneys, George Rogers of Birmingham and John W. Brown of Boaz, head bowed in murmured conversation as a parade of witnesses took the stand. After court was adjourned for the day, Ann approached Elizabeth Kilpatrick to offer her condolences and encouragement. Elizabeth was charmed by the kindhearted, pretty blonde, commenting that what would truly lift James's spirits would be a letter from Ann to him in jail.

So, Ann wrote to him. Having been denied bond, James remained in the Marshall County jail in Guntersville, and while jail is never an ideal or desired location, James's time there was particularly harrowing. He was off the mountain, miles away from the community that sympathized with and supported him. Guntersville was enemy territory for the Kilpatricks— Sheriff Zeke Boyles and Chief Deputy Washington Bennett had been respected and admired by many in the close-knit lake town, with families who were grieving their loss and law officers who wanted justice and revenge for the untimely deaths of their fellow enforcers. James spent his seventeenth birthday behind bars, just ten days after the shooting. The guards did not actively abuse or assault him; instead, they played a long game, using more subtle ways to make James pay. Instead of providing three meals a day, the jailers served him just one meager portion daily with a glass of hot water on the side. They left James's cell door unlocked, not out of any generous impulse or trust but in hopes that he would try to escape so they could shoot him.

As the summer heat intensified, James roasted in his small cell, often soaking a towel in the toilet bowl and draping it over his head and shoulders to cool off. He dreamed of hot biscuits slathered in gravy and cool wind in his face, the bustling activity of the farm, the antics of his seven siblings. He missed his family, especially his father, whose funeral he had not been allowed to attend. He replayed in his mind the events of May 17, trying to focus on the details he knew he would inevitably be asked to recall when he testified in court. He imagined how different his circumstances would be if the altercation with the troublesome tenant farmers had never occurred, if that large, black car had never pulled up in front of his house, if the sheriff had simply accepted Aubrey Kilpatrick's verbal promise to pay his bond on Friday morning. James's unlikely savior was the new sheriff of Marshall County, Jesse Camp, who had been appointed to the office by Governor Gordon Persons a week after Boyles was killed. When Sheriff Camp visited James at the jail in Guntersville, he was shocked and incensed at the boy's condition. When James was booked into custody in Gadsden on May 18, he weighed around 120 pounds, but by the end of the month, his weight had dropped below 100 pounds. Starved, kept in virtual isolation, taunted by the guards, and weakened into immobility and listlessness, James thought he was going to die, but Camp took pity and demanded that James be properly fed and clothed. Camp also made sure James received potable water, a clean blanket and pillow, and a haircut. While the new sheriff may have saved James's life during those long, numbing days in the county jail, Ann Scott was the one who sparked his desire to live.

One Sunday in the fall of 1951, Elizabeth Kilpatrick made her customary visit to the jail to see James, but on this particular day she was accompanied by the young woman whose letters had become a lifeline for James. The author of those treasured letters stood outside his cell door, a flesh-and-blood girl, hope incarnate. Suddenly, James felt self-conscious. His skin, usually infused with health and color from all the time spent outdoors farming and riding horses, had become pale and sallow; his normally wiry but muscular frame was gaunt and emaciated. The door to his cell was solid steel with a small opening through which food and bedding could be passed, and James was glad that all Ann Scott could see of him were his eyes. He looked into her blue eyes, and he was lost—or perhaps found.

Today, the notion of love at first sight evokes both wistful longing and cynical scorn. Twenty-first-century skeptics could easily psychoanalyze what engendered the immediate, intense attraction between these two teenagers. Ann Scott was not only clean, well groomed, and polite; she was also lovely to such a degree that she could have graced the cover of *Seventeen* magazine or caught a film scout's eye at the Schwab's soda counter in Hollywood. She was a nice girl, a good daughter from a respectable family, the kind of young lady who did not go out with bootlegger's sons. However, James was not the archetypal bad boy, despite his father's reputation and illegal dealings. While the hardscrabble life of farming, bootlegging, and conforming to his mercurial father's demands and expectations may have toughened James into a caricature of rural southern masculinity, as he sweated in that tiny, bleak cell, James was no doubt traumatized, frightened, desperately lonely, and uncertain about his future.

Regardless of the numerous complex psychological reasons that might explain why James experienced this profound epiphany, what transpired between him and Ann during that first meeting was the same powerful emotional response that poets, playwrights, novelists, and lyricists have written about for millennia. Even though James had probably not studied any Shakespeare during his brief, obligatory stint in school, he would have felt the thrill of recognition if he had read Romeo's praise of Juliet's eyes: "... her eye in heaven / Would through the airy region stream so bright / That birds would sing and think it were not night." Shakespeare also wrote that "the course of true love never did run smooth," and this sentiment would have struck a chord as well in James Kilpatrick. By Thanksgiving of 1951, he had been convicted of second-degree murder for the slaying of Sheriff Zeke Boyles and sentenced to seventeen years in prison. And Alabama's judicial system was not through with him yet, not by a long shot.

The love story of Ann Scott and James Kilpatrick may have had an unlikely and unconventional beginning, but one obstacle that they did not encounter was resistance from Ann's parents. The idea of a bright, obedient young girl going to her parents and saying, "I've been writing letters to the boy who's in jail for shooting the sheriff, the police chief, and two deputies, and I think we're in love" would certainly quiver the antennae of most twenty-first-century parents, but Orb and Tiny Scott, like many on Sand

Mountain, did not see James as a ruthless criminal who had committed cold-blooded murder. Several members of the Boaz community, including ministers, Sunday school teachers, neighboring farmers, and business owners, had come forward to testify to James's good character, praising him as a dutiful and loyal son, a hard worker, and a protective big brother to his seven siblings.

In a recent reminiscence, Ann Scott Kilpatrick recalled that although James helped his father procure, bottle, and sell Tennessee moonshine to thirsty customers in a dry county, James "never had a taste for liquor" and did not imbibe throughout his life. "The closest James ever came to being drunk," Ann laughed, with a twinkle in her bright blue eyes, "was from smelling the fumes when he was pouring it into the bottles." Paradoxically, the Baptists and Methodists in the Double Bridges community may have openly denounced the evils of drinking alcohol, but when it came to private consumption and even bootlegging, they were willing to look the other way. While Orb and Tiny Scott may have secretly worried about their daughter's blossoming romance with a boy no doubt headed for prison, they never expressed any misgivings. Instead, when James was eventually released from jail on bond in May 1952, a year and a day after the shooting, the Scotts drove Ann to a celebratory gathering in James's honor out at the Kilpatrick farm. Hundreds of friends had turned out to welcome James home, the makeshift tables groaning with food and the sounds of laughter and good-natured back-slapping floating through the clean Sand Mountain air.

As thrilled as James was to be reunited with his family, his father's absence saddened him and reminded him of his mother's burdens as the head of a teeming household. The outbuildings slumped with neglect; weeds sprouted among the untended crops. But his heart lifted at the sight of Ann, standing bashfully at the edge of the boisterous crowd. As the well-wishers began to drift away, James told his mother that he wanted to go to the Scotts' house to pay his respects—after all, like any boy of that era and place, James knew that one of the most important rituals of courtship was calling on a young lady at her parents' home and meeting her father and mother. Whatever anxieties they may have had about this young man's future, the Scotts welcomed him into their home and, as Ann remembered fondly, "treated him like the son they never had." Sitting in the swing on the sun-dappled porch, holding hands, and occasionally sneaking glances at each other, Ann and James felt like any other teenage couple, the weight of time and troubles temporarily suspended in the glow of their newfound love.

Although James had already been convicted of second-degree murder for killing Sheriff Boyles, he still had to stand trial for the deaths of Leonard Floyd and Washington Bennett. His third trial, which began on January 28, 1952, had abruptly ended on January 30 with the declaration of a technical mistrial after his attorney, George Rogers, suffered severe injuries in an automobile accident and was unable to represent his client. A fourth trial was on the docket for July. Despite the cloud of legal proceedings hanging over him, James attempted to carry on as normally as possible, taking a job driving cars to an auto sale and going on dates with Ann. He was by no means free, but he made the most of what freedom he had. At the end of Sunday dinners at the Scott house, James would slip a five-dollar bill under his plate as a gesture of appreciation for Tiny's home-cooked meals.

James basked in the love and attention the Scotts lavished on him, finding a haven that sheltered him from the dread of his impending trials and the cares of helping his mother and siblings survive. Like the other teenagers in Boaz, Ann and James went to movies at the Shady Side Drive-In and the Rialto Theater, and they stopped at the College Inn in Boaz for burgers and shakes. Ann Kilpatrick remembers "getting some hard looks" from the occasional Boaz town-dweller when she and James went out in public— after all, here was the young man who had, without question, shot and killed the town's former chief of police, and the new chief, J. C. Sanders, had been on the job only a year when James was freed on bond from the Marshall County jail. From the outside looking in, James and Ann's courtship must have seemed like the typical teen romance, two attractive young people obviously smitten with each other. But apart from his tender affections for Ann, inside James was a roiling cauldron of anxiety and worry, for his sweetheart was not the only woman who occupied his thoughts during those tenuous months.

∞

A photograph of Nellie Elizabeth Pankey Kilpatrick taken in the late 1920s shows a young girl on the brink of womanhood with an oval face and large, expressive eyes. Her dark hair, center parted, is pulled away from her face, and she seems shy (if not a little skeptical) about having her picture taken. While not exactly a glamorous flapper, Elizabeth looks like many young women of her time, but her life was quite different than, say, Zelda Sayre's or Tallulah Bankhead's. Born in 1913, Elizabeth and her family moved from Catoosa County, Georgia, to Etowah County, Alabama, where they worked as tenant farmers close to the town of Sardis. Little is known about her life until she married Aubrey Evelyn Kilpatrick on December 16, 1932. Aubrey and Elizabeth welcomed their first child, James David, on May 27, 1934, and three children followed in quick succession: Billy Joe (1936), Harold Elvin (1937), and Jeretta Ann (1938). After a brief childbearing hiatus, Elizabeth gave birth to Russell (1945), Lyndall (1947), Jettie Faye (1948), and Daniel Columbus (1950). Later generations of the Kilpatrick family would refer to the siblings as the "First Four" and the "Second Four," with a span of sixteen years separating the oldest and the youngest of Aubrey and Elizabeth's children.

Like many farming families of that time and place, the Kilpatricks considered their large brood not only a blessing but a labor asset as well. While certainly not wealthy or even part of the genteel middle class of Marshall County, the Kilpatricks were hardly impoverished—Aubrey owned over two hundred acres and was able to not only hire itinerant workers as needed but also provide housing and equipment for several long-term tenant farmers. Unless widowed or abandoned, few women were heads of households, and the division of labor within nuclear families traditionally dictated that the patriarch controlled the family's finances while the women managed the domestic affairs. Life on a farm was grueling and demanding for everyone involved. Agrarian life has its own rhythms, mercilessly requiring constant obeisance from the humans who depend on the land's bounty. At sunrise, cows needed milking, and eggs had to be gathered from chicken coops. All the living creatures had to be fed, a task typically performed by the women of the household. Sometimes biscuits, bacon, dried salt pork, and cornbread would be prepared in the morning and left on the kitchen table all day for intermittent grazing, a cloth laid over the plates to protect the food from flies. There were crops to be planted, tended, and harvested, and, in the Kilpatricks' particular case, moonshine to be bottled and sold.

The life of a farm wife in rural north Alabama in the first half of the twentieth century might seem shockingly retrograde or perhaps even primitive to twenty-first-century Americans, conditioned as most people are to expect a 1950s housewife to be vacuuming the carpet of her immaculate home while wearing a smart dress, kitten heels, and a string of pearls. A tube of lipstick from the local Woolworth's might be the extent of a farm wife's cosmetics collection. The "foundation garments" popularized by the era's hourglass-shaped film stars were not practical for the sheer physicality of farm life—who would want to bother with a girdle while trying to simultaneously cook enough food for ten people, scald and can vegetables, wring a chicken's neck, or snatch up a wayward child? While some young women from rural areas in Alabama left home to attend college, usually at predominantly or exclusively female institutions such as the State Teachers College in Livingston or Judson College in Marion, few sought education beyond a high school diploma. On Sand Mountain, girls were more likely to finish high school than boys, but the same principle often applied to the former as to the latter: help was needed at home and in the fields. Most young women fully expected to marry in their teens, and an unmarried woman in her mid- to late twenties was often derided as a "dried-up old maid."

Providing a full and faithful account of Elizabeth Kilpatrick's struggles is tricky, especially the tragic turn her life took after May 17, 1951, because the stereotype of the long-suffering, self-sacrificial mother has been a staple of folk, gospel, bluegrass, and country music for decades. It's like trying to drive a car down a well-traveled dirt road—the wheels can slide so easily into the ruts and grooves worn by other travelers. From the Carter Family's "Can the Circle Be Unbroken" to Jimmy Dean's "I.O.U." to Merle Haggard's "Mama Tried," songs about a mother's tireless devotion and unconditional love (even when the thankless and rebellious children ended up in prison) were so popular that in 1975, songwriter-satirist David Allan Coe turned all the customary tropes on their heads in "You Never Even Called Me By My Name," playing a lyrical shell game by incarcerating Mama and having her drunken son drive his pickup truck in the rain to collect her. Aside from Coe's comic subversion, every southern mama is a saint, either praying for the wild child who turns out to be the only hell she ever raised or lying awake at night listening for coughs or creaking floorboards.

Yet, as with many stereotypes, there is a kernel of truth behind the clichés. Part Victorian angel in the house, part daughter of Eve, a rural southern matriarch was expected to sublimate any metaphysical or material desires of her own for the sake of her husband's and children's needs. Pulitzer Prize–winning Alabama writer Rick Bragg wrote lovingly but with unflinching honesty about his mother's life of privation, first from being married to a man who spent "years drinking more whiskey than water," and then from trying to raise three boys and make ends meet after that man walked out the door. In his 1997 memoir *All Over but the Shoutin'*, Bragg writes, self-effacingly, that his book "is not an important book," that "anyone could tell" the stories he tells:

Anyone who had a momma who went eighteen years without a new dress so that her sons could have school clothes, who picked cotton in other people's fields and ironed other people's clothes and cleaned the mess in other people's houses, so that her children didn't have to live on welfare alone, so that one of them could climb up her backbone and escape the poverty and hopelessness that ringed them, free and clean.

As Bragg describes his mother, the scaffolding of clichés falls away, revealing a real woman driven by hardship and hope to give her children the opportunities she never had. For women like Margaret Marie Bragg, the hard times came about incrementally, like the proverbial frog in the gradually heating pot. For Elizabeth Kilpatrick, her life changed suddenly and radically overnight. Her man didn't walk out on her, but he was gone all the same.

While Aubrey Kilpatrick may have been a proud peacock in full plumage, Elizabeth, although strong willed and fiercely protective of her home and children, was content to be the less conspicuous peahen. She treasured her reputation as one of finest cooks in the Double Bridges community, and she could ride a horse just as capably as any man. The sheer physical toll of multiple pregnancies and births, especially in a time when prenatal care was nonexistent and most children were born at home, had diminished some of her youthful vigor, but a woman in her place and time with her responsibilities did not get to lie abed with the vapors. She may not have known where all her children were all of the time, and on occasion, extra children from neighboring farms showed up just in time for dinner. One frequent visitor to the Kilpatrick home, a boy named Fred Howard Burns, eventually moved in to live. His mother was terminally ill and staying with relatives, and his father drove a taxi, often working at night. Unable to care for his son, the elder Burns asked Aubrey and Elizabeth if Fred Howard could reside with them. There were no agencies involved or custodial agreements drawn up—Fred Howard simply brought a few belongings, including his gun and his dog, and melded into the multitude of Kilpatricks.

In the spring of 1951, the Kilpatrick family anticipated two significant events: they were preparing to move into a new house, and Elizabeth was expecting a ninth child. The youngest child, Danny, had just turned one in January of that year; the next youngest, Jettie Faye, was three years old and had been born deaf. Despite the efforts of one of Alabama's most remarkable women, Helen Keller, to raise awareness about the sensory impaired, early education for differently abled children was unavailable on Sand Mountain, in part due to the area's poverty and geographic isolation, but also because of the widely held opinion that home was the best place for all children, regardless of the degree to which they could see, hear, walk, or talk.

The descriptors during that time may seem jarring to modern ears: just as "idiot," "imbecile," and "moron" were once clinical terms used to describe a specific range of intellectual abilities, "crippled," "hard of hearing," and "dumb" were deemed acceptable expressions for someone whose physical abilities fell within a certain range. An article in the May 3, 1951, issue of the *Albertville Herald* told the inspiring story of a young man who, despite being unable to hear or talk, was the first deaf Alabamian to reach the solo stage of flying, had earned his private pilot's license, and was working toward a degree in aeronautical engineering at the University of Alabama. The headline read, "Deaf and Dumb Makes Good Record at University." Private flying lessons and a college degree were not in the cards for Jettie Faye Kilpatrick. For most farm children on Sand Mountain, formal education was aspirational at best, completely disregarded at worst. A child who needed instruction beyond the most rudimentary basics was deemed better off learning domestic skills or a trade. In 1951 Jettie Faye was only three, so she was still safely ensconced within the protective cocoon of her large and loving family.

Elizabeth Kilpatrick knew the man she had married had rough edges that no amount of gentleness could smooth. Perhaps that was part of his charm—he was brash and swaggering enough to be considered a man in full; he was just vain enough to cut a dashing figure without seeming like a backwoods fop. Like the ungovernable horses he preferred, Aubrey could be erratic and capricious. Although husband and wife worked alongside each other on the farm and in the bootlegging business, there were spheres that each controlled. Aubrey managed the land and the tenant farmers and sharecroppers who cultivated their allotted acreage; he made the runs to and from Tennessee to get the moonshine. Elizabeth tended to the children and oversaw the cooking and cleaning, with the oldest daughter, Jeretta, learning at her mother's elbow the duties that would be expected of her when she eventually married. If there was a conflict with a rival bootlegger or one of the sharecroppers, Elizabeth may have listened to her husband's complaints, but she would have never interfered.

Their lives followed a rhythm as predictable as the seasons themselves. There were the occasional trials and tragedies—the death of an ailing parent, a sick child, blighted crops, a surprise visit from local law enforcement or ABC agents—but in May 1951, with construction on the new house nearing completion and a new baby on the way, Elizabeth must have felt like her life was complete. She was thirty-seven years old, watching her oldest child grow into a capable young man and carrying what would surely be her last child. Even though childbearing and childrearing had dominated almost half her life, she perhaps envisioned a future in which she and Aubrey would be surrounded by scores of grandchildren, their home the nexus of family gatherings and holiday celebrations. Aubrey would not live to enjoy the newer, larger house, nor would the unborn child, a boy.

No one would have ever said that Elizabeth Kilpatrick led a pampered or privileged existence, but the trajectory and patterns of her life were at least familiar to her and her community. Even helping her husband distribute the illegal moonshine (and adding her own innovative touches like the peach syrup) was not an aberration from Sand Mountain customs since much of Marshall County was in covert but tacitly accepted rebellion against the dry laws anyway. Aubrey's volatility spiked each day with fraught energy, like the thrumming of a low-voltage wire, adding a frisson of excitement (and, on occasion, trepidation) to the otherwise ordinary routines of farm and family life.

After the shooting, virtually nothing was the same. One of the first obstacles Elizabeth had to confront was the sudden lack of income. Her husband was dead and therefore not making moonshine runs up to Tennessee, thus eliminating that supplemental cash. Even though the spring crops had been planted, two of the Kilpatricks' most loyal and hardworking sharecroppers, Tom Upton and Fred Goble, were in jail, and the Whiteheads had decamped suddenly after the shootout, for obvious reasons. Aubrey had had the foresight to take out a life insurance policy on himself, and the double-indemnity clause on the policy paid double if the bearer was killed by accidental means, including murder. Even though the $25,000 Elizabeth received would have been considered a sizeable sum in 1951, it diminished quickly as the legal fees accumulated. No bond had been set for James's release, and besides, Marshall County Circuit Court judge J. S. Stone had repeatedly denied bond appeals. And there was the matter of securing a lawyer. Adamant that her boy have the best legal representation in the state, Elizabeth contacted Birmingham attorney George Rogers under the advisement of Boaz businessman Dures Thomas, who had read in the area newspapers about Rogers's reputation for winning seemingly unwinnable cases. Relatives, neighbors, and friends brought food to the Kilpatrick home, but many people in the wider community felt that they had to tread lightly—after all, even though Aubrey had been one of their own, Leonard Floyd had been Boaz's chief of police, a World War II veteran, a husband,

and a father to two children. Aubrey had made enemies around Marshall, DeKalb, and Etowah Counties, and there were many who believed he had gotten what he deserved.

Regardless of what people thought about Aubrey or even James's actions after his father's death, Elizabeth was the one who had to bear the brunt of the abuse that came in the aftermath. Being Aubrey Kilpatrick's wife and the mother of eight children had never been easy, but the cataclysmic shift that occurred that May night had weakened Elizabeth psychologically and physically. One minute she was standing patiently in front of her husband as he sat in a rocking chair, removing his boots, the house silent as the younger children slept. Then came the crunch of gravel under tires as a car made its way along the drive, pulling just a few yards from the front of the house. The next minute, she was running to the door, hearing the shots ring out, watching her husband sink to the ground, screaming his name. More shots followed; more men fell. The car left, quickly gathering speed as it raced away from the gunfire and mayhem, abandoning two of the original passengers because they were beyond any help that a fast getaway could afford them. The children, awakened by the gunfire, were sobbing and shrieking in terror, except for Jettie Faye, whose inability to hear was, in that instance, a mercy. She slept through the entire incident. Hoping to offer her dying husband some relief as he labored to breathe, blood and spittle bubbling from his mouth, Elizabeth placed a pillow under Aubrey's head and went in the house to call a doctor. Dr. H. E. Barker arrived on the scene within thirty minutes, but his ministrations were for naught. Clearly, Zeke Boyles and Leonard Floyd were dead—nothing to be done there. Soon after, even as Barker leaned over to check his vital signs, Aubrey gave a few last gasps and died. For a moment, Elizabeth sat beside her husband, stroking his hair away from his high, pale forehead. Then she had to turn to the business of the living as the law arrived in full force, coming to take her three oldest children to jail.

There's an old saying, dating back to the late 1400s in England, that describes a makeshift solution to unexpected difficulty or dearth: "That'll do in a pinch, and the pinch is on." Elizabeth Kilpatrick was surely in a terrible pinch, more like a crushing vice, but she was resourceful and determined. On the recommendation of family friend Dures Thomas, Elizabeth secured the services of attorneys George Rogers and John Brown, who immediately filed the change-of-venue request. She buried her husband. Unaccustomed to the complexities of the legal system and social services, she had to leave her comfort zone of home and community to regain her sons Billy and

Harold, who had been taken into custody the night of the shooting. She had young children, ages ranging from twelve years to eighteen months, to attend to at home, including little Jettie Faye, who required special care. While there were many sympathetic and compassionate neighbors and relatives who offered emotional and financial support in the aftermath of the shooting, there were others who saw Elizabeth and her children as despised extensions of the outlaw Aubrey Kilpatrick. She received death threats, although no one ever acted on them.

A week after the shooting, Opal Floyd, the widow of Boaz police chief Leonard Floyd, paid a visit to the Kilpatrick farm. Of the men who had driven out to arrest Aubrey, Floyd had been the peacemaker. He knew the Kilpatrick family well, and despite Aubrey's reputation for fighting and bootlegging, Floyd considered the family hardworking and good-hearted members of the community. When he had learned that Sheriff Boyles intended to serve the warrant on Aubrey so late at night, well after the younger children would have gone to bed, he had tried to convince the sheriff and his deputies to let Aubrey turn himself in the following morning. Aubrey Kilpatrick may have been belligerent, violent, and stubborn, but Floyd knew him as a man of his word. Yet Boyles would not be deterred from his mission, which was to give the bootlegger his comeuppance, the lateness of the hour and a house full of children and guns be damned.

As an elected official, a sheriff wielded a significant amount of power over appointed law enforcement officials in a county's municipalities. When Zeke Boyles called Leonard Floyd's house on the night of May 17, Floyd had little choice but to go to the Boaz police station to accompany the sheriff and his deputies, despite his reluctance and misgivings. It ended up costing him his life—one of James Kilpatrick's rifle bullets found him as he struggled to free himself from some barbed wire on the ground just outside the car. He never even unsnapped the holster on his Sam Browne belt to remove his gun. One might have expected Opal Floyd to feel bitterness, anger, and resentment toward the mother of her husband's killer. Instead, the two women commiserated with each other and mourned their losses. Opal Floyd wanted justice for her husband's death, to be sure, but she also saw in Elizabeth a fellow traveler on a long, uncertain road of suffering. The trials and the assigning of blame were yet to come, but on that late May afternoon, they were just two widows with fatherless children, their lives irreversibly changed by an hour of tragedy.

It is true, as Shakespeare wrote in *Hamlet*, that "when troubles come, they come not single spies but in battalions." Physically and emotionally exhausted by the onslaught of shocks, Elizabeth had yet more to endure. Her firstborn was wasting away in the county jail in Guntersville, denied both bail and sufficient food. In July 1951 James stood trial for killing Leonard Floyd, but after four days of testimony, Judge J. S. Stone ordered a mistrial, which may have seemed like a reprieve of sorts but only delayed the inevitable. In August, Harold, the third oldest, had to undergo emergency surgery for a ruptured appendix. (Needless to say, the Kilpatricks did not have health insurance.) Elizabeth watched as her oldest daughter, Jeretta, transformed from a bubbly twelve-year-old girl into a careworn woman, aged beyond her years by taking care of four younger siblings during their mother's illnesses and absences. In September of that year, Elizabeth delivered a stillborn child, a boy. Although the family was finally able to move into the long-anticipated new house, there was no happiness in achieving this goal, only grief, the palpable sense of loss, and an empty cradle.

Even with the generous contributions of friends and family, Elizabeth Kilpatrick realized that paying the growing legal bills for James's defense was going to require the sale of the family's assets. By January 1952, the Kilpatrick estate was out of probate, which allowed Elizabeth to sell property to pay debts. A legal notice in the January 3 issue of the *Boaz Leader* announced that "Elizabeth Kilpatrick, as the administratrix of the estate of A. E. Kilpatrick, deceased" would sell "personal and real property belonging to said estate for the payment of debts against said estate." Two weeks later, the sale began: "Four mules; 12 horses; 1 milch cow, 2 yearlings; 1 tractor; 1 2-horse wagon; tractor equipment, etc., all farming tools." The days of the family working on the land were over; with James in jail, Billy already eyeing the military recruitment posters around town, Harold slowly recovering from a near-fatal bout of appendicitis, and the tenant farmers scattered, all the male support needed for maintaining over two hundred acres of land was dwindling away, leaving Elizabeth with little choice but to get what money she could from the sale of the property, equipment, and livestock. Ultimately, she was faced with the hardest choice of all—leaving the farm and neighboring community that had sheltered her through most of her married adult life and finding a low-skill job that would provide a regular paycheck.

Elizabeth had no driver's license. She had never learned to drive. She had always depended on her husband or one of her boys to operate the cars or trucks the family owned, and she could hardly ride a horse into town to get to work. Besides, all the horses had been sold. In 1947 Wayne Poultry, a chicken processing plant, had opened a facility in Albertville, roughly five miles from the Kilpatrick farm. Leaving the younger children in the care of Jeretta, Elizabeth rose before dawn, not to ready herself for a day of working in the house or on the farm, but to begin the long walk into Albertville to scald and pluck dead chickens on an assembly line. She worked the day shift, which allowed her to at least be at home with the children at night, but these hours meant that she had to walk the five miles home in the dark. Elizabeth was not a timid woman—after all, she had been married to a hard-drinking, gun-brandishing, law-defying bootlegger for twenty years— but traveling alone on foot down a lonely, dark, country highway made her feel vulnerable and exposed. She never knew if approaching headlights signaled a vehicle carrying a friend or a foe, so she hid in roadside cornfields or woods until the car passed. Only then would she continue on her long walk home, her body weary and worn and her heart heavy.

The day Elizabeth Kilpatrick met Ann Scott and encouraged the young girl to write to her jailed son was one of the most fortuitous events of James and Elizabeth's lives. It marked the beginning of a deep and abiding friendship between the two women, and they leaned on and sustained each other in the difficult years to come. And the next few years were indeed difficult—not only was James convicted of first-degree manslaughter, sentenced to ten years in prison, and incarcerated until 1957, but Elizabeth also watched helplessly as her family fell apart. Billy left to join the army while James was in prison, sending money home whenever he could. In what must have been one of the most painful decisions of her life, Elizabeth arranged for Jettie Faye to live at the Alabama School for the Deaf in Talladega. At only six years old, Jettie Faye became a residential student at the institution, sixty miles away from the only home she had ever known. Elizabeth was unable to visit her youngest daughter with any regularity, and for months Jettie Faye was inconsolable, crying for her lost family and feeling abandoned by her mother. Elizabeth knew that sending Jettie Faye to Talladega would give her a chance at a better life; the teachers at the Alabama School for the Deaf helped their pupils cultivate a wide range of skills that would enable them to live independently and secure gainful employment. But how could Elizabeth explain this to a little girl, living in a world of silence, who had suffered the loss of her father and her oldest brother and was then sent to live among strangers? At least Lynda, Russell, and Danny—three of the "Second Four"—had some degree of normalcy, as much as their vastly altered circumstances allowed, by being able to live at home and continue their schooling. But nothing in the Kilpatrick family would ever be the same again.

Robert Adams, a *Birmingham News* photographer, snapped a picture of Elizabeth Kilpatrick and five of her children during James's first trial in July 1951. Probably excited at the prospect of having her picture taken for the newspaper, Jeretta smiles shyly at the camera, holding an anxious-looking Jettie Faye on her lap. Little Russell, only five years old, peeks from behind his older sister, while Lynda, wearing a very adult expression of impatience, glares over her mother's shoulder. Danny, the baby, sprawls shirtless against his mother's chest. The only person in the picture not looking toward the photographer is Elizabeth—her face is turned away, hand outstretched as if to comfort Jettie Faye with her touch. The caption reads, "A mother listens: Mrs. Aubrey Kilpatrick, widow of one of the slain men and mother of one of the defendants, listens intently with some of her other children in the courtroom in Albertville yesterday during questioning of jurors." On that hot July day in 1951, Elizabeth would indeed listen as the prosecution and the defense battled to determine her oldest son's fate. The tribulations were constant and unrelenting, but the trials had just begun.

Aubrey Kilpatrick, circa 1947. (Photo courtesy of
Marty and Rhonda Kilpatrick)

Aubrey Kilpatrick, circa 1950. (Photo courtesy of
Marty and Rhonda Kilpatrick)

(*from l. to r.*) Marshall County chief deputy Washington Bennett, Sheriff Ezekiel "Zeke" Boyles, and Deputy James Lang, January 1951. (Photo courtesy of the *Guntersville [Ala.] Advertiser-Gleam*)

Ann Scott Kilpatrick, 1953. (Photo courtesy of Marty and Rhonda Kilpatrick)

Marshall County sheriff Ezekiel "Zeke" Boyles and Mrs. Eva Boyles.
(Photo courtesy of the Marshall County Archives)

The Kilpatrick family and friends on a horseback ride into the town of Boaz. (Photo courtesy of
Marty and Rhonda Kilpatrick)

Marshall County Circuit Court judge J. S. Stone. (Photo courtesy of the Alabama Department of Archives and History. Donated by Alabama Media Group. Photo by Robert Adams, *Birmingham News*)

(*from l. to r.*) Tom Upton, James Kilpatrick, and Fred Goble, July 1951. (Photo courtesy of the Alabama Department of Archives and History. Donated by Alabama Media Group. Photo by Robert Adams, *Birmingham News*)

(*foreground*) Mrs. Opal Floyd and children, Linda Floyd and John Arthur Floyd, July 1951. (Photo courtesy of the Alabama Department of Archives and History. Donated by Alabama Media Group. Photo by Robert Adams, *Birmingham News*)

(*foreground*) Jeretta Kilpatrick, Jettie Faye Kilpatrick, Russell Kilpatrick, Linda Kilpatrick, Elizabeth Kilpatrick, and Danny Kilpatrick, July 1951. (Photo courtesy of the Alabama Department of Archives and History. Donated by Alabama Media Group. Photo by Robert Adams, *Birmingham News*)

James Kilpatrick and Elizabeth Kilpatrick, April 1953. (Photo courtesy of the *Guntersville [Ala.] Advertiser–Gleam*)

James Kilpatrick working in the prison laundry at Draper Penitentiary, circa 1956. (Photo courtesy of Marty and Rhonda Kilpatrick)

# CHAPTER 7

# The First Trial

Lawyers are storytellers—not in the sense that they create fictions intended to mislead, but rather that they must create a narrative that convinces a jury of a defendant's guilt or innocence. Kate Coscarelli of the American Bar Association observes that the "tools attorneys use every day to perform their work are the very guts of good storytelling: artful and careful use of words and the craft of organizing complicated thoughts and themes into reasoned prose that is backed up with citations and evidence." Sometimes the narratives presented by the defense and the prosecution seem to be describing wholly disparate people and events. In James Kilpatrick's first trial, each side had a different tale to tell. The prosecution's story was this: Aubrey Kilpatrick was a known criminal, a bootlegger with a violent streak who, at every turn, had defied local and state officials in their attempts to enforce the law. On May 17, 1951, knowing he was going to be served with a warrant, Aubrey had compelled his oldest son, James, and two loyal sharecroppers to set up an ambush for the anticipated officers. When the officers had arrived, Aubrey had threatened to kill them and then acted on that threat by firing at them before they had a chance to exit the car. Only after they had been fired on did Deputy Washington Bennett, with a single shot in self-defense, kill the thirty-nine-year-old farmer.

What followed Aubrey's death was the crux of the prosecution's argument: young James, armed with a .30-caliber carbine, stepped out from a hiding place and gunned down Sheriff Zeke Boyles, Police Chief Leonard Floyd, and Deputies Washington Bennett and James Lang. Here the word "ambush" played a crucial role in defining the defendant's actions that night, just as it had figured prominently in many of the newspaper accounts of the shooting. The prosecutors knew that they had to present James not as a shocked and grieving sixteen-year-old avenging his father's death but as a cold-blooded murderer, a man-boy who had been raised to be as rash and dangerous as his father and a fledgling criminal who lay in wait with a semiautomatic rifle and the skill and compulsion to use it. They had to portray James as a ruthless automaton, nourished on violence and primed to kill, who had expressed little remorse in the aftermath for his actions.

The defense would tell a different story, one that flipped the prosecution's narrative into a tragic account of a boy—a child, really—so traumatized at the sight of his father's bleeding body on the ground that, out of fear for his own life and, more importantly to him, the lives of his mother and younger siblings, had reacted out of sheer primal instinct to the danger posed by four strangers arriving late at night in an unmarked car and shooting his father in front of the family home. In Rogers's telling, James Kilpatrick was not a bad seed blooming darkly from tainted soil; he was instead a good boy caught up in a conflict not of his own making. Rogers knew that convincing a jury comprised of law-abiding Marshall County residents would require evoking powerful emotions of family loyalty and home protection. Would not any young man—any "red-blooded American boy," as John Brown, the Boaz attorney who served as Rogers's second chair, asserted in a closing argument—have reacted in the same manner? Wouldn't such circumstances cause an otherwise stable, rational boy to lose his mind, at least temporarily? Initially, Rogers submitted a plea of not guilty by reason of insanity, but he withdrew it on the first day of the trial. Such a defense carried its own complications and consequences.

As Casey Cep points out in *Furious Hours: Murder, Fraud, and the Last Trial of Harper Lee*, "Insanity isn't an easy thing to prove, and it is often the defense of last resort. The belief that madness can be exculpatory is an ancient one—so ancient that it was carved into the Code of Hammurabi seventeen hundred years before the birth of Christ, alongside the notion of proportional retaliation, *lex talionis*, an eye for an eye." In Alabama, the legal code outlining the insanity defense had originally conformed to the standard set by the M'Naghten Rule, which had originated in Great Britain in 1843. Daniel M'Naghten (sometimes spelled "M'Naughten") had murdered Edward Drummond, secretary to Sir Robert Peel, in an assassination attempt targeting Peel. M'Naghten's defense counsel, Alexander Cockburn, took the unconventional stance of assembling medical experts to testify that M'Naghten's mental condition had been the central factor in the commission of this crime. When Cockburn addressed the court and jury, he laid the groundwork for the modern insanity defense:

I shall call before you members of the medical profession—men of intelligence, experience, skill, and undoubted probity—who will tell you upon their oaths that it is their belief, their deliberate opinion, their deep conviction, that this man is mad, that he is the creature of delusion, and the victim of ungovernable impulses, which wholly take away from him the character of a reasonable and responsible being.

The court found M'Naghten insane, and he was hospitalized for the remainder of his life. The M'Naghten ruling established the precedent that certain mental diseases or defects could impair an individual's ability to form *mens rea*, or the intent to commit an act and have a desired consequence, as required by the law.

Most U.S. states used M'Naghten as the standard for the insanity defense (and some still do), although challenges arose in the late nineteenth century and continued into the twentieth. An 1886 case in Alabama, *Parsons v. State*, questioned the precedent set by M'Naghten: was the insanity criterion, based on archaic medical theories, an adequate test of legal responsibility given the advancement of knowledge since that ruling? The case was certainly a strange one, even by late nineteenth-century standards. A woman named Nancy Parsons, aided by her mentally challenged daughter Joe (who was referred to in court documents as an "idiot," a now mercifully defunct clinical term used to describe someone whose mental development never exceeded that of a two-year-old child), had shot and killed her husband, Bennett Parsons, in January 1885. Nancy claimed that her husband had used "supernatural powers" to inflict her with disease, and she believed the only way to free herself from this debilitating influence was to get rid of her tormentor once and for all. During the initial trial, the defense argued for an instruction that the defendants were not guilty if their acts are "offspring or product of mental disease"; then the defense proposed an instruction that the defendants were not guilty if "moved to action by an insane impulse controlling their will or their judgment." Unconvinced, the jury convicted the mother and daughter of second-degree murder.

The subsequent appeal went to the Alabama Supreme Court, where Associate Justice Henderson Somerville authored an opinion essentially overturning M'Naghten. Contained within his opinion were two significant alterations to the M'Naghten ruling: first, that even a person who knew right from wrong could not be held legally responsible if she or he had lost the power to choose between right and wrong and to avoid the act—the phrase "irresistible impulse" thus entered the legal lexicon to describe this loss of agency—and, second, that the alleged crime was so connected with mental disease as to have been the "product of it solely." With both factors in mind, the court assigned responsibility for the crime to the mental illness despite the defendant's ability to distinguish right from wrong.

Could George Rogers convince a jury composed of twelve pragmatic, no-nonsense men, most of them devout Christians who firmly believed in both free will and retributive justice, that James Kilpatrick had suffered from this "irresistible impulse," triggered by the trauma of seeing his father lying bleeding in front of their home, and consequently lost the power to choose between right and wrong? Would claiming that James suffered from a preexisting mental illness that destroyed his ability to control his actions in a moment of extreme duress be a Pyrrhic victory, perhaps keeping him out of prison but sending him to a mental institution for years? Such a defense was risky. Juries had become less receptive to the insanity defense, regarding it as a loophole conjured by legal mumbo-jumbo and promoted by what George Wallace later derisively called "pointy-headed intellectuals" to get killers off the hook.

To most people, insane meant crazy, and that stigma would stick. Crazy people walked imaginary dogs and talked to unseen companions and ran around screeching and babbling with no pants on. Whatever else the people of Marshall County thought about James Kilpatrick—avenging angel or heartless murderer—they would not buy the idea that he was insane, regardless of how many psychiatrists and mental health experts Rogers assembled to testify. Rogers withdrew the insanity plea and opted instead to argue that James was not guilty by reason of self-defense and protection of his home. That approach, Rogers knew, would resonate more viscerally and fundamentally with men for whom the sanctity of home and family was everything. The ferocity of protecting the ones you loved could be a kind of madness unto itself. George Rogers was staking his professional reputation—and perhaps James Kilpatrick's life, for the death penalty was definitely alive and well in 1951—on this assumption.

Opal Floyd waited outside the main courtroom inside the Marshall County Courthouse in Albertville on the morning of July 23, smoothing her best dress over her hips and dabbing her forehead and cheeks with a handkerchief. Already the humidity shimmered over the streets and blurred the tree lines on the edge of town. Her right hand kept moving toward the wedding ring on her left hand, nervously twisting the thin gold band as she waited to be called to the stand. Her two children, John Arthur, nine, and Linda, four, stood solemnly on either side, occasionally reaching up to pluck at her skirt or touch her arm for reassurance. The families of police officers know that their loved ones do a dangerous job, that each day ushers in the possibility of a knock on the door or a phone call imparting bad news. But before May 17 of that year, Opal may have believed that her husband was somehow safe from danger, safer than most men in his position, because he had escaped death before and on a much larger scale.

Their lives together had begun happily and uneventfully. On Christmas Day in 1937, eighteen-year-old Opal Annie Coppett had married eighteen-year-old Leonard James Floyd, and the two newlyweds assumed that their lives would follow the path of their forebears—farming and raising their children in a familiar community where generations of Coppetts and Floyds had done much the same. Such a life would be demanding but simple, no great expectations of wealth or fame but cocooned within the embrace of family and the comfort of the known. But history intervened, as it had for thousands of other Americans who initially viewed the growing unrest in Europe and Asia as far away and not vitally connected to their own lives. On September 16, 1940, after France had fallen to the Nazis in June, the United States instituted the Selective Training and Service Act, which required all men between the ages of twenty-one and forty-five to register for the draft. Leonard Floyd dutifully signed up on October 16, 1940.

In 1942 Opal and Leonard welcomed their first child, a boy with his mother's dark hair and his father's shy smile. The new family's bliss was interrupted, however, when Leonard's number came up for service in July 1943. Suddenly the abstract war halfway across the world took on solidity and urgency. What felt concrete, what felt real—cool soil under bare feet, the heft of a toddler balanced in the crook of an arm, the solid warmth of bodies embracing in a narrow bed—would have to be consigned, at least temporarily, to memory, something to sustain Leonard during the months away from his wife and son.

Equipped with an M1903 Springfield bolt-action rifle, two grenades, an ammo supply pack, and a combat knife, Private Leonard Floyd served as a rifleman in the United States Fifth Army in Italy, a unit that experienced some of the fiercest combat in World War II. In the spring of 1944 Floyd was wounded east of Anzio during intense fighting. For the injuries he sustained in action against the enemy, Floyd would receive a Purple Heart, but as he lay gasping and writhing in agony in the Italian dirt, far away from his north Alabama farm, he would have traded all the medals the army had to give just to be home with his wife and son. His wish was partially granted—after two months in the 8th Evacuation Hospital near Galluzzo, Italy, Floyd returned stateside, but to Florida, not Alabama. The Army Service Forces had established convalescent centers for returning soldiers across the country, and Floyd arrived at Welch Convalescent Hospital in Daytona Beach in December 1944, just in time for his seventh wedding anniversary. His honorable discharge from the army coincided with his twenty-sixth birthday, March 10, 1945.

Coming home, especially after almost two years of combat and convalescence, was not easy for Leonard Floyd. Opal and her young son had lived with her parents while Leonard had been away, and little John Arthur was already walking and talking by the time father and son were reunited. The world had changed since Floyd left to fight in Europe, and the old ways of making a living off the land had changed as well. Between 1940 and 1945, the number of Americans living on farms had decreased by five million, or 15 percent of the farmers prior to World War II. The industrialization of agriculture was well under way, and the end of the war ushered in a technological boom in agricultural machinery and research. Farmers would have to be educated in the new methods of agricultural production. On June 22, 1944, before the war had ended, President Franklin D. Roosevelt signed into law the Serviceman's Readjustment Act, also known as the G.I. Bill. The law offered four major benefits for returning servicemen: job counseling and placement; employment insurance (if needed); guaranteed home and small-business loans; and four years of college education or vocational training. Embedded within the last provision was agricultural education and training, which allowed veterans to receive training and payment while they worked on their own farms or on rented land.

Across the country, especially in the Midwest and South, vocational agriculture training programs sprang up, and the Floyd family moved to Boaz, Alabama, to take advantage of Marshall County's model training program. Like other participating trainees, Floyd could receive subsistence payments of ninety dollars a month while working under supervision on a farm as long as he followed an approved farming program and met the program's requirements. Not only was the knowledge gained during this training program crucial for farming in this brave new world of agricultural production, but the Floyds desperately needed the additional stipend, especially since their family had increased by one with the birth of Linda, their daughter, in 1947.

Being a part of this learning community afforded Floyd the chance to be of service to his neighbors, just as he had served his country. In July 1948 Floyd and eighteen of his fellow trainees put their newfound knowledge to practical use when they aided one of their own, a Boaz farmer named C. E. Kemp, who had been unable to tend his crops for several weeks due to illness. The men arrived at Kemp's farm with plows, planters, cultivators, and a tractor. Within six hours the team had plowed eight acres of cotton, sacked up two acres of sweet and Irish potatoes, and planted seven acres of grain sorghum. Despite the program's emphasis on the use of modern farming technology, some tried-and-true methods just couldn't be resisted—one of the men loaded up four mules and brought them to Kemp's farm to assist in plowing. Without these trainees' help, the Kemp family would have suffered the loss of a year's crop and therefore a year's income. The world may have changed, but the unified kindness of neighbors had not.

The Floyds had found a new home in Marshall County, and Leonard was able to maintain his generational ties to farming. He joined the local soil conservation board and several civic organizations. Perhaps because his own military service had been cut short by injury, Floyd felt compelled to put the discipline and skills he had learned in the army to use for the betterment of his community. Returning veterans often found careers in law enforcement, then as now, and Floyd became a member of the Boaz Police Department in 1949. By the age of thirty-two, he had worked his way up the ranks of the Boaz police force, and the city council appointed him chief. As police chief, Floyd gained the reputation as a peacemaker, often defusing liquor-fueled brawls and domestic disputes with calm persuasion. He had seen—and experienced—what men with weapons could do to one another. He knew that men like Aubrey Kilpatrick conducted illegal business on their farms, but as long as violence didn't break out, the young chief of police was willing to look the other way. He cultivated relationships within the community with the same equanimity that he embraced when cultivating the land. Floyd eschewed the public liquor pourings favored by the county sheriffs, instead maintaining a low profile, seeking to gain the community's trust.

When the young police chief learned of Aubrey Kilpatrick's altercation with the Whiteheads, he realized that he could not turn a blind eye in this instance; however, hoping to deescalate an already tense situation and avoid an explosive showdown between the strong-willed sheriff and the trigger-happy bootlegger, Floyd suggested that Aubrey be allowed to wait until the next morning to post bond on the warrants issued against him. Everyone would be calmer, Floyd reckoned, if they all got a good night's rest, if they went home to their wives and children and remembered that Aubrey, too, had a wife and eight children who would be in harm's way if the bootlegger were confronted at his house. These suggestions fell on deaf ears. When Sheriff Boyles called the chief and told him to meet him and his deputies at the Boaz police station, Floyd felt he had no choice but to go. Maybe he imagined a scenario where, once at the Kilpatrick farm, he could help negotiate a peaceful resolution that satisfied all parties involved. He strapped on his Sam Browne belt, the one that he had purchased after the war as part of his new police uniform, and kissed his wife goodbye, assuring her that he would be careful. He had already seen his children off to bed. Perhaps he would have an exciting story to share at the breakfast table the next morning. He did not come home that night, or any night afterward.

As she stood outside the courtroom door, waiting for the bailiff to call her name, Opal Floyd held her daughter's hand and gazed out the window at the curious, milling throng on the courthouse lawn. How cruel, she mused, how very cruel, that her husband had survived a war in a distant land, only to be shot and killed by a sixteen-year-old farm boy roughly three miles from the Floyd family home. The bullet he had bested in Italy had found its way to him, fatally, across an ocean and many miles.

Despite the almost festive atmosphere outside the Marshall County Courthouse, where hundreds of people from surrounding towns and counties gathered in hopes of gaining access to the proceeding or getting tidbits of gossip from those who had made it inside, the testimonies on the first day of the trial focused on the rather mundane business of establishing the location of the shooting. There was a brief episode at the beginning of the trial that caused some excitement but produced little in the way of hard evidence—when Opal Floyd took the stand as the first witness, four-year-old Linda was with her, frightened and crying. Whether it was an intentional ploy by the prosecution to evoke the jury's sympathy or simply Opal's desire to comfort her child, George Rogers nonetheless objected strenuously, and little Linda was sent out of the courtroom to sit in the lobby with her older brother. Circuit Solicitor L. P. Waid initiated the questioning, verifying Opal's relationship to the deceased, the date of his death, and the position he occupied at the time of his death. Rogers probed a little deeper, asking Opal if she had gone with her husband at any point on May 17 to the Kilpatrick farm or if she had known of her husband's whereabouts throughout that day. Once he had ascertained that she did not know what events had transpired prior to the shooting, she was allowed to leave the stand.

The other witnesses that day included C. B. Sartain, the county engineer for Marshall County; *Gadsden Times* photographer Leon Reeves; and Walter L. Allen, criminal investigator for the Alabama Department of Public Safety. Maps, photographs, and elaborately detailed blueprints of the crime scene, which included the Kilpatrick house and the surrounding area, were admitted into evidence, with each witness testifying as to the location of everything from the house and outbuildings to trees to power poles and farming equipment. From time to time, Rogers objected with what would become a catchphrase of sorts: "Illegal, irrelevant, and immaterial!" The spectators grew restless, with so many people wandering in and out of the courtroom that Judge Stone eventually asked court officers to lock the door. The most exciting element of that day's testimonies, other than the appearance of Floyd's sorrowful widow, had been when the men in the courtroom had been asked to remove their hats from pegs on the wall so that a large map could be pinned up as an exhibit. People yawned openly or discreetly behind handheld fans advertising the local funeral home; several jurors fidgeted and perhaps wished they were outside on the courthouse lawn, enjoying a ham sandwich wrapped in wax paper and a cold drink. But the next day of the trial would feature the man who could give a firsthand account of the shooting, the "lone survivor," as the newspapers described him—Deputy James Lang.

When Zeke Boyles ran for sheriff in 1950, one of his campaign promises had been to increase the number of deputies from areas in Marshall County besides Guntersville. Sheriff Boyles and Chief Deputy Bennett were both from Guntersville; James Lang was from Albertville, known as "The Heart of Sand Mountain" and the most populous municipality in Marshall County. Like Deputy Bennett and Chief Floyd, Lang had fought in World War II, which meant that three of the four men who rode out to the Kilpatrick farm on the night of May 17 had survived encounters with an enemy far superior in numbers, strength, and weaponry than Aubrey Kilpatrick. Yet what the Axis fighters had failed to do in Europe and the Pacific, one farm boy in Alabama had managed to do in just a few minutes: Floyd had been killed, Bennett had been mortally wounded, and Lang had been critically injured. Unlike Floyd, who had joined the police force in Boaz after his military service, Lang had been a member of the Albertville Police Department when he was called up by the U.S. army for active duty in 1944. Upon returning home from the war, Lang went back to policing, but he also supplemented his income by driving what the locals called "a rolling truck," delivering groceries and other household goods to homes around town. He had confided to a few family members that he hoped to take advantage of the G.I. Bill's educational funding and return to school, perhaps to become a teacher or a lawyer. At thirty, he was the youngest of the shooting victims.

When James Lang took the stand as the first witness on the second day of the trial, he was considerably paler and thinner than he had been seven months earlier when he posed for an official photo with Boyles and Bennett. Lang was still recovering from his wound, a through-and-through shot that had entered and exited cleanly but had still passed through his right lung. He had been hospitalized in Gadsden from May 17 until the first week in June, after which he had gone home to convalesce. The day before, the judge often had to ask the courtroom audience to quiet down or sit still, but when Lang took the oath to tell the truth, the whole truth, and nothing but the truth, so help him God, a tense silence fell upon the crowd of spectators. They sat up, leaned forward, and listened carefully to Lang's testimony.

Circuit Solicitor L. P. Waid began his examination of the witness by establishing the day and time of the officers' visit to the Kilpatrick farm. Although the previous day's testimonies had offered none of the high drama the public and reporters clamored for, the tedious introductions of maps, land plats, and house blueprints into evidence had laid the groundwork for Lang's crucial testimony as well as the accounts provided by subsequent law enforcement officials. Lang testified that he had been driving the sheriff's car, which held Boyles, Bennett, and Floyd, and that they had picked up Billy Kilpatrick and Fred Howard Burns as they approached the Kilpatrick farm. Then, according to Lang, he maneuvered the car up the Kilpatricks' driveway, stopping between ten and fifteen yards from the front of the house. Lang explained that he could see into the house through a front window where Aubrey Kilpatrick was sitting at a table. On the table were two guns, which Kilpatrick picked up as he rose to walk out the front door of his house. Lang stated that Kilpatrick "came directly toward the car" and said to its occupants, "Don't get out of the car. I will kill you." In Lang's telling, none of the officers attempted to exit the car; instead, he asserted that Sheriff Boyles had responded, "Aubrey, don't use those guns. We want to fix up a bond here and get this fixed up. . . . Please don't use those guns." Despite the sheriff's efforts to placate the armed bootlegger, Lang claimed,

Kilpatrick slowly backed away from the car, lifted his pistols, and started firing.

Even though James Kilpatrick was the one on trial, the elder Kilpatrick's actions prior to his death had direct bearing on the sequence of events that followed. The question of who fired first was of paramount importance in all of James Kilpatrick's trials. If the prosecution could show that Aubrey, with little provocation other than the appearance of lawmen on official business, had begun shooting first, then James's subsequent actions seemed less nobly motivated and more closely aligned with the ambush narrative promoted by local investigators and recounted in many newspapers. In this proposed scenario, James Kilpatrick was finishing what Aubrey had started, a son about his father's business. Deputy Lang's testimony was intended to support the prosecution's argument that the four lawmen had been waylaid and taken completely by surprise.

Lang testified that Aubrey fired two shots, causing Lang to "lean over in the seat," while Washington Bennett "jumped out on the right" and fired one shot. That single bullet struck Aubrey center mass, but he was still able to fire three more shots after he had been hit. But inconsistencies emerged in Lang's testimony concerning the timeline. At first Lang claimed that all the officers were still in the car when Aubrey began shooting, and only after Aubrey had fired twice did Washington Bennett quickly open the passenger door, jump out of the car, and return fire. Almost immediately, however, Lang contradicted himself by saying that Bennett was already out of the car "when Aubrey was backing back in position to fire." When Waid pressed Lang to explain what had happened to the two boys in the car, Billy Kilpatrick and Fred Howard Burns, Lang reiterated his original stance: "The boys, after Kilpatrick, Aubrey, had fired twice and Bennett jumped out, opened the door and got out, the boys got out and run toward the house. I didn't know what become of them." Lang also maintained that he had first espied James Kilpatrick coming up a trail on the west side of the house just as Aubrey was moving into position to fire: "I seen him when the old man was backing back." Then, according to Lang, bullets seemed to be everywhere.

As the remaining officers exited the car, with Lang and Floyd getting out on the passenger side, a volley of shots rang out. Lang was hit just a few feet from the car, and Floyd went down next to a large oak tree in front of the house. Neither Lang nor Floyd drew their weapons—Lang, because he was injured and seeking cover, Floyd, because he was dead. Lang testified that he had not seen James Kilpatrick fire the shots that hit him and Floyd, but he added that as the boy approached his father, who was lying close to the front steps, the younger Kilpatrick whirled, ducked behind the corner of the house, and fired two shots at Washington Bennett. While James Lang was not exactly eloquent in his testimony, his sparse words nonetheless painted a tragic picture: the sounds of gunfire, seemingly coming from all directions; the horrified son, tentatively making his way toward his dying father; the wounded deputy, staggering toward the nearest house to get help.

When George Rogers began his cross-examination of James Lang, he knew he had to shift the jury's attention away from the descriptions of James Kilpatrick systematically picking off the officers who had arrived to arrest his father. To support James's plea of self-defense and protection of home and family, Rogers needed to convince the jury that the officers had acted in bad faith, that the shootout which transpired after the officers drove out to the farm was not a calculated ambush but instead the defensive actions of a man and his son who had been tricked by a dishonest sheriff. Again, James Lang offered contradictory testimony. At first, he stated that he and Bennett had offered to let Aubrey Kilpatrick come in the following morning to make bond. Rogers repeated the question to make sure that the jury grasped the implications of what Lang was saying: "You left [Aubrey] with the understanding that if you wanted him he would come in and make bond?" Lang responded in the affirmative.

Later in the cross-examination, however, when Rogers again raised the issue of the agreement, Lang denied having made the statement. The courtroom erupted—spectators gasped and murmured excitedly, with one man shouting, "You said it! You know you did!" Astonished, Rogers exclaimed, "Didn't you tell the jury a minute ago that Kilpatrick told you and you made arrangements with him to come in the next morning if a warrant was gotten for him?" Lang continued to insist that he had not testified as such, and with the judge calling for order in the courtroom, Rogers changed tactics. He had gone far enough in sowing seeds of doubt in the jurors' minds regarding Aubrey's alleged deal with the lawmen.

In a time when a man's word was his bond, even if that man was a known criminal with a checkered past, for representatives of the law to offer that man a mutually satisfactory compromise and then renege on that agreement would have been viewed as the worst kind of treachery, the sort of authoritative overreach that justified retaliation. While the legal basis of such an argument was shaky, Rogers knew from successfully defending many apparently guilty clients that juries often relied more on their personal beliefs about morality and justice than codified law when weighing a defendant's guilt or innocence. The jurors in this trial (who all would have been men since women were not allowed to serve on juries in Alabama until 1965) were predominantly farmers and small business owners who had been born and raised in Marshall County. Rogers knew that men like these didn't take too kindly to anything that threatened the sanctity of home and family, even if that perceived threat came from officers sworn to uphold the law.

Rogers's new angle was this: Zeke Boyles and his crew had not only exhibited wanton disregard for the sleeping children in the Kilpatrick household, but they had also taken one of the wanted man's children and a child who was for all intents and purposes under the care of the Kilpatrick family from the farm, driven them to town and back with no clear objective, and returned to confront Aubrey with the children still in the car. Aware of every nuance conveyed by the words he spoke, Rogers asked Lang, "Now, then, when you got out there and before you got out there, you stopped the car containing this little twelve-year-old boy of Mr. Kilpatrick's on the highway, didn't you?" The "little twelve-year-old boy" was Billy Kilpatrick, who was in fact fifteen at the time of the shooting. Why had Rogers knocked three years off Billy's real age? Surely it wasn't ignorance because Rogers was, if anything, a man with a stellar memory for details. Neither the judge nor the prosecuting attorneys corrected him, which probably meant that they did not know Billy's age. As with so many elements of this case, Rogers understood the power of transforming the two older Kilpatrick boys and their friend into innocent children who had been pulled into the machinations of their elders, not a "lead-slinging gang" armed to the teeth and lying in ambush. In this rendering, Billy Kilpatrick and Fred Howard Burns became two little country boys with their dog out on a possum hunt, never mind that they were carrying loaded shotguns, driving a car, and away from home close to midnight.

Rogers did not ask Lang why the officers had forced the boys to get into the car with them, but two possible reasons could be deduced: perhaps the lawmen were worried that Billy and Fred had been posted at the end of the driveway close to the highway entrance to the Kilpatrick farm as lookouts, or maybe the men saw the opportunity to question the boys as to Aubrey's intentions. Throughout this line of questioning, Rogers hinted at a more nefarious motive—maybe the men in the car wanted leverage against Aubrey, which made the boys bargaining chips in what would doubtless be a dangerous standoff. After all, Boyles and his men had secured the warrants they needed to arrest Aubrey Kilpatrick, so why make the boys get into Boyles's car, ride to Boaz, circle the police station without stopping, and return to the farm? When Lang stated that the boys had been in violation of the law by having a "concealed weapon," Rogers, with his usual biting sarcasm, asked, "What kind of concealed weapon? A shotgun? How did he have it concealed? In his pocket or how?" Before Lang could answer, one of the prosecutors, Claude Scruggs, hastily objected, and Judge Stone sustained the objection. The prosecution knew they had to tread lightly where gun rights were concerned, especially in northern Alabama. The last thing the prosecution wanted to do was cause the jury to envision roving lawmen seizing firearms from people on their own land.

George Rogers's strategy of emphasizing his defendant's youth could have easily backfired. His description of James Kilpatrick as a "sixteen-year-old child," repeated so often as to almost become a mantra, was intended to remind the jury that James's age affected and determined his legal status. Since the establishment of the first juvenile court in Cook County, Illinois, in 1899, states had recognized that children who commit crimes are different from adults; as a class, they were considered less blameworthy, and they possessed a greater capacity for change. But few Marshall County jurors would have taken that bait. Technically, James Kilpatrick was a minor, but he was no child. While James was sixteen at the time of the shooting, he turned seventeen ten days later. At seventeen, boys had gotten parental consent to enlist to fight in World War II. In 1951 Alabama sixteen-year-olds could get married with their parents' permission. Farm boys like James assumed adult duties upon reaching adolescence, and most rural youth grew up using guns and driving trucks well before the law sanctioned such activities. Many of the men deciding James Kilpatrick's fate had been brought up in a similar fashion, taking on the responsibilities and consequences of manhood, especially if their fathers had left them in charge during the war. In their minds, if a boy picked up a gun and used it to kill another person, he forfeited any claim to childhood.

The succession of witnesses who came after James Lang revealed another hole in the surviving deputy's testimony. The chain of custody involving the weapons used in the shooting had been sloppy. By the various officers' admission, the crime scene had been hardly well preserved, with scores of law enforcement officials, reporters, and well-intentioned neighbors, friends, and members of the Kilpatrick family roaming freely about the property in the aftermath, touching and moving bodies and guns. Someone, perhaps Elizabeth Kilpatrick, hoping to provide some small comfort to her dying husband, had placed a pillow under Aubrey's head, and Aubrey's nickel-plated .44 had been removed from the scene and hidden under a mattress inside the house. The county coroner, Howard "Moose" Hardin, had secured Aubrey's favorite gun only after James himself had revealed where the pistol was stashed away. Washington Bennett's gun, a snub-nosed .38 Smith & Wesson, had been recovered from the floorboard of Boyles's car after the two deputies had made their desperate flight from the Kilpatrick farm to the Boaz police station, whereupon the assistant chief of police, J. C. Sanders, had unloaded the gun and placed it and the shells in a desk drawer. One of the first officers on the scene, Highway Patrolman W. W. Locke, had picked up the pieces of Zeke Boyles's shattered .38 Smith & Wesson and carried them around in his pocket before handing them over to Hardin. Although the grip had been splintered when the gun was presumably shot out of Boyles's hand by James Kilpatrick's .30 carbine, the cylinder assembly was intact. Despite James Lang's testimony that none of the officers had fired their weapons except for Washington Bennett's one fatally accurate shot, Highway Patrolman E. B. Robbins stated, under oath, that Boyles's gun had been fired twice.

The introduction of this finding into evidence threatened to unravel the prosecution's carefully constructed account of that night's events. When had Zeke Boyles fired his gun, and at whom? Had one or both shots initiated the exchange of gunfire, or had Boyles fired in response to Aubrey Kilpatrick's shots into the car's windshield? When James Lang had fallen over in the front seat of the Pontiac, had it been a panicked reaction to Aubrey's shots at the car, or had he been warned by the sheriff, who was sitting in the back seat behind Lang, to duck so that Boyles could get a clear shot, from inside the car, at the armed bootlegger who stood a few feet from the driver's side? Had Lang intentionally omitted the fact that his boss had fired his gun— not once, but twice—at Aubrey Kilpatrick, or had Lang, amid the chaos and fear for his life, blanked out the memory of anyone but Washington Bennett firing his weapon? The front of the courtroom was papered with maps and photographs, the witnesses had offered their testimonies of what had transpired before and after the shooting, and James Lang had recounted what now seemed either an unwittingly flawed or a deliberately selective memory of that night's events. The next day—Wednesday, July 25—would introduce evidence that had the power to clarify and quantify the details of the case beyond observation, speculation, or recollection. What maps and memory could not prove, science could.

CHAPTER 8

# The Scientists

History has not been nor will it ever be kind to Thomas E. Knight Jr., the former attorney general and lieutenant governor of Alabama, who served as the lead prosecutor in the infamous Scottsboro Boys trials of the early 1930s. Knight bullied witnesses, adamantly defended the court's refusal to include Blacks and women on its juries, and even resorted to cheap showmanship to convict Haywood Patterson of raping Ruby Bates and Victoria Price, at one point even whipping a pair of Price's tattered and soiled panties out of his briefcase ("evidence" that had not been disclosed to the defense) and tossing the "step-ins" onto the lap of an astounded juror. Defense attorney Samuel Leibowitz objected ferociously, stating that "this is the first time in two years any such step-ins have ever been shown in any court of justice," to which Knight, grinning, replied, "They are here now." Knight's courtroom histrionics and showboating, aided and abetted by the systemic racism that permeated not only Alabama and the Deep South but the nation in general, led to a series of hung juries, mistrials, retrials, and two hearings before the United States Supreme Court. Eventually, in 1937, the charges against some of the Scottsboro Boys were dropped, and over the subsequent years all of the defendants were released; decades later, in 2013, Alabama's parole board voted to grant posthumous pardons to the last three Scottsboro Boys.

Nothing can excuse Knight's role in one of the most egregious miscarriages of justice in American history, but if any iota of silver lining can be mined from this dark cloud, it would have to be the recognition, prompted in large part by Knight, that the gathering of evidence needed to be guided by more objective and scientific methods; mere self-exculpatory and subjective witness testimony would no longer suffice. Midtrial panty-throwing aside, Knight had grown frustrated with what he considered the mishandling of evidence in the case against the Scottsboro Boys, and he, like most of America at that time, had been following the trial of Bruno Hauptmann, the man tried and convicted in 1935 of abducting and murdering Charles Augustus Lindbergh Jr., the twenty-month-old son of Charles and Anne Morrow Lindbergh. In a 1973 monograph titled *Alabama's Master Plan for a Crime Laboratory Delivery System*, the Lindbergh case is cited as the impetus for the formation of a "scientific State agency with the specific duty of assisting law enforcement and the courts in the investigation and adjudication of criminal matters." Unlike the Scottsboro trials, the Hauptmann criminal proceedings presented scientific evidence in the form of handwriting and document comparisons as well as the forensic analysis of tool marks made on the wooden ladder that the prosecution claimed Hauptmann had used to climb to the Lindberghs' second-floor nursery and abscond with their sleeping son. In a rare instance of foresight, Knight, newly elected as Alabama's lieutenant governor, supported the establishment of the Department of Toxicology and Criminal Investigation, and in 1935 the Alabama legislature approved Act 225, which outlined the duties, budgetary allotment, and facilities for the new agency. The location of the agency was at Alabama's foremost agricultural school, chartered in Auburn in 1859 as East Alabama Male College and renamed in 1899 as the Alabama Polytechnic Institute (API).

Locating the fledgling state toxicology laboratories at API was no arbitrary decision. In the early twentieth century, Alabama's "state chemist" wore an astounding array of scientific hats, serving not only as director of the State Department of Agriculture's feed and fertilizer assay laboratory and dean of the School of Chemistry at API but also as the official state analyst of foods and vital organs in cases of human poisoning. As Brent Wheeler laments in his history of Alabama's Department of Forensic Sciences, "No funds, facilities, or remuneration were provided . . . for this purpose." At his own expense, the overtasked chemist traveled around the state performing his various duties. Needless to say, many cases fell through the cracks, not due to lack of effort but instead because of the dearth of support and resources. Like the head upon which lies the heavy crown, the unlucky API faculty member who was appointed to assume these duties usually did so reluctantly, and in 1930 chemistry professor Cliff Hare (whose half-century relationship with API began when he played on the school's first football team in 1892) found himself burdened with the combined duties of teaching and research as well as the legal obligations that came with serving as the state's toxicological point man. In that grand academic tradition of relegation, Hare assigned the toxicology duties to Hubert W. Nixon, who was then working in the Agricultural Laboratory. Nixon then enlisted the assistance of a brilliant and enthusiastic colleague, Carl J. Rehling, a native of Cullman, Alabama, who had received his BS in chemical engineering at API in 1929 and was serving as an instructor in analytical and organic chemistry at his alma mater. Both Nixon and Rehling were instrumental in launching the state's new toxicology agency, even going so far as to earn LL.B. (bachelor of laws) degrees from the Thomas Goode Jones School of Law in Montgomery so that they both could fully comprehend the intersection of jurisprudence and science. In fact, Nixon found the legal world so compelling that he eventually resigned from his post as state toxicologist to practice law full time, and in 1945 Rehling took over Nixon's position.

Now armed with a PhD in chemistry from the University of Wisconsin, Dr. Rehling embraced his new duties with the zeal and commitment of a medieval Crusader, calling himself the "Crime Doctor" and his forensic assistants the "Crime Crew." By 1951, the year in which what newspapers around the country would call "the Marshall County gun battle" occurred, Rehling was already nationally recognized as a leading forensic investigator. That May, Rehling examined the bodies of Aubrey Kilpatrick, Marshall County sheriff Zeke Boyles, Boaz police chief Leonard Floyd, and Deputy Washington Bennett, carefully and methodically analyzing their wounds to determine what bullets from which guns had ended each man's life. His role in the subsequent trials was not only pivotal for young James Kilpatrick but also for the "Crime Doctor" himself, cementing his legacy as one of the great forensic detectives in Alabama history.

Born in 1907 to Fred and Wilhelmina (née Engel) Rehling, Carl John Rehling grew up in the thriving and close-knit German community in Cullman, Alabama. While most early Alabama settlers claimed ancestral ties to Ireland, Scotland, and England, German immigrants who followed Johann Gottfried Cullmann's siren song of a utopian community with a shared vision of hard work and prosperity converged on the tract of land purchased by Cullmann from the Nashville–Montgomery Railroad in 1872. An antimonarchist revolutionary from Bavaria, Cullmann was twice ruined—both politically and financially—by the ongoing conflicts in his native country, and, as young men have done throughout history, he left his homeland in search of greater opportunities abroad. Since the United States was in the middle of fighting itself in 1864, Cullmann decided to go to London and wait for the end of the American Civil War. He had heard the horror stories of immigrants forcibly conscripted into serving either the Union or the Confederacy, and he had seen enough fighting in the Revolutions of 1848 and the subsequent upheavals that destabilized Europe in the mid-nineteenth century. He felt compelled to make a new life in America, but his wife did not. She and their children remained behind in Germany.

After the Civil War ended in 1865, Cullmann traveled first to New York City, then to Philadelphia, and he eventually settled in Cincinnati. There, with his broad educational background and business acumen, Cullmann set up an apparently lucrative law practice, which enabled him to procure the capital to fulfill his dream of establishing a prosperous colony of German Americans and German immigrants. He set his sights on northern Alabama, where the land was cheap and available after the Civil War. A skilled land speculator and promoter as well as a shrewd businessman, Cullmann (who was given the honorific of "Colonel" by the railroad company after it made him a land agent) convinced thirteen German families, most of them from Cincinnati, to make the journey by train or down the Ohio and Tennessee Rivers to become part of *Die Deutsche Kolonie von Nord Alabama*.

What began as a trickle soon turned into a flood. By 1874, the settlement was incorporated, going by the name of Cullman (with one "n"), born of land excised from the surrounding counties of Blount, Winston, Morgan, and Walker. In 1877 the town met the state's population requirements to become a county, and Colonel Cullmann's dream became reality. Between 1871 and 1895, Cullmann enticed more than a thousand German Americans to leave other parts of the country and move to north Alabama. Among them were the Rehling family from Cincinnati and the Engel family from Kankakee, Indiana. One of the Rehling sons, Fred Adolph, went to work as a carpenter for W. A. Schlosser and Company, one of north Alabama's most sought-after and successful builders. From 1910 to 1930, Schlosser transformed downtown Cullman from a crude frontier rail town into a picturesque, bustling commercial district, complete with a printing company, several bakeries, a drugstore, and an opera house. Working for W. A. Schlosser and Company carried a certain cachet among members of Cullman's German community—only highly skilled artisans were hired, and the company's carpenters, bricklayers, stonemasons, and glaziers were considered the best in the region.

In October 1906 Fred Rehling married Wilhelmina "Minnie" Engels, who was six years his senior and had arrived in Cullman with her family in 1881. Carl John was born a year later in 1907 and Henry Walter five years later. Like many of the German American settlers in Cullman, the Rehling family emphasized thrift, hard work, civic involvement, and academic excellence. Both Rehling boys were stellar students and attended Alabama Polytechnic

Institute in Auburn, with Carl earning a bachelor's and a master's degree in chemistry. From his boyhood spent fishing and skinny-dipping in Eight-Mile Creek to his academic achievements both as an undergraduate and graduate student at API and a PhD candidate at Wisconsin, Carl Rehling developed into a twentieth-century Renaissance man. His parents inculcated in him a voracious intellectual curiosity and a commensurate appreciation for all facets of knowledge. He was a talented painter, writer, and singer. Like many polymaths, Rehling applied his scientific and creative talents to solving problems—and solving crimes.

Even before assuming the directorship of the State Toxicology Laboratory at API, Carl Rehling had already gained notoriety for making the department one of the most advanced forensics labs in the country at a time when even the FBI's Technical Crime Laboratory was only a decade old. Under the careful tutelage of Hubert Nixon, Rehling studied the effects that various substances and instruments had upon the human body: the rate at which flesh decomposes in water or heat, the source of fibers found embedded in postmortem wounds, the way poisons like strychnine and arsenic affect the central nervous system, how microscopic evidence from a bullet could save a man from the electric chair. Nixon and Rehling did not see themselves as extensions of law enforcement officials or prosecutors or politicians; instead, Nixon referred to the facility as a "'truth detection' laboratory . . . [f]or the microscopic and chemical examinations we are doing here are designed to uncover the truth, whether it tends to incriminate or clear any particular person in connection with a crime."

During World War II, with all state agencies ordered by Alabama governor Chauncey Sparks to contribute to the war effort, the lab assisted the Counter Intelligence Corps and conducted scientific experiments in conjunction with the pilot training program at Maxwell Air Force Base in Montgomery. Just before the end of the war, however, Nixon discovered that his passion for the law had overtaken his fascination with science, and he resigned as director of the State Department of Toxicology to hang out his shingle in Auburn. The logical successor for the position was Nixon's assistant Carl Rehling, who took over as director at the end of August 1945. For the next thirty-three years, Rehling and his "Crime Crew" made local, state, and national news for analyzing evidence that led to convictions as well as exonerations, the former satisfying the public thirst for justice and the latter much appreciated by the wrongfully accused. Following his mentor's lead, Rehling stayed true to keeping the lab unbiased and apolitical: "It is not our purpose to prove guilt or innocence but to present the facts."

While the 1951 shootout on Sand Mountain ranked among Rehling's more high-profile cases, it was hardly the most sensational. In 1948 Rehling uncovered the truth behind what appeared to be a fairly cut-and-dried case of murder. An Alabama woman had died of a gunshot wound to the heart, and investigators concluded that she must have been the victim of a burglary gone wrong or even a revenge attack by her former husband. All the evidence pointed toward homicide: the fuse that controlled the lights in the woman's house had been disabled, drawers had been pulled out and their contents strewn across the floor, and her purse sat empty beneath a front-porch window. According to an article in the November 21, 1948, issue of the *Montgomery Advertiser*, "At first blush, officers thought that it was just another sloppy job of murder." However, as Rehling and his assistants conducted their forensic investigation, they soon realized that the woman's death was not a homicide—it was, as Rehling put it, "a rather intricate and weird job of suicide."

Science alone did not lead Rehling to this answer. His greatest gift, one that inspired over three decades of assistants and analysts to work alongside him loyally and tirelessly, was an all-encompassing vision that drew upon objective, empirical facts and logical deduction complemented by an uncanny understanding of human behavior and an almost cinematic imagination. In this case, a small, circular abrasion on the woman's right thumb caught the attention of Rehling's assistants during the autopsy. The toxicologist knew what could make that kind of mark. When the woman had held the gun to her own chest, she had not positioned her index finger on the trigger, as would have normally occurred if aiming at an opposing target; instead, she had depressed the trigger with her right thumb, the other four fingers clasping the back of the gun, and as she fired, the pistol had spun around and left the circular abrasion. Other details about the scene led Rehling to reconstruct the woman's sad, angry self-destruction—the instinctive tucking of her injured thumb inside her right fist, even as she lay dying, was preserved in rigor mortis, and fingerprints divulged her careful and deliberate manipulation of clocks in the house to cover the time of her death. She had created her own mise-en-scène, a final act of desperation or vengeance to incriminate someone other than herself. But the tableau didn't fool Carl Rehling.

He shot bullets into bales of cotton and tanks of water and through sheets of steel and tin. He took cars apart, from door panels to bumpers to bench seats. He rushed to construction sites to examine bodies that had fallen from great heights. He made impressions of various stab wounds in the flesh of fresh cadavers. What he did not know, he learned. What he could not learn in a classroom or laboratory, he discovered by conducting field experiments. Rehling ignored the most common and pernicious myths surrounding scientific research. While he was brilliant, innovative, and, most important of all, incessantly curious, he did not succumb to the modern fetishization of the lone genius working in isolation. He did not hesitate to turn to those who knew more than he did about a subject, putting aside his ego to glean whatever new knowledge he needed from his fellow scientists. He saw scientific exploration as the work of a community of seekers, not the products of a singular mind. He also did not regard scientific research as a male-only realm; he actively recruited women to work in his lab as chemists, handwriting specialists, and fingerprint analysts. When he desired to enhance his department's scope to include postmortem examinations, he brought on board Dr. Herman Jones, a member of the biochemistry faculty at API who had pursued graduate studies in anatomy, pathology, and physiology. With a vision rare in bureaucratic organizations, Rehling assembled a plan and a team to conduct criminal investigations in Alabama, and by the end of his tenure as state toxicologist, crime labs had been established in every major city in the state.

When the American Academy of Forensic Sciences was founded in 1948, Alabama's toxicology department had been operating on all cylinders for over a decade. The word *forensic* comes from the Latin word *forensis*, meaning "public, to the forum or public discussion; argumentative, rhetorical, belonging to debate or discussion." Until the twentieth century, the term "forensics" had been used primarily to refer to academic competitions in speech, debate, and drama. High school and college forensics teams competed in events that included persuasive and informative speaking, individual and duet acting, storytelling, and debate activities. When paired with "science," the word's old etymological roots expanded into a new, modern meaning: forensic science became the phrase used to describe the application of scientific methods and principles to questions of law. The objectives of forensic science, however, are neither new nor modern. The ancient Egyptians removed and examined the internal organs of the dead. With one of the most famous murder victims in history as his subject, the Roman physician Antistius conducted the postmortem examination of Julius Caesar in 44 BCE. In true forensic fashion, Antistius delivered his findings to the Roman people in the place for important political announcements: the Forum.

*Xi Yuan Ji Lu*, or *The Washing Away of Wrongs*, by Tz'u Sung, was a thirteenth-century Chinese treatise on the inspection of bodily injuries and corpses and is considered the first textbook of forensic science. Intended as a handbook for coroners, *Xi Yuan Ji Lu* was both an etiquette guide ("A coroner must not avoid performing an autopsy just because he detests the stench of corpses") and a procedural manual ("A coroner must refrain from sitting comfortably behind a curtain of incense that masks the stench, letting his subordinates do the autopsy unsupervised, or allowing a petty official to write his autopsy report, otherwise any potential inaccuracy is unchecked and uncorrected"). It also advanced a moral and judicial code, as intimated in the document's title: "Should there be any inaccuracy in an autopsy report, injustice would remain with the deceased as well as the living. A wrongful death sentence without justice may claim one or more additional lives, which would in turn result in feuds and revenges, prolonging the tragedy. In order to avoid any miscarriage of justice, the coroner must immediately examine the case personally."

The Scientific Revolution of the seventeenth and eighteenth centuries produced not only the Newtonian principles of classical physics but also startling discoveries about the nature of noncelestial bodies, especially those done in by exsanguination, poison, and a variety of other nasty ends. In 1773 Swedish chemist Carl Wilhelm Scheele developed a chemical test to detect the presence of arsenic in corpses. In 1814 Spanish chemist Mathieu Joseph Bonaventure Orfila, often called "The Father of Forensic Toxicology," published *Traité des poisons,* the first scientific monograph on using quantitative analysis techniques to test for poisons. Some of the discoveries and innovations focused on the cause of death, but others sought to identify the causal agents, namely, the humans who had, out of hot passion or cold calculation, taken the life of another human. Dignitaries in ancient Babylonia and China used thumbprints and fingerprints on clay tablets as signatory seals, recognizing the unique characteristics of individual impressions, but it was not until the nineteenth century that investigators began utilizing fingerprint identification to solve crimes. Sir Francis Galton, a cousin of Charles Darwin and an anthropologist by training (and, more ignobly, a fervent champion of social Darwinism, eugenics, and scientific racism), pioneered the use of fingerprinting in criminal investigations. By studying fingerprints to look for hereditary traits, Galton discovered two important features: first, that no two fingerprints are exactly alike, and second, that fingerprints remain the same over an individual's lifetime. In 1892 Galton published the aptly titled book *Fingerprints,* which presented his findings that are still used today—a person's fingerprints can be identified by distinctive patterns of loops, whorls, and arches. Over the centuries, through intentional experiments or happenstance discoveries, scientists assembled an arsenal of techniques and methods to apprehend miscreants, giving rise to a new breed of crime fighter—the forensic investigator.

While Carl Rehling was an expert in all the various ways to determine cause of death and track down someone suspected of foul play, the expertise required of him for James Kilpatrick's trials was ballistics. Rehling was, indeed, number one with a bullet. On July 25, 1951, the third day of testimony in James Kilpatrick's first trial, the state toxicologist took the stand. Rehling's presence thrilled the courtroom onlookers, who anticipated the type of tense drama they enjoyed in the *Perry Mason* and *Martin Kane, Private Eye* radio shows that were wildly popular at that time. Rehling identified a fragment of a bullet taken from the body of Boaz police chief Leonard J. Floyd as having been fired from a .30-caliber carbine found on the scene. Rehling's testimony was the first to link James Kilpatrick to the specific weapon used to shoot Floyd. While most of the spectators in that rural Alabama courtroom would have been familiar with the types of guns used in the shootout, the science of reuniting a bullet with the weapon that fired it seemed very modern, sophisticated, and even arcane.

Forensic ballistic analysis, also called "forensic firearm examination" and "forensic fingerprinting," was both an old and new method for identifying whether a certain type of ammunition had been fired from a particular gun. The first recorded account of ballistic analysis being used to solve a crime occurred in 1835, when Londoner Henry Goddard linked a bullet recovered from a victim to the culprit. Goddard (not to be confused with the American Henry Goddard, the eugenicist who wrote the infamous 1912 book *The Kallikak Family: A Study in the Heredity of Feeble-Mindedness*) was one of the last members of the Bow Street Runners, a nickname given to London's first professional police force. Founded in 1749 by Henry Fielding, perhaps better known to modern litterateurs for his picaresque coming-of-age novel *The History of Tom Jones, a Foundling*, the Bow Street Runners signaled a distinct shift from the custom of allowing private citizens, professional "thief takers," and part-time, local, and often underpaid constables and night watchmen to apprehend, accuse, and prosecute lawbreakers toward a more regulated, legitimized group of law enforcement officials.

Although by 1835 the Bow Street Runners had essentially been rendered redundant and obsolete by the Metropolitan Police Act of 1829, investigators like Henry Goddard were applying scientific techniques to crime solving rather than relying solely on the interrogation of subjects and the interviewing of witnesses. In this first recorded account of ballistic "fingerprinting," Goddard examined the bullet removed from a murdered victim's body during an autopsy and discovered a small flaw that, in his estimation, was not the result of being fired or entering the victim's body but instead occurred during the bullet's manufacture. Especially in an era when bullets were usually handcrafted by gunsmiths for private use rather than mass produced, Goddard's technique, while rather reductive and flawed, got the results he wanted: after a suspect had been identified, Goddard searched the man's residence, found a bullet mold with a corresponding defect, cast several bullets using this mold, and ascertained that the suspect's mold was indeed the source of the fatal projectile. Confronted with this evidence, the suspect confessed to the murder.

Roughly three decades later, ballistic analysis played a vital role in several high-profile shootings in the United States, perhaps most famously in the investigation into the shooting of Thomas Jonathan "Stonewall" Jackson. As Jackson and his aides were returning to camp after the Battle of Chancellorsville on May 2, 1863, members of the 18th North Carolina Infantry regiment, doubtless fatigued and trigger-happy, mistook Jackson and his men for Union troops and opened fire on them. Amid the darkness, confusion, and gunfire, Jackson was shot three times—once in the right hand and twice in the left arm, injuries that by modern standards would hardly be fatal. However, the delay in medical treatment, the rough handling and jostling Jackson experienced as his men attempted to move him to safety, and unsanitary field conditions led to the amputation of the general's left arm, and, even after Jackson, his doctor, and his friends believed he was on the mend, sepsis set in, and Jackson died of pneumonia on May 10. Whether out of procedural thoroughness or the hope of exonerating the Confederacy's own soldiers in the wounding and eventual death of a general who had already achieved legendary status, the surgeons who amputated Jackson's arm recovered one of the bullets and turned it over to Confederate officers, who examined it and determined its caliber and design, both of which were, much to their dismay, consistent with Confederate, not Union, guns. The man whom military historians regard as one of the most gifted tactical commanders in U.S. history and who had stood "like a stone wall" at the First Battle of Bull Run had fallen because of that ironic euphemism, "friendly fire."

By the twentieth century, ballistic analysis became even more precise and exact with the comparison microscope, invented in 1923 specifically for the purpose of comparing bullets. Like human fingerprints, gun barrels have their own distinctive markings, known as riflings. When a gun is fired, small imperfections inside the barrel leave a unique pattern of marks on the bullet. All guns are manufactured with a rifling pattern unique to that gun, some turning right, some turning left, depending on the manufacturer's specifications. If an examiner has the weapon used in the commission of a crime, she or he can fire test bullets and compare them to the bullets or slugs found at the scene or procured through postmortem wound examination.

As Dr. Rehling testified in James Kilpatrick's first trial in July 1951, he did indeed have the weapons discharged in the shootout, including the .30 carbine, the .44 Smith & Wesson pistol, and the two .38 Smith & Wesson handguns that were fired at the scene. For the benefit of the court and jury, Rehling explained the basic principles of ballistic analysis:

> [I]dentification depends upon an identification of the tooling pattern which every bored gun barrell [sic] possesses. Each bullet that is fired from a certain gun barrell [sic] will bear the marks or pattern of marks produced by the toolings in that barrell [sic].

Using microscopic analysis, Rehling was able to determine which bullets from which guns had found their way into each slain man's body, for not only had he examined the bullets and the guns, but he had also examined the bodies. From the spine of Aubrey Kilpatrick, who had once sat straight and tall in the saddle, he removed the lead slug that had entered in the upper-left chest area midway between the armpit and the midline of the body, three inches above the nipple line. Even if Aubrey had survived the gunshot, he would have been paralyzed from the chest down. But in its path through his body, what Rehling referred to as "inward ranging," the bullet had torn through Aubrey's left lung, resulting in a fatal hemorrhage. That singular bullet, Rehling testified, had come from the .38 special of Washington Bennett, the deputy who had emerged from the right side of the Pontiac and fired across the top of the car. Bennett had succumbed to his own fatal injuries only a few hours after the shooting, so he was not present in that stiflingly hot courtroom to tell his side of the story. Where Bennett could not speak, science spoke for him.

Since James Kilpatrick was on trial in July 1951 for the death of Leonard Floyd, much of Rehling's forensic testimony focused on the way Floyd had died. In many ways, the account of Floyd's death painted James in the most damning light—unlike Bennett, who had been shot while engaged in the exchange of gunfire, Floyd, although armed (as one would expect of a police chief serving a warrant to a man known for, as Sheriff Boyles had once said, "being too handy with a gun"), had never drawn his weapon. Upon exiting the car, Floyd had gotten tangled in a loop of barbed wire on the ground, and as he struggled to free his pants leg, he had been shot in the back. Dr. Edward W. Venning, a Guntersville physician who had witnessed Rehling's postmortem examination of Leonard Floyd, took the stand during the July trial and recounted the details of Floyd's autopsy. Aside from the bullet that killed him, Floyd's wounds were mostly superficial: an abrasion on his forehead and a scrape on his left knee, as if he had fallen on a rock as he crumpled to the ground. As Venning explained, a bullet wound in the back, six inches down from the shoulder and four inches from the side, had severed the spinal cord. Death was instantaneous. Throughout Rehling's and Venning's testimonies, Floyd's widow, seated in the courtroom gallery among the other perspiring spectators, had wept into her hands.

In this first and subsequent trials, Rehling returned to the stand to testify as the state's forensic specialist, delivering his findings in the same calm, polite, and erudite manner. Since he had performed autopsies on all the slain men, Rehling held the pieces of the lives that had been shattered on that May night. Rehling had known none of these men while they were alive. It must have been hard for a man filled with so much respect for life, so much intelligence, so much passion for knowledge, a man who read voraciously and possessed such artistic skill and sang so beautifully, to stand under the cold lights of a tiled examination room and gaze upon the still bodies whose personalities, hopes, and desires had been extinguished by death. But Rehling was not alone in his investigations. The team that he had so assiduously and patiently mentored had gone forth like disciples to direct forensic labs of their own around the state. As knowledgeable as Rehling was about ballistics, he willingly ceded his role as the expert to Cecil D. Brooks, the director of the branch toxicology lab in Birmingham. Like Rehling, Brooks was a graduate of Alabama Polytechnic Institute in chemical engineering and a recognized authority in handwriting analysis, chemical research, and ballistics. He had worked with Rehling in the primary toxicology lab, and in 1943 he had moved from Auburn to Birmingham to head up the state's third established crime analysis facility. Alabama was proud of its local talent, proclaiming in a 1943 *Birmingham News* article that "since 1935, Alabama has not found it necessary to call on Chicago for a ballistics expert, nor on Washington for a handwriting expert." When Brooks took the stand in July 1951, he corroborated Rehling's testimony about the types of weapons that caused the deaths of Aubrey Kilpatrick and Leonard Floyd as well as the bullets that had been fired into Boyles's car. But Brooks added a detail that up to that point in the trial had not been broached: one of the occupants in the car had fired—from inside the car.

Expert testimony in trials, especially complex scientific analysis, can be both illuminating and confusing. The mere presence of specialists whose names are followed by a string of letters indicating advanced degrees can impress a jury, but more often than not, jurors react far more favorably to testimony given by people they know, members of the community who, despite having a level of knowledge beyond most citizens, live in the area, shop at the local businesses, send their children to school in town, or worship at nearby churches. Rogers had wisely inserted Dr. Edward Venning's testimony in between Rehling's and Brooks's, mainly because Venning was a local doctor who had been practicing in the area for over twenty years. While Venning had not performed the autopsies on Aubrey Kilpatrick, Zeke Boyles, Leonard Floyd, or Washington Bennett, he had observed Rehling's work, and the people of Marshall County knew and trusted Venning. The ballistics analysis, however, required not only a knowledge of the weapons themselves but also of the chemical and physical reactions that occurred when a gun was fired into metal, glass, or flesh. The men on the jury knew guns, had grown up handling firearms. But knowing how to shoot a gun or even being able to identify types of guns by make and manufacturer does not make one a ballistics expert any more than knowing how to drive or repair a car makes one an automotive engineer. While many of the jurors were doubtless shrewd and capable men, even the most educated among them would have found the scientific jargon daunting.

George Rogers had to walk a fine line between interpreting and translating the expert testimony for the jury's benefit and putting words into Rehling's and Brooks's mouths and thereby drawing the prosecution's objection for leading the witnesses. As aggressive and tenacious as Rogers could be in a courtroom, at times stretching the facts to suit his arguments, it was one thing to subtract a few years from the Kilpatrick children's ages; it was quite another to attempt to distort expert testimony, especially with the experts themselves on the stand to refute any misrepresentations. All it would have taken was a simple "No, that's not right" to destroy Rogers's credibility with the jury, even if they did not fully understand the complicated testimony themselves.

When Rogers began questioning C. D. Brooks about the possibility of a shot fired from inside the car, the attorney proceeded with uncharacteristic caution:

*Rogers*: I want you to tell this jury from what seat, front or back, the two shots that were fired from the inside were fired, in your opinion as an expert.

*Brooks*: It was shot with the gun forward of the back of the front seat.

*Rogers*: What I am trying to get is—

*Brooks*: A person could have been behind there holding his hand in the front seat.

*Rogers*: You are telling the jury, if I understand—see if I have got this correct—you examined the car and found two holes from the inside of the left front glass?

*Brooks*: Yes.

*Rogers*: You are also telling the jury in your opinion as an expert, that from the position of those holes, the location of the holes, the location of the glass when it was broken and the way it looked from a close study of the glass, you are telling the jury the gun that fired the shot that made the holes in the window of that car were fired from the front seat, whether the man was sitting on it or not, he was either sitting on it or holding it over it?

*Brooks:* Yes.

The trial transcript does not indicate the reaction that this revelation had upon the spectators, the prosecutors, or the judge, nor did the reporters in the courtroom covering the trial make any mention of the impact that this information elicited. Perhaps no one fully realized the import.

It ended up being all for naught—at least for the first trial. On Thursday, July 26, Circuit Judge J. S. Stone declared a mistrial. During a cross-examination of character witnesses on July 25, Special Prosecutor Claude Scruggs commented in open court that he did not think character witnesses' testimony should be admissible unless Rogers agreed to put the defendant, James Kilpatrick, on the stand. Rogers had made another motion for a mistrial earlier in the week, and Judge Stone had denied the motion. In that instance, Rogers based his motion on Howard "Moose" Hardin's contact with the jury during the trial. On the night of the shooting, Hardin was the coroner for Marshall County, which meant that he had not only examined the victims' bodies but also participated in the chain of custody for the weapons involved in the shooting. He was the one who retrieved Aubrey Kilpatrick's extra pistol, wrapped in a sack, from the slain man's pocket, and he had removed Aubrey's nickel-plated .44 from underneath the mattress where it had been hidden.

Like the office of sheriff, county coroner was an elected position, making Hardin the acting sheriff upon Boyles's death. In essence, because of the unusual circumstances, Hardin was both coroner and sheriff as he assisted in the crime scene investigation. A month later, after Alabama governor Gordon Persons had appointed Jesse Camp as Marshall County's new sheriff, Hardin then became chief deputy sheriff. These multiple duties complicated Hardin's role in the trial, and when Rogers learned that Hardin had been in contact with the jury outside the proceedings, he pounced upon the potential conflict of interest. Rogers explained to Judge Stone that Hardin had, "in company with another deputy, kept the jury until the late hours of the night on Monday, July 23, and had also been in the private room of the jury on at least one occasion, and had been very active in helping and keeping the jury in spite of the fact that he was a witness in the trial of said cause and testified on the next day, July 24, at length in the trial of said cause." Hardin was recalled to the stand, where he admitted that he had, in his capacity as chief deputy, taken the jurors to supper, although he claimed that at no time had the case been discussed. After a cursory examination, the judge declared that Hardin's actions had caused no harm to the case, overruled the motion for a mistrial, and the trial continued.

Rogers's next motion for a mistrial, however, hit the mark. He had subpoenaed several upstanding members of the Boaz community—ministers, Sunday school teachers, neighboring farmers from the Double Bridges area—to serve as character witnesses on James Kilpatrick's behalf. When Rogers began introducing these witnesses, Claude Scruggs, largely silent during most of the trial since L. P. Waid was serving as lead counsel, objected that the content of the character witnesses' testimony was no substitute for the testimony of the defendant himself, who was not slated to take the stand during the trial. Rogers immediately requested a mistrial on the grounds of Scruggs's remarks, and Judge Stone overruled the motion. But the hasty ruling must have nagged at the judge at the end of the day, for he reviewed the law that night, poring over statutes and legal precedents that could either refute or support Rogers's motion.

Rogers was right—by demanding in open court that the defendant take the stand, Scruggs had violated James Kilpatrick's Fifth Amendment right against self-incrimination: "No person . . . shall be compelled in any criminal case to be a witness against himself." On July 26, Judge Stone declared a mistrial:

It is with great reluctance that I do this. I know the jury wants to get this case over with, and I also want to. But under my constitutional oath I have no choice. The boy deserves a fair trial. If I were to let the case continue and the jury returned a verdict of guilty, and if it were appealed to the supreme court, the supreme court would not uphold the jury's verdict on the grounds that the boy had not had an impartial trial. I don't believe Mr. Scruggs made the remark with the intention of influencing the jury, but nevertheless I am forced to declare the case ended in a mistrial.

The mistrial granted James Kilpatrick a brief reprieve, but only from the immediate threat of conviction in the first trial. While the other two men accused in the killings, Tom Upton and Fred Goble, had been released on bond, James remained in the Marshall County jail, having been denied bond by Judge Stone.

The stress of the first trial as well as the three months since the shooting had taken a tremendous toll on all the families involved. As the summer wore on, the widows, children, and grandchildren of the slain officers mourned their losses and pressed for justice, the adults in particular feeling that a cruel trick had been played on them by the legal system. After the buildup prior to the first trial, the mistrial seemed like a step backward. Angry supporters of the sheriff, his deputies, and the Boaz chief of police clamored for swift retribution. The Kilpatricks were not without their own suffering. Several frustrated members of the community projected their hostilities onto the bootlegger's family, sending death threats to the Kilpatrick farm and penning heated letters to local newspapers.

August rolled into September, and James, despite the improved conditions of his confinement, began to suffer from bouts of gastrointestinal distress and headaches that required medical attention. On September 2, 1951, Elizabeth Kilpatrick delivered a stillborn child, a boy. Some whispered that the loss was a blessing in disguise, especially since Elizabeth already had seven children at home in her care, but the compounded grief of all that she had endured and still faced was almost too much to bear. Photographs taken of Elizabeth by newspaper reporters after the first trial revealed a careworn, defeated woman who looked two decades older than her thirty-seven years. The wheels of justice, however, ground mercilessly forward, and in October 1951 Judge J. S. Stone called for a special term of the Marshall County circuit court to try James Kilpatrick for the murder of Ezekiel Boyles. November would bring another grim harvest.

# CHAPTER 9

# The Second Trial

November in north Alabama is fickle. Some days the relentless sun beats down, the only relief a light breeze lifting the hair from a sweaty neck or brow. The harvest is over, and the fields lie fallow, covered in brown stubble, under azure skies. Eventually a cold front rolls in across the plains, sinking downward toward the South, where it slams into the warm, moist air rising from the Gulf of Mexico. Then the skies darken, and the gentle breezes become changelings, twisting and shrieking and taking the roofs off houses. After the lines of storms pass, cooler air sweeps in, the short-lived autumn rudely forced and violently birthed. People begin to anticipate Thanksgiving and shop for Christmas. Such was the case in November 1951 as those who lived in Marshall County prepared for the year-end holidays. Civic clubs in Albertville, Boaz, and Guntersville scheduled turkey shoots and Christmas tree lightings. Ministers at area churches closely eyed their congregations' heavily expectant mothers-to-be in anticipation of a newborn to play baby Jesus in that year's nativity performances. Although not many rural denizens of Sand Mountain had televisions yet, those who did had fallen in love, like the rest of the country, with a feisty redhead named Lucy and her Cuban bandleader husband, Ricky Ricardo. On the screens at the Rialto and Princess Theaters in Boaz and Albertville, a drenched, muscular Marlon Brando bawled "Stella!" and a pale, wide-eyed Vivien Leigh murmured about depending on the kindness of strangers. In the county jail in Guntersville, James Kilpatrick steeled himself to stand trial for the murder of Sheriff Ezekiel Boyles.

Other than the company of the occasional drunk brought in to sleep off his bender or a thief caught stealing chickens, James had spent his days in jail alone. Tom Upton and Fred Goble, the two sharecroppers who had been arrested along with James, had made bond in August, a month after the first trial. Ann Scott continued to write to him, and his mother, once she was well enough to travel after losing the baby boy in early September, visited on Sundays when she was able to find someone to drive her down the mountain to Guntersville. The jailhouse guards, admonished by the new sheriff, grudgingly brought James his meals and clean water but for the most part left him to his thoughts. He had not testified in the first trial. Even though Claude Scruggs, one of the two special prosecutors, had made a tactical mistake when he commented in open court that the character witnesses meant nothing without the defendant taking the stand, James's attorney George Rogers knew that a seed had been planted in the jurors' minds, jurors who would then go out into the community and talk about how that Kilpatrick boy with his fancy Birmingham lawyer had weaseled out of a conviction. A mistrial was only a temporary reprieve, but Rogers fully intended to make use of what he and John Brown, his co-counsel, had gleaned from the first trial's testimonies and the prosecution's questions. For the November trial, James would have to take the stand, but George Rogers was ready.

James was not. His health had continued to decline while he was in jail, in part because of the meager rations but primarily because of his extreme emotional distress. He may have been raised to be fearless and stoic, and his family, community, and even the legal system may have considered him a man, but he was still in many ways a boy. Through the open windows of the jail, James could hear the Marshall County High School marching band practicing for their halftime performance at the homecoming game in the middle of November, the strains of "Stars Fell on Alabama" floating through the crisp air. Occasional giggles pierced his loneliness as high school girls passed the jail on their way to admire the new dresses in the window of the Quality Store in downtown Guntersville. Sometimes he picked up the excited babble of children as they begged their parents to let them visit "Toy Land" at Kennamer Hardware, stocked and ready for early holiday shopping. James could not help but think about his brothers and sisters up on Sand Mountain, how much Jeretta would love a pretty new dress or how delighted the younger ones would be with shiny, store-bought toys. His heart ached, his head throbbed, and his stomach roiled. Dr. B. N. Lavender, an Albertville physician, checked on James throughout October, eventually prescribing what James later described as "nerve pills"—more than likely barbiturates—to calm him down and help him sleep. Regardless of the outcome of the upcoming trial, James knew he would be spending Thanksgiving and Christmas of 1951 in the Marshall County jail. He knew, too, that because of his actions, the Kilpatricks were not the only ones facing their first Thanksgiving and Christmas without a father. Guilt and grief brooded over and with him in his cell as he waited for November 12 to arrive.

∞

The atmosphere in and around the courthouse in Albertville on the day the second trial began lacked the oddly carnivalesque mood that had surrounded the earlier trial. The weather had turned cool, and low clouds hinted at rain. With the summer heat gone, the courthouse windows could be closed, which meant that any spectators on the lawn would be unable to hear George Rogers's thunderous objections coupled with his declarations of "irrelevant, illegal, and immaterial!" The curious teenagers who had gawked and mingled outside in July instead sat in high school classrooms, concentrating on learning about the periodic table or Sherman's March to the Sea, or, more likely, throwing spitballs at each other or carving their initials into the tops of wooden desks. Still, the crowds came, surging into the courthouse in hopes of securing a seat or squeezing in among the standing spectators. Chief Leonard Floyd had been much loved and respected in Boaz, but Sheriff Zeke Boyles was a legend in north Alabama. The man whom the citizens of Marshall County had elected sheriff three times had left a mixed legacy. Some remembered him with great esteem and admiration; to his supporters, he was a big man with a big smile, an inveterate jokester and backslapper, tirelessly devoted to serving and protecting the people of Marshall County. Others, however, regarded him as a politically driven braggart who treated the law with self-serving malleability, a hot-tempered hypocrite as liable to tip illegal whiskey down his throat in private as he was to pour it on the ground in public. Regardless of whatever respect or scorn individual citizens held for Zeke Boyles, he had been their sheriff, and he had been killed in the line of duty. There was a reckoning at hand, and the crowd at the courthouse wanted to be there to witness it.

George Rogers smoothed down his tie with one hand and ran a hand over his Brilliantined hair with the other. Even though the air in the courtroom was decidedly cooler than it had been in July, the defense attorney mopped his sweaty brow with a starched handkerchief only slightly discolored by the oily, brown hair pomade. He had taken up residence during the trial at a boardinghouse in Boaz coincidentally run by one of James Kilpatrick's aunts, making sure to pay over the usual price and to leave a dollar or two under the plate after each meal. Although the Kilpatrick case occupied almost all his time and energy, especially his continued push to obtain James Kilpatrick's release on bond, he followed closely the news coming out of Phenix City, a town on the Alabama–Georgia border roughly 160 miles south and east of Boaz. An up-and-coming young politician named Albert Patterson, along with longtime Phenix City resident and businessman Hugh Bentley, was fighting a losing battle to break the grip of organized crime as gambling, prostitution, illegal liquor sales, and drug trafficking brought mayhem and fear to the small town. Denounced by U.S. secretary of war Henry L. Stimson as "the wickedest city in America," Phenix City had become an iniquitous playground for soldiers stationed across the Chattahoochee River at Fort Benning, and the vice and corruption had prompted Major General George Patton to propose using his tanks to raze the city to the ground. The violence in Phenix City peaked in 1954 after a series of bombings (in 1952 Bentley's home was dynamited, his family only narrowly escaping) and the assassination of Patterson outside his law office in Phenix City, culminating in the declaration of martial law. With his reputation as a never-say-die, top-notch defense attorney cemented, in part by his widely publicized efforts on behalf of James Kilpatrick, Rogers would eventually take on the challenge of defending Archer "Arch" Bradford Ferrell against charges of conspiring to murder Albert Patterson in Phenix City. But on that cool, overcast November morning in 1951, the tempest downstate seemed half a world away. George Rogers seated himself at the defense table next to his co-counsel, John Brown, organized his notes, and began the process of selecting the jury.

The Honorable J. S. Stone took his place at the bench as the jury prospects filed into the courtroom. He knew these men—farmers, salesmen, shopkeepers, grist mill owners—and he knew the lives they led, the values they held, and the way their minds worked. But there were always surprises. The right to trial by jury in criminal cases is guaranteed by the Sixth Amendment to the U.S. Constitution as well as the laws of every state. From a selected panel of jurors, known as a venire, the trial judge begins by asking a series of questions to ensure the jurors' eligibility. After ascertaining that none of the potential jurors were members of the grand jury that had indicted the defendant, had been indicted within the last year for a felony or charged with homicide, or were related by blood or marriage to the defendant or the deceased sheriff, Judge Stone asked if any of the men had a fixed opinion as to the guilt or innocence of the defendant that would bias their verdict. As happens with many venire inquiries, this question elicited several responses. Three prospects claimed that regardless of any evidence presented in the trial, their minds were made up, with one man commenting that he could not in good conscience serve on the jury: "By what I heard and what I read and what I heard other folks say. Such as that." One by one, the jury pool shrank. Then the judge inquired whether any of them had any reservations about capital punishment.

Even though many of these men had been brought up in the Old Testament eye-for-an-eye tradition, several averred that, even if presented with overwhelming evidence of the defendant's guilt, they adamantly opposed the death penalty. One potential juror, a Church of Christ minister from Guntersville, stated that the doctrine of his faith prohibited him from condoning the death penalty, but such sentiment was rare on Sand Mountain. Alabama had (and still has) a reputation for prolific executions. From 1900 until 1951, the state of Alabama had put over two hundred convicted criminals to death, switching from hanging to electrocution in 1927. Alabama's electric chair, known as "Yellow Mama" because it had been painted with traffic line paint borrowed from the state highway department, sat grimly at Kilby Prison outside Montgomery. George Rogers was determined to keep his client from becoming the youngest person in state history to sit on Yellow Mama's deadly lap.

The jury had been sworn and seated, but the trial could not begin yet, not without the man whose testimony had been so pivotal in the first trial—Dr. Carl Rehling, the state toxicologist. November 1951 had been a busy month for Rehling. Not only had he announced the week before James Kilpatrick's second trial that he would be establishing a branch crime laboratory in Montgomery (labs already existed in Auburn, Mobile, and Birmingham), but he was also traveling from town to town, scheduling an inquest in Prattville for a hit-and-run victim, conducting an autopsy on a man whose skull had been shattered by an adjustable wrench during a fight in Gadsden, and examining a bundle of bones hunters had found in a sack in the woods outside Clanton. Even with the new satellite labs, Rehling was very much in demand, and he saw each investigation as an opportunity to learn. The first interstate highway in Alabama would not open until the end of the 1950s, and the elaborate four-lane system that eventually crisscrossed the state was in the distant future, so Rehling rattled along two-lane blacktop highways and narrow dirt roads in his 1946 Ford sedan, a worn Shell Oil Company highway map of Alabama spread out on the passenger seat. Although he had lived in Auburn for much of the past twenty-five years, Rehling still considered north Alabama home, but his duties kept him on the road throughout the week, sometimes performing scientific analyses, sometimes taking the stand as expert witness in a trial.

On Monday, November 12, the day James Kilpatrick's second trial was scheduled to begin, Rehling had been detained by another murder investigation, the case of the unfortunate Gadsden man who had been done in with his own adjustable wrench. Sand Mountain loomed in the distance as Rehling presented his evidence in Etowah County concerning the death of Robert Lee Spinks, but he would not be able to make his way up U.S. Route 241 to Albertville until Tuesday, November 13. After the prosecution declined to proceed in Rehling's absence, court was recessed for the day. Judge Stone instructed the jury to stay with the sheriff at all times and warned them not to wander off or get lost, adding with a particularly grim choice of words, "If any of you get separated, it will be fatal."

From the beginning, James Kilpatrick's November 1951 trial proceeded in a far more deliberate and methodical manner than the July trial. Just as the summer heat and humidity had given way to autumn's cool austerity, in November the prosecution and the defense faced each other less like duelists and more like chess players. The whole atmosphere of the first trial had felt like a tinderbox—passions were still running high only ten weeks after the shooting, and the excitement of the swarming crowd inside and outside the courthouse had heightened the antagonism between the two opposing sides. Frustrated by the mistrial in July, the prosecution had become wary. Claude Scruggs's offhand comment concerning the viability of character witnesses was a misstep that could not be repeated, which meant that the defense could bring to the stand upstanding community members, ministers, Sunday school teachers, and local business owners who would all testify that James Kilpatrick, while not exactly a Boy Scout, was a good-hearted, hardworking, respectful young man. Likewise, Rogers and Brown knew that Scruggs's comments, however legally problematic they had been, had sounded a bell that could not be unrung: James Kilpatrick, now six months away from turning eighteen, would not merely be seated at the front of the courtroom with his back to the gallery, silent and intently listening as men in suits and ties presented opposing accounts of his actions on the night of May 17. He would have to rise, take the witness stand, face the crowd, and relive, through his own words, what he had done.

∞

If all the world's a stage, as Jaques sadly but wisely observes in Shakespeare's *As You Like It*, then the courtroom is the nexus of art imitating life as well as life imitating art. The stage (and, in modern times, the screen) and the courtroom explore the same human verities and foibles: the consequences of provoked passions or cool calculations, greed, betrayal, pride, vaulting ambition, revenge. The spectators in the courtroom are the audience, with the specially selected jury weighing the actions of the accused and passing judgment. The jury, like the chorus in Greek tragedies, thus becomes the embodiment of the desires and fears of the polity, the average citizens. A trial has a protagonist and an antagonist, although these roles are not fixed but fluid, depending on who is steering the plot. The prosecution clearly wants the jury to see the victim as the protagonist and the defendant as the antagonist, while the defense seeks to transpose that characterization. The burden of proof is on the prosecution, for they must establish guilt beyond a reasonable doubt, but the defense has the equally daunting task of calling into question the actions of a victim who, if dead, can't offer a counterargument. The tension in a play relies on the assemblage of the dramatis personae, whose order of appearance dictates the rise of suspense and the resolution of conflict, just as the artful presentation of witnesses in a trial helps each side unveil the narrative it wishes to tell. Of course, a trial is not scripted in the same way a play is—in this way, trials resemble improvisational theater more than formally rehearsed stagecraft—although witnesses are usually rigorously coached and taught to anticipate particular questions or directions of inquiry. In a trial, instead of memorizing and reciting, the participants provide the lines, and the court reporter reproduces the proceedings as a transcript that reads like a play.

For James Kilpatrick's second trial, George Rogers needed to reconstruct his client's persona. Rogers could not change the basic facts of the case or the identifying details of the defendant (full name, address, age, and such), but he could alter his strategy from the previous trial, which meant employing new tactics. In the July trial, Rogers had conspicuously and repeatedly referred to James as a "sixteen-year-old child." With James sitting quietly at the defense table throughout the first trial, neatly dressed in a plaid shirt that his mother had ironed and delivered to him each morning, the cowlick on the crown of his head visible to the spectators in the gallery, such a description did not seem far-fetched. He was of average height and slightly built, with a lean, earnest, boyish face, his clear, smooth skin barely (and rarely) needing a razor. This time, however, a man—not a frightened, naïve little boy—would stand before the court and respond to questions that led to the indisputable fact that he had shot four men, killing three of them and gravely wounding the fourth. These four men had not been late-night customers seeking to quench their thirst for Aubrey Kilpatrick's illegal moonshine, nor were they a gang of criminals planning to rob the farm. They were an elected county sheriff, his trusted deputies, and a decorated war hero who had sworn to serve and protect the people of Boaz as their chief of police. The blood-stained warrants that then-coroner Howard "Moose" Hardin had removed from the dead sheriff's breast pocket the night of the shooting would be introduced into evidence and displayed in the courtroom as documented, legal proof, regardless of dubious timing or private vendetta, that the officers had had the right to be at the Kilpatrick farm. What George Rogers had to insinuate—deftly, carefully, and convincingly—was that James Kilpatrick had believed he had the right to shoot at them.

Nowhere in Rogers's questions or statements does the phrase "Castle Doctrine" appear, but this ancient principle, dating back to the Roman Republic, has been the basis of laws concerning self-defense in America since colonial settlement. The inviolability of the home and the duty of the paterfamilias to protect those under his care became part of English common law in the seventeenth century, beginning with Sir Edward Coke's assertion in his 1628 legal treatise *The Institutes of the Laws of England* that "a man's house is his castle, *et domus sua cuique est tutissimum refugium* [and each man's home is his safest refuge]." The power of the paterfamilias as well as the definition of what constituted a "castle" evolved over the centuries, both concepts deeply and historically entrenched in feudal hierarchies, slavery, and class divisions. By the eighteenth century, the definition of a "castle" had been broadened to include any domicile, royal or not. In 1763, sounding dangerously democratic, Prime Minister William Pitt, known as "The Great Commoner" (before he accepted a peerage to become the first Earl of Chatham, a decidedly uncommon move), declared the sacrosanctity of even the humblest abode: "The poorest man may in his cottage bid defiance to all the forces of the crown. It may be frail—its roof may shake—the wind may blow through it—the storm may enter—the rain may enter—but the King of England cannot enter."

After the American Revolution, the laws of the new nation, derived liberally from English common law, recycled castle doctrine as a justification for self-defense, retaining the democratic flavor given to it by Pitt. From the eighteenth century onward, the emergent U.S. states incorporated some variant of castle doctrine principles into their laws. Broadly interpreted, such laws dictated that every mansion, bungalow, cabin, shack, and sod dwelling could be considered a "castle," and any head of household from the wealthiest plantation master to the lowliest sharecropper was a paterfamilias. In the late nineteenth and early twentieth centuries, particularly in southern and western states, castle doctrine served as the centerpiece of not only laws concerning self-defense but also general resistance to centralized authority. Henry Grady, proponent of the New South, delivered an address called "Against Centralization" at the University of Virginia in 1889 in which he encouraged his audience to "Exalt the citizen" and "Teach him that his home is his castle, and his sovereignty rests beneath his hat." As the wave of populist sentiment swept through the South, vestiges of the cries for states' rights that swirled around the Civil War, Louisiana governor (and, later, U.S. senator) Huey Long proclaimed "every man a king" with "castles and clothing and food for all." Thus Aubrey Kilpatrick's home, derided as it was in newspapers as a "ramshackle house" and a "rundown dwelling," was his castle, he was its king, and the inhabitants therein were his responsibility and under his protection.

In short, George Rogers didn't have to describe, define, or even overtly invoke castle doctrine—the principles it embodied were as natural to the jurors as the air they breathed. After initially submitting a plea of "not guilty by reason of insanity" on James Kilpatrick's behalf in the July 1951 trial, Rogers changed the plea to "not guilty by reason of self-defense and protection of home and family," a strategy he maintained throughout all the trials. But although castle doctrine could be used as an affirmative defense in the case of criminal homicide, one of the most significant exclusions to claiming the justifiable use of deadly force against an intruder was if the person or persons were law enforcement officers acting in an official capacity, such as serving a warrant. Sheriff Boyles and the accompanying officers were indeed performing a lawful act—they had duly investigated a criminal complaint and obtained, from a sworn justice of the peace, a legal document that authorized the arrest of Aubrey Kilpatrick. So how could Rogers argue, under the auspices of castle doctrine, that James Kilpatrick was not guilty by reason of self-defense and protection of home and family? He would have to convince the jury that James—when he had heard the shots outside, emerged from his house, saw his father on the ground "in his own life's blood," went back inside to retrieve his carbine, and subsequently opened fire on the men getting out of the car—had not known that they were the law.

In his opening statement at the November 1951 trial, Rogers asserted that "at approximately midnight or a short time before midnight, a car loaded with four men drove up into the yard of his [James Kilpatrick's] father's home." After hearing gunshots, James "ran outside" and "saw some tall man he did not know holding [his] twelve-year-old brother by the arm as a shield and shooting in the general direction of the front door of his father's house." In case any nuance may have been missed, Rogers said clearly and succinctly to the jury, his gaze level and penetrating, "At no time did James Kilpatrick know that the men in the yard were officers or the purpose of their visit at or near midnight on the night of May 17, 1951." Later in this same opening statement, Rogers reiterated that "at no time did the defendant, James Kilpatrick, know that the men who were killed were officers of the law until after the shooting." The defense attorney's word choices carried their own nuances. By repeating the phrases "his father's house" and "at or near midnight," Rogers evoked an almost mystical scene: the inviolate refuge of a man and his family besieged by unknown assailants at an hour when any ordinary citizen would be tucked into bed. Even if the men were officers who carried a warrant, they were in an unmarked car, one of the occupants had shot James's father virtually at the threshold of the family's home, and James did not know who the men were.

Despite the powerful emotional appeal of the defense Rogers was constructing, there were flaws in its foundation. The testimonies of the surviving officer (James Lang) and the justice of the peace (R. L. Turner) verified that proper procedures were followed in obtaining the warrant. Nothing within the law specified when a warrant should be served or in what manner. The issue of a "no-knock warrant," currently under such scrutiny and criticism after a series of tragic civilian deaths, had not been codified in 1951, although by 1958, the U.S. Supreme Court had ruled in *Miller v. United States* that one could not be lawfully arrested in one's home by officers breaking in without first giving notice of their authority and purpose. The arresting officers who drove up to the Kilpatrick house had not attempted to enter the house per se; according to testimony from both sides, the officers had not even exited the car when the shooting began, although who shot first was the central point of contention between the prosecution and the defense. Rogers tried, frequently and at times desperately, to suppress both stated and implied reasons for the officers' visit, objecting that events which transpired several hours prior had no bearing on James Kilpatrick's actions "at or near midnight" of May 17. But the ambush narrative, so prominent in the newspaper coverage of the shooting and propagated in cafés and barbershops and over dinner tables throughout Marshall County, cast James Kilpatrick's reaction in a less noble and far more sinister light.

Had Aubrey Kilpatrick not been a bootlegger "known for his fiery temper and his willingness to fight on short notice," as the *Birmingham News* had described him, or as "handy with a gun," as Sheriff Boyles had commented publicly only two months before the shooting, the incident with the Whiteheads might not have seemed so portentous. Surely the jurors, many of them landowners and landlords themselves, had dealt with recalcitrant or even destructive workers. Threats of eviction were seldom met with contrition and acceptance, and the Whiteheads had the reputation throughout the area for being difficult tenants. After the fight with Whiteheads, Aubrey was clearly on edge about the potential for further violence; otherwise, he would not have sent James and Fred Goble with guns to guard the barn. George Rogers just as easily could have argued that Aubrey—and subsequently James—might have thought the car rolling up to the front door around midnight contained William Whitehead and a few of the young toughs he was known to consort with, seeking revenge on Aubrey for injuring and humiliating Whitehead and David Dean earlier in the day, waiting until late at night to catch Aubrey off guard.

Such reasoning was not beyond logical consideration. If Aubrey Kilpatrick had been anyone else, the incident might have been judged as a case of heightened tempers and mistaken identity gone horribly, tragically awry. But he was who he was, and, in the eyes of the community, James was procurate to a dangerous and volatile paterfamilias. It didn't help matters at all, therefore, when William Whitehead's mother took the stand and testified that, immediately after the dustup between Aubrey and her son, James had dared her to "call Zeke and all the sheriffs" and declared he "wanted to kill all the damn sons of bitches."

The Whiteheads had been noticeably and inexplicably absent from the witness list for the first trial in July, and none of the family members appear to have been subpoenaed. Existing court documents contain no information about this omission. Whatever the reason, they did not testify in the first trial, but Burnice Whitehead, known familiarly as "Fannie," and her twenty-one-year-old son William both took the stand in the second trial. While William had nothing particularly damaging to contribute, answering most of the questions with a laconic "Sure did," George Rogers objected mightily to any inclusion of testimony about that afternoon's events: "Attempt to go into the details of a prior difficulty. Would not have any bearing on this. It is too remote in that it occurred, allegedly, approximately eight hours before the alleged homicide occurred on which this indictment is based."

One small victory that Rogers won, however, occurred during his cross-examination of William Whitehead. During James Lang's testimony, immediately before Whitehead took the stand, the deputy had claimed that the justice of the peace was awake and dressed when he and the two

Whitehead sons had shown up at the Turner house to obtain the warrant. Whitehead's testimony contradicted Lang's statements—instead of Turner being "up" and "fully clothed and dressed" as Lang had testified, Whitehead asserted that Turner was "in the bed" when Lang knocked at the door and in "his night clothes" when he came to the door. It was a minor detail, to be sure, but it cast doubt on Lang's account of the events leading up to the shooting. Whether he was either intentionally altering the facts or merely misremembering what had transpired prior to being critically wounded at the Kilpatrick farm, Lang had unwittingly handed Rogers a chisel to chip away at the clarity of the deputy's memory. Rogers clearly hoped that the contradictions would lead the jury to scrutinize the urgency Zeke Boyles had felt was necessary to serve arrest papers on Aubrey Kilpatrick regardless of any previous agreements made by his deputies or the lateness of the hour. But if William's words were a chisel that Rogers thought he could use in James Kilpatrick's favor, Mrs. Whitehead's testimony was a sledgehammer that shattered Rogers's carefully wrought construction of the defendant as a virtuous defender of his family, surprised by violence into reacting with justifiable force against a clear and present threat.

When Fannie Whitehead took the stand, George Rogers launched a volley of objections to her testimony to thwart the negative impression of Aubrey and James Kilpatrick that she was sure to create. After the judge overruled a series of Rogers's objections, Special Prosecutor E. G. Pilcher instructed Mrs. Whitehead to "tell the jury what James Kilpatrick said" when she had threatened to call the law. Mrs. Whitehead responded, "I told him he ought not to have his guns out there. That I would have to go call Zeke. He said, 'Go ahead. Call Zeke and all the sheriffs.' Said he wanted to kill all the damn sons of bitches." With a dramatic pause for effect, even as audible gasps rose from the courtroom spectators, Pilcher reiterated, "Said go ahead and call the sheriff? He wanted to kill all the damn sons of bitches?" Judge Stone banged his gavel and called for order in the court, but the damage had been done. All Rogers could do was object, somewhat desperately and feebly, that Pilcher was "leading and suggesting. Telling her what he wants her to say." Satisfied and triumphant, Pilcher ended his questions and returned to the counsel table.

Suddenly the polite farm boy with the guileless face didn't seem so nice. No one could call George Rogers a quitter, and although Mrs. Whitehead's words had rattled the jury, Rogers had an arrow in his quiver to deflate her credibility. He began his cross-examination bluntly: "Who did you first tell that to?" When Mrs. Whitehead faltered, appearing not to understand the question, Rogers pressed, "Who did you first tell? What officer? What officer did you first tell it to? That you say you heard James say that?" The witness admitted that she had not initially relayed James's words to an officer; instead, she said, pointing at the counsel table where the prosecution sat, "I told that little man." The "little man" was Pilcher. She also pointed to L. P. Waid, the circuit solicitor, stating, "And that other fellow behind there." In case the jury could not see at whom she was pointing, Rogers clarified, "Waid?" The woman who had boldly proclaimed that she had heard James Kilpatrick boast that he would "kill all the damn sons of bitches" now seemed tentative and unsure in the face of Rogers's barrage of questions. "Was it before the other trial?" Rogers demanded. Mrs. Whitehead admitted that it was not. "In other words," Rogers continued, "you didn't testify to that at the last trial, did you?" Pilcher objected, and when Judge Stone overruled, Rogers made quick work of tightening the snare. When exactly, Rogers persisted, had Mrs. Whitehead informed any official that James had threatened to kill the sheriff and his deputies if they came to serve a warrant? Mrs. Whitehead responded tersely, "About a week ago."

"About a week ago" would have been the beginning of November 1951, roughly six months after the shooting had occurred. Why had Mrs. Whitehead waited half a year to drop the bombshell that could cost James Kilpatrick his freedom and possibly even his life? Rogers wanted the jury to consider this belated admission in all its implications: had the omission of this information in the previous trial simply been an oversight, or had Mrs. Whitehead been encouraged by overzealous prosecutors to give embellished testimony? The timing was suspicious, as was the woman's admission that she had withheld the statement until an eleventh-hour visit by Pilcher, Waid, and, as she further testified, Deputy James Lang.

Perhaps realizing that she had inadvertently undermined the dramatic impact of her claim, Mrs. Whitehead became sullen and defensive, stubbornly insisting that she had only felt compelled to tell her recent visitors about James Kilpatrick's threat because no one in the aftermath of the shooting had thought to ask her. Incredulous, Rogers repeated his question: "You didn't tell the state investigators or the deputy sheriffs, you didn't tell anybody until this man here come and talked to you that you heard any such statement as that?" Mrs. Whitehead exclaimed, "I didn't tell no lie!" Rogers backed off. He wouldn't score any points with the jury for badgering a poor, illiterate sharecropper's wife; he could only hope that the twelve men would infer that the woman had been manipulated (or even subtly coerced) into making a false claim. Rogers wrapped up his cross-examination of Mrs.

Whitehead by asking her, "You don't feel very kindly toward the Kilpatricks, do you?" She grudgingly replied, "I haven't got anything against them. I am not mad at them. The children never harmed me or done a thing toward me in my life." Whether she included James as one of the Kilpatrick children against which she bore no hard feelings was left unaddressed, and she was allowed to leave the witness stand. The verdict would reveal the degree to which her words had left an impression on the arbiters of James Kilpatrick's fate.

The Whiteheads were not the only first-time witnesses in James Kilpatrick's second trial. Dr. Hampton Ephraim Barker, the Boaz physician whom Elizabeth Kilpatrick had called to her home immediately after the shooting, had not testified in the July trial. He had treated members of the Kilpatrick family on various occasions, stitching up wounds and tending to the types of injuries typically incurred on farms. He had delivered all eight of the Kilpatrick children in a time and place when most babies were born at home, and he had watched the children grow up. He had a son the same age as James Kilpatrick. Doctors in rural communities often made house calls, but the frantic phone call he had received from the Kilpatrick residence close to midnight on May 17, 1951, had nothing to do with a croupy child or a tenant farmer kicked by an ornery mule.

When Dr. Barker arrived at the Kilpatrick farm, he found a chaotic scene—bloody bodies lay on the ground in front of the house; Elizabeth was bent over her husband, keening in distress; and several of the Kilpatrick children were weeping and screaming. Another tenant farmer, Fred Goble, paced nearby, cradling a shotgun. With the calm dignity he was known for throughout the Boaz community, Dr. Barker sat at the front of the courtroom in November 1951 and responded to E. G. Pilcher's examination, describing in detail the position of Aubrey Kilpatrick's body in relation to the house ("His feet were up the hill. His head was downhill toward the old road just below the house") and the bootlegger's dying moments ("He looked like he was dead. I thought he was until I saw him gasp just three or four short breaths"). The doctor also testified that Aubrey Kilpatrick "had a large pistol in his right hand," which Barker removed and "handed . . . to one of the members of the family." Presenting an unloaded .44 Smith & Wesson to Barker, Pilcher asked, "In your judgment, is that the gun you took out of the hand of Aubrey Kilpatrick?" Barker positively identified the gun as Aubrey Kilpatrick's—the gun the doctor had given over to twelve-year-old Jeretta Kilpatrick, who had then run inside the house to hide the gun under a mattress.

Dr. H. E. Barker was a highly educated man and greatly respected in Marshall County. He had earned his medical degree from Emory University in Atlanta and served as president of the medical staff of the Boaz-Albertville Hospital and director of Marshall County's Health Unit. Despite the vast social and educational gulf that must have separated Barker from most of his patients in the largely rural community of Boaz, he had not hesitated to rush to Aubrey Kilpatrick's farm when the distraught bootlegger's wife had phoned him close to midnight. He was a man who took his oath and commitment to his patients seriously. He was also a man not inclined to sensationalism or grandstanding, which made his testimony about James Kilpatrick's state of mind after the shooting even more compelling and more believable than Fannie Whitehead's. When Pilcher asked if James had made any statements to Dr. Barker while he was examining the bodies of Aubrey Kilpatrick, Zeke Boyles, and Leonard Floyd, Barker offered a heart-wrenching description:

> He was crying, nervous and upset. And he was angry at the officers because they had shot his father. He said his father didn't even have any gun in his hand. They shot him—got the draw on him and shot him before he had a chance to defend himself. And then he said he shot at them. He shot two of the sons of bitches and hit another one but he, or two of the men, got away but he knew he hit one of them.

After the doctor finished speaking, murmurs, muffled sobs, and the sounds of clearing throats filled the courtroom. At the defense counsel table, James Kilpatrick lowered his head and wept.

A pattern emerged in the second trial that would grow more pronounced and inflammatory in the trials that followed: while all the prosecutors were seasoned, capable attorneys, E. G. Pilcher was clearly the most aggressive of the lot, the one best suited to go head-to-head with George Rogers. Whatever the two men's relationship might have been like outside the courtroom, when they were in front of the jury, their intense and apparent dislike for each other whetted the gallery's appetite for high drama and spectacle. Sometimes the two opponents' rapid-fire exchanges and thinly veiled insults drew laughter from the spectators, causing Judge Stone to rap his gavel and demand order in the court. On more than one occasion, Pilcher exhibited a mean streak that could have possibly turned the jury against him. During his cross-examination of Dr. Barker, George Rogers asked the physician, in reference to Elizabeth Kilpatrick, "Do you know whether or not she sometime later miscarried?" Pilcher objected, adding,

"So what if she did. That wouldn't have anything to do with it." Rogers retorted, "I know it is all right with you if she did," drawing a rebuke from Judge Stone for the two attorneys to "direct [their] remarks to the Court." As harsh as Pilcher's comment seems, a murder trial is not Sunday school, and neither Pilcher nor Rogers claimed to be choirboys.

Pilcher had been hired by the Alabama Sheriffs' and Peace Officers' Association, founded in 1933 as an organization representing law enforcement throughout the state, to serve as a special prosecutor in July 1951 when James Kilpatrick stood trial for the death of Boaz police chief Leonard Floyd, in November 1951 for Sheriff Zeke Boyles, and in October 1952 for Chief Deputy Washington Bennett. Pilcher earned every penny. He knew just where the line of propriety and judicial conduct was drawn, and if his toe sometimes crossed that line, the results he gleaned were well worth the risks he took. Pilcher clearly relished taking the lead, especially when the witnesses on the stand provided particularly incriminating and sensational testimony. It was during the cross-examination of the character witnesses that Pilcher did the most damage to Rogers's argument that James Kilpatrick's actions on the night of May 17 were an aberration, that the otherwise well-mannered, respectful farm boy had resorted to violence only to protect his family and himself. That's the double-edged sword of introducing character witnesses—the defense intends for these testimonies to present the defendant in the best light possible, but a wily prosecutor can turn the tables and cause the jurors to see the defendant more negatively than if they never heard supporting testimony at all.

And that's exactly what Pilcher did. While Rogers's examination was limited to asking the character witnesses how they knew James Kilpatrick and whether his reputation was good or bad, Pilcher had the advantage of introducing otherwise inadmissible prior "bad acts" during his cross-examination. In other words, if a witness states an opinion about the defendant's character or reputation, the prosecutor may ask the witness whether she or he has heard about the defendant committing any violent acts, even if these acts did not result in arrests or convictions. Pilcher was walking a legal tightrope, but he knew from nearly three decades of courtroom experience that jurors tend to focus on and retain concrete examples of negative behavior more so than positive but vague generalities.

Even as respected local business owners, teachers, Sunday school superintendents, and pastors testified to James Kilpatrick's good character and reputation, Pilcher undermined the veracity of their claims with a series of questions designed to expose the defendant as a bully who terrorized anyone who crossed him. Pilcher asked Sam Bruce, a DeKalb County commissioner and cotton gin owner, if he had heard about James holding a gun on Marshall County deputies. Bruce responded that he had not. Pilcher then inquired if Bruce knew "about the time he [James] took this boy off the school bus down there and whipped him." Again, Bruce replied that he had not. Pilcher persisted: "Did you know he shot at Lonnie Holcomb there in his yard?" Bruce once again denied having heard about any such incident. In his redirect examination, Rogers tried to deflect attention away from the intimations that James, like his father, was a "little too handy with a gun." If Pilcher could tar James with the brush of gossip and rumors, Rogers could counter with some editorializing of his own. Two could play that game. Before Bruce was dismissed from the witness stand, Rogers said, "I will ask you whether or not if James didn't take the lead among his seven brothers and sisters and if he didn't operate that farm himself and take a man's place about the farm?" The blatantly leading remark drew an objection from Pilcher, which Judge Stone sustained, but Rogers had met Pilcher's parry with a thrust of his own.

To each successive character witness that took the stand, Pilcher asked variations of the same four questions:

1. "Have you heard out there he and his father were selling whiskey?"
2. "Did you hear about the time he pulled a boy off the school bus and whipped him while his father held a gun on the driver?"
3. "Did you know that he shot at Lonnie Holcomb there in his yard?"
4. "Did you hear about the time he held his gun on Sheriff Grant's deputies out there?"

George Rogers, exasperated by Pilcher's repeated references to alleged (but unsubstantiated) incidents, began his redirect examination of the Kilpatricks' neighbor Kermit Gerrard with, "Did you ever hear that James fell off a horse and the horse run off and he threw a rock at it?" Laughter erupted in the courtroom as Ed Scruggs objected, and Rogers snapped, "It's not any more improper than what he has been asking." The questioning of the character witnesses was beginning to sound like an absurdist play, with the jurors growing restless and probably desensitized to any import that the testimony might convey. But the atmosphere suddenly became electrified as Billy Kilpatrick, James's younger brother and one of the few eyewitnesses to the shooting, entered the courtroom and made his way to the witness stand.

Like James, Billy was slight and rangy and had the same lean, angular features of his older brother. Fifteen years old at the time of the shooting, Billy had just turned sixteen in October. With his older brother, James, in jail and his younger brother Harold recovering from an emergency appendectomy, Billy had assumed the duties of the eldest male in the Kilpatrick household, and times had been exceedingly hard on the family. He had not testified in the July trial, so his appearance in the November trial marked the first time he was able to recount publicly the events of May 17. Rogers guided him through his movements prior to the shooting: the evening possum hunting with his friend Fred Howard Burns, the encounter with Sheriff Boyles and his men, the strange ride into Boaz and back, even the release of the dog at the mailboxes at the end of the driveway. Billy described the car pulling within a few feet of the front of the Kilpatricks' house and seeing his father sitting in a rocking chair near the open door. Jurors leaned forward intently as Billy recounted his father rising from the chair and stepping out the front door. While James Lang had testified that Aubrey had threatened the officers with a menacing "Don't get out, or I'll kill you," Billy stated that his father had merely told the men to "go on back to town." Then Billy made the most shocking statement that had been uttered in the trial to that point— when Rogers prompted him to tell what happened next, Billy said, "And the driver shot him and he fell on the ground."

The driver? Both James Lang and Billy Kilpatrick had verified that Lang was the one driving the car, with Washington Bennett in the front passenger seat, Zeke Boyles sitting behind the driver's seat, and Leonard Floyd positioned behind Bennett. After Billy and Fred had gotten into the car, they sat between Boyles and Floyd, with Fred perched on Billy's lap. The back seat of a 1950 Pontiac Chieftain is roomy, practically cavernous compared to today's automobiles; both the front and back seats are styled as benches, undivided by a console. The seat tops lack headrests, this feature not incorporated into standard automobile manufacture until the 1960s. How much could Billy have seen, given that he was not a tall boy, sitting in between two large men and holding another teenaged boy on his lap? Billy's claim that the driver had shot his father seemed to have surprised even Rogers (although the lawyer had more than likely orchestrated this exchange), who responded, "The driver did what?" In a louder voice, Billy replied, "And the driver shot him. When he [Aubrey] started down he got his gun." Suddenly a new narrative took shape, one that challenged James Lang's previous testimony that Aubrey Kilpatrick had emerged from the house, uttered his threat, and immediately fired twice at the car. But this narrative was not without its serious flaws.

Besides the possibility that Billy's view had been partially obstructed, the likelihood that James Lang had shot Aubrey Kilpatrick had already been disproven in earlier testimony from expert witnesses. On the night of May 17, Lang had been carrying a .32-20 Smith & Wesson military and police revolver, and both Cecil Sanderson, an investigator for the Alabama Department of Public Safety, and C. D. Brooks, assistant state toxicologist, had testified that Lang's weapon had never been fired and that the two shots that had come from inside the car had been from a .38. Lang had avowed that he had never fired or even unholstered his revolver. Yet someone had fired a gun—a .38—twice from the interior of the driver's side window, and Brooks had explained how his ballistic analysis had determined that the two shots had been fired by a gun held by someone sitting behind the driver and leaning over the front seat. In his earlier testimony, Lang had equivocated when Rogers asked four times whether a shot had been fired from inside the car: "Not that I know of." Lang gave the same response when Rogers inquired if Sheriff Boyles had ever fired his gun. Amid the definite affirmations or negations with which Lang responded to other questions, this singular ambiguity seemed suspect. One matter was certain: someone had fired twice from inside the car through the driver's side window, and it hadn't been James Lang.

Besides the startling declaration that James Lang had been the one who shot Aubrey Kilpatrick, the rest of Billy's testimony revealed little about his brother's involvement in the subsequent shootout. Although he maintained that Chief Deputy Washington Bennett had grabbed Billy as he exited the car, Billy claimed that not once during all of the shooting did he see his older brother. Instead, Billy asserted, he saw James in the house "after it was over." To emphasize the vulnerability of the home's inhabitants, Rogers had Billy give the names and ages of each child inside the house. In Rogers's descriptions, Billy himself was a victimized child, a young boy left fatherless because a hotheaded sheriff had forced a confrontation. During cross-examination, Circuit Solicitor Waid managed to elicit little more from Billy than an admission that the only member of the Kilpatrick family he had seen shoot a gun was his father. Waid abruptly ended the questioning, apparently frustrated with the lack of headway he was making with such an integral witness but also wary of bullying a young boy in front of a jury. L. P. Waid was an elected official who had to be mindful of his comportment when representing his circuit. On the other hand, being the "hired gun," so to speak, gave E. G. Pilcher more latitude to go after witnesses aggressively.

The last witness to take the stand on Wednesday, November 14, was one who inspired both compassion and contempt among people throughout the county. Elizabeth Kilpatrick, Aubrey's widow and James's mother, also had not testified in the first trial, although she had been present in the courtroom for all of the testimony before the mistrial had been declared. Photographers had clustered around her, snapping pictures that appeared in newspapers across the state, and her discomfort at being the center of attention showed in every image of her, usually seated with a phalanx of children surrounding her. She never smiled; she spoke in a low voice, often with her hand hovering near or covering her mouth. The reason for her shyness became painfully apparent during her time on the witness stand. At several points during her testimony, Rogers, Judge Stone, or a member of the prosecution prompted her to "talk out" so the jurors could hear her. Finally, Rogers pleaded with her, "These gentlemen, Mrs. Kilpatrick, before they know, have got to hear what you say or else you might as well not testify." Embarrassed, Elizabeth admitted, "I am talking about as loud as I can with no teeth." She had just turned thirty-eight years old, but seventeen years of almost constant childbearing and a lack of consistent dental care had left her virtually toothless. But she was determined to speak out in defense of her boy, her firstborn, who sat nodding at her encouragingly from the defense counsel table.

Elizabeth Kilpatrick was not a worldly or sophisticated woman, and her life had been circumscribed by and filled with caring for her husband and children. Everything she knew about the law had been learned the hard way. When James and Billy were toddlers, she had roused them from sleep, loaded them into a relative's car, and ridden to the jail to retrieve Aubrey after a run-in with ABC agents. That visit would not be the only one during her eighteen years of marriage. Despite the precarious and shifting sands of her life with Aubrey Kilpatrick, she had made a loving home for her family. She had watched her husband die in front of this home, and she had stood by helplessly as lawmen had taken her three oldest sons off to jail. She had lost one child. She was not about to lose another. Despite her discomfort at sitting in front of a crowded courtroom, jurors and spectators alike staring at her with curious avidity, Elizabeth answered each of George Rogers's questions politely and succinctly, her hand fluttering like a semaphore around her mouth. And the questions were excruciatingly detailed—Rogers guided her through virtually every moment of May 17, from the afternoon when the deputies came to speak with Aubrey (Elizabeth was not present for the conversations and testified that she did not know anything about the reason for their visit) until the aftermath of the shooting, when she realized that Billy had escaped to safety. She also claimed that from the time her oldest child had entered the house after guarding the barn and getting a drink of water at the kitchen sink until after the shooting had stopped, she had not seen James at all.

Like her second-born child, Elizabeth told the court that the first shots had been fired from the driver's side window of the black Pontiac: "He didn't get two steps from the door until a bullet came from the window and hit him." Since the "least ones were in bed," she recounted, only Jeretta, twelve at the time, had immediately rushed to the door. Gunfire continued, Elizabeth testified, seeming to go on "for a long time, I guess longer than it was." When Rogers asked Elizabeth if she had gone out to her husband after the shooting had stopped, she responded, "Lord, no," adding: "No, I went down after the doctor got there, [then] I went out. I was afraid to go." County Solicitor Ed Scruggs moved to exclude the last part of her statement, and reluctantly, Rogers agreed to the exclusion. Only after Elizabeth had called the doctor did she see James, who had entered the house and began "rubbing the head of his daddy's bed, crying and taking on." Despite eliciting several objections from the prosecution, Rogers was satisfied at that point with the images Elizabeth Kilpatrick's testimony had evoked: the stealthy arrival of Zeke Boyles and the other officers, the first gunshots coming from inside the car, a shocked wife and mother who "fell to praying" and possibly even passed out, a houseful of terrified children wailing in alarm, one son grieving demonstrably at his father's bed, and another son emerging, mercifully unscathed, from the darkness. Rogers wrapped up his questioning and turned Elizabeth over to E. G. Pilcher for cross-examination.

This trial, like the one that came before it and the ones that came after it, was not about who killed Aubrey Kilpatrick. It wasn't even about whether or not James Kilpatrick had shot four men, killing three of them; James had never denied the crimes of which he was accused. But determining who shot first was vital to establishing James's defense that he was responding to a viable threat and acting to protect himself and his family. While Pilcher was not exactly gentle with Aubrey Kilpatrick's widow during his cross-examination, he did not harangue or belittle her. Instead, like Rogers, he guided her through the events that had transpired just prior to midnight on May 17, occasionally prodding her to clarify significant details. When he asked her if she had seen the shot she alleged came from the car, she responded, "Couldn't nobody help but seeing—fire came with it." He then asked if she had seen who had fired the shot. Unlike Billy, who had claimed that from his vantage point inside the car he had seen James Lang shoot at Aubrey, Elizabeth stated that she did not know if "the man sitting under the wheel" had fired. When Pilcher began asking about the gunfire that had ensued after Aubrey had fallen, Elizabeth's responses became more guarded and circumspect, her whispered replies of "I don't know" and "I didn't see that" causing everyone in the courtroom to crane forward to hear, yet she never wavered from her avowal that at no time had she witnessed James, with or without the .30 carbine, in the yard where the officers were.

Pilcher was getting nowhere. The day had been long and exhausting for everyone involved, and the mid-November daylight was turning to dusk. It was close to six o'clock—dinnertime—and the spectators and the jury were growing restive and hungry. The amount of information the jury had had to take in that day was varied and complicated, ranging from State Toxicologists Rehling's and Brooks's explanations of human anatomy and ballistics to the array of character witnesses to the highly emotional testimonies of Billy and Elizabeth Kilpatrick. Even Rogers and Pilcher, both normally fiery and theatrical, seemed a little wilted and subdued. Everyone needed food and rest, especially since the next day would present the moment the people had been waiting for. On Thursday, November 15, 1951, at 9:00 a.m., James Kilpatrick would take the stand.

# CHAPTER 10

# The Reckoning

James Kilpatrick was sick. Despite the "nerve pills" that Dr. Lavender had prescribed to smooth the spikes of his constant anxiety, the young defendant had lain awake on his cell cot all night, staring at the underside of the urine-stained mattress on the bunk above him. A relative had delivered his favorite plaid shirt—one of two "Sunday-go-to-meetin' shirts" he owned— the crisply starched collar and cuffs evidence of his mother's loving care. Before the lights in the Marshall County jail were shut off for the night, James had unfolded the letters Ann Scott had written to him, the paper soft and the edges dog-eared from frequent reading. Would he ever get to talk to her without iron bars between them? Hold her hand without a jailer shouting, "No touching!"? George Rogers was working diligently not only on the current trial but also on an appeal to the Alabama Supreme Court for James's release on bond, which Judge Stone had denied in circuit court. For three days, James had sat in the Marshall County Courthouse in Albertville, listening as witness after witness had spoken either for him or against him or simply delivered the cold, objective facts of his case. He had watched with fierce pride as his younger brother Billy had taken the stand and given his account of what had happened on the night of May 17, knowing that despite Billy's bravado, the second-born Kilpatrick child had been intimidated and frightened, especially when Circuit Solicitor L. P. Waid peppered him with rapid-fire questions. He had clasped and unclasped his hands underneath the defense counsel table as his mother, alternately timid and defiant, had testified that the first shots had been fired by one of the officers in Zeke Boyles's black car and that she had not seen James during the shooting. And now it was his turn to put his hand on the courtroom Bible and swear to tell the truth, the whole truth, and nothing but the truth. It was time, at last, for him to tell his side of the story.

When the court convened at 9:00 a.m. on Thursday, November 15, George

Rogers was fit to be tied. Before the jurors were called in and seated, Rogers noticed that two chairs had been placed next to the rail in front of the jury box. Sitting in one chair was Eva Boyles, the widow of the slain sheriff; perched on the arm of her chair was five-year-old Donnie Hodges, Zeke Boyles's grandson. In the other chair sat Marion Boyles Hodges, one of Zeke and Eva's two daughters. The three made a tragic tableau—after a hysterectomy the previous February, only three months before losing her husband, Mrs. Boyles had suffered a blood clot that led to the amputation of one of her legs, and her crutches leaned against the rail that separated the jury box from the prosecution's table. Little Donnie, certainly too young to be present at a murder trial, particularly one that featured graphic details about his grandfather's death, looked around solemnly and occasionally slipped his small hand into the crook of his grandmother's arm. Marion Hodges worked in the Marshall County clerk's office and therefore had a legitimate excuse for sitting at the prosecution's table, but Rogers knew that the combined, multigenerational presence of the grieving, disabled widow, her daughter, and her grandson in short pants was too blatantly prejudicial to be ignored.

Rogers declared to the court that "it will be impossible for [James Kilpatrick] to obtain a fair and impartial trial of this cause with that situation existing. That such situation is produced solely and only for the purpose of creating sympathy on the part of the jury in the opinion of counsel representing the defendant." Rogers suggested that the judge "require the above-mentioned parties to vacate the special seats provided for them." Judge Stone agreed. But Rogers had a sympathy card of his own to play, which he introduced on the heels of his complaint about the conspicuous positioning of the Boyles family. After the jury was seated in court, Rogers announced that "this defendant has just come from the doctor's office and he is sick and may have to stop the proceedings at any time for a few minutes." The courtroom stilled, and everyone watched in silence as the seventeen-year-old defendant took his place on the witness stand.

Anyone who had known James Kilpatrick prior to the night of May 17, 1951, would have been shocked by his appearance. His lean angularity had morphed into gauntness. Never a large boy, James's diminished frame seemed shrunken inside his neatly pressed shirt. The ruddy good health that usually brightened his face had faded into a pale sallowness accentuated by purplish half-moons underneath eyes sunken by sleeplessness, illness, and anxiety. Observers in the courtroom noted a slight tremor as he placed his hand upon the courtroom Bible, and his voice quavered as he began answering George

Rogers's questions. At first the questions were simple and straightforward, designed to put James at ease. Rogers asked James where he lived, how old he was, and with whom he shared his home. As the inquiries became more pointed, moving closer to the time of the shooting, James grew increasingly agitated, prompting Rogers to ask, "Do you feel all right?" James closed his eyes. The courtroom, which had previously seemed so airy and cool on that November morning, now felt oppressive and claustrophobic.

When Rogers prompted James to tell the jury about the conversation between his father and Deputy Washington Bennett that had taken place the evening just prior to the shooting, James recalled his father, stubborn and proud, leaning in to tell Bennett, "I won't go to jail with you because of them sorry tenants," and Bennett responding, "I won't blame you." These two men, who were having such a civilized and agreeable discussion on a balmy, late spring evening, would be instrumental in each other's deaths less than six hours later. Bennett would fire a single shot that severed Aubrey's spinal cord and fatally perforated one of his lungs; not long after, the dying man's sixteen-year-old son would fire his own weapon, that made-for-war carbine, wounding the deputy so grievously that he would not live to see the sun rise. As if down a long corridor lined with echoes, James heard his defense attorney's inquiry concerning how he was feeling and County Solicitor Scruggs's interjection of "He will let us know. He said he would give a signal." James opened his eyes, cleared his throat, and responded, "Yes, sir. I feel all right. I can go on."

And go on he did. When George Rogers asked about the first time he had known someone other than a family member was in the front yard, James answered, "When the gun fired." Rogers pressed on: "What did you do, if anything, when you heard the first gun fire?" James recalled that his mother had screamed, "They shot Aubrey," and that he had "run out the door around to the east corner of the house." Between Rogers's gentle prodding and James's testimony, the pair reconstructed the scene as James had experienced it: the sounds of gunfire, his mother's screams, his first foray outside the house to investigate, his observation that a "tall man" seemed to be holding his younger brother Billy by the arm, his retreat into the house to grab his rifle, and his return to the yard, where he "began to shooting." At times James faltered, admitting that he did not remember details such as the exact movements of the men emerging from the car or precisely what time the next morning he had given a statement to officers after his arrest: "I was scared." When Rogers asked if he was still frightened, James murmured, "Yes, sir. I am." Surprisingly, the prosecution did not object. At the end of his examination, Rogers asked, "You want to rest a little while?" but James insisted he could "go a little longer." Now it was Special Prosecutor E. G. Pilcher's turn to cross-examine James.

Rogers had taken a linear, chronological approach in his examination—he had questioned James about the order of events, beginning with the deputies' visit to the Kilpatrick farm on the evening of May 17 and ending with James's arrest and transport to the Etowah County jail in Gadsden. Pilcher, however, employed a different strategy. He opened his cross-examination by seeming to be sympathetic, solicitously assuring James, "If you get to feeling bad, let us know. We will stop." The cross-examination proceeded in fits and starts—when Pilcher began questioning James about the Kilpatrick family's prior relationship with the Whiteheads, Rogers objected with his trademark "Immaterial, irrelevant, and incompetent!" Each time Pilcher asked James about the events that occurred prior to the arrival of Sheriff Boyles and the other officers, Rogers repeatedly objected, causing Pilcher to peevishly snap, "I wish you would keep quiet"; in true schoolyard fashion, Rogers retorted, "You keep quiet." Despite Rogers's incessant objections and Pilcher's frustrated attempts to get James to answer questions, a very significant discrepancy emerged as James testified, an inconsistency which, if noted by attentive jurors, would unravel Rogers's entire defense: had James ever been fired upon, leading him to return fire in self-defense?

According to the ballistics reports, as well as the testimony given by Alabama state patrolmen R. H. Parker and W. W. Locke, Sheriff Boyles's gun, a .38 Smith & Wesson, had fired two shots from inside the car. What was left of his gun contained four intact bullets of a full load of six. James Lang had never fired his gun; neither had Leonard Floyd. Rehling and Brooks testified that the bullet which struck Aubrey Kilpatrick came from a .38 Smith & Wesson, but the ballistics analysis verified that it was Bennett's .38, not Boyles's, that had fired the bullet. Acting Boaz police chief J. C. Sanders confirmed that he had found Bennett's pistol in the passenger floorboard of the black Pontiac Chieftain after Bennett and Lang had made their desperate drive to the Boaz police station: "There was five shells in the gun. There was six and one of them had been shot."

The problem was mathematical—James claimed that the reason he had gone back inside his house to get his .30 carbine was because Bennett had fired at him while holding Billy's arm to keep him from running away ("There was a tall man holding my brother"). Pilcher even made James leave the witness stand to provide a demonstration in front of the courtroom:

*Pilcher:* I want you to stand right down here, if you don't mind, and you be the man holding your brother. I will be your brother. Show this jury how the man was holding your little brother.

*Kilpatrick:* He had him like that shooting over the car.

*Pilcher:* Did he have him by the left hand?

*Kilpatrick:* Yes, sir.

*Pilcher:* Was he shooting in your direction?

*Kilpatrick:* No, sir. He was shooting toward Father.

*Pilcher:* What was the boy doing?

*Kilpatrick:* Twisting, scrambling, trying to get loose.

Up to this point, Pilcher had appeared compassionate, almost kindly, toward the young defendant, but he was slowly building toward the inevitable conclusion that if Bennett had shot at James, even once, the chamber of Bennett's gun would have had more than one bullet discharged.

Like a shark circling a terrified swimmer, Pilcher began to home in on what was essentially the linchpin of James's claim of self-defense. Pilcher asked, "After you came out of the house and saw the man holding your little brother and shooting over the car, what did you do then?" James answered, "I don't remember just what I did say. I asked him what he was doing. What do you mean, or something like that. I wouldn't say it was in that words." Pilcher then inquired, "Did he respond to you hollering at him?" James replied, "He fired at me." Pilcher then asked the question that would be instrumental in the verdict that would be handed down the next morning: "Did you see the gun point at you?" And James responded, "Yes." More than seven times in the testimony that followed, Pilcher returned to the moment that James had witnessed "the tall man" holding his brother Billy by the arm. Each time, with only slight variations, the special prosecutor asked James who had shot at him and when the shot had been fired. Each time, James answered that "the tall man" had aimed his gun at him and discharged his weapon. But the cross-examination was wearing James down; perhaps he sensed that Pilcher was closing in on some vital, incriminating point, but James remained determined to stick by his original account. James's responses became confused: "I don't remember. I was scared"; "I don't know which one shot at me. A tall fellow is all I know"; "They was so much shooting going on, I don't know whether they was shooting at anybody." The circle tightened, and James was caught helplessly at its center. The damage had been done. All George Rogers could do was to redirect the visibly shaken defendant to one last question: "Out there that night was it dark enough for you to be able to discern and be able to see and tell what was what?" James weakly replied, "I couldn't tell what."

James Kilpatrick's testimony was consistent with what he had told the investigators in the early morning hours of Friday, May 18, 1951. Sitting in the Etowah County jail, surrounded by armed officers and lacking any representation, either by an adult relative or an attorney, James had described to the attending officers and Circuit Solicitor L. P. Waid the following:

> I went in the back room to get me a drink, and when I heard a gun fire, I went out the back door and went around, and I seen my brother there that a fellow had by the arm. . . . It was getting dark, and he shot over the car. I hollered at him, and he turned around and fired at me, and I come back to the house and I don't know which room I went in, but I got a gun. I believe it was that carbine. I don't know how many times I shot. They asked me last night, but I couldn't tell them how many times I shot, nor which way. I don't know. All the kids were screaming and hollering, and my mother was and I don't know nothing about that. How many I shot or which way . . . I was just shooting. I don't know what I was shooting at. That's all. I was just scared and I just was shooting.

This statement, taken by Etowah County court reporter Thomas Callen, had been read to the court on the previous day, thus entering it into the official trial record. James had not been primed or coached in any way, and no lawyer was there to caution or silence him as he poured out his story. When Rogers and Brown signed on as James's defense attorneys, they would have known that this statement existed and that it would be used in court. James had sat in court during the ballistics testimony and heard several officers and Drs. Rehling and Brooks testify that Deputy Bennett, the "tall man" who had grabbed Billy Kilpatrick to protect him or detain him or (more nefariously) use him as a shield in the escalating gunfight, had fired only a single shot, and that shot had found its mark in Aubrey Kilpatrick's chest. Why had James so persistently and adamantly claimed that Bennett had shot at him?

One can only speculate why James stuck by his story, even as it condemned him. Maybe after hearing the shots as he drank water in the kitchen, James had run outside just as Bennett fired his .38 across the roof of Sheriff Boyles's car and struck Aubrey. Simultaneously, Aubrey, fatally wounded and collapsing to the ground, had managed to fire three shots into the bottom of the car. In the darkness and panic and confusion, James had mistaken his father's last three shots as coming from Bennett's gun, especially since James had shouted at the men, presumably causing Bennett to turn in his direction. Believing he was being fired upon, James had gone back into the house, taken the .30 carbine, run out the back door and around the side of the house, and began shooting at the officers assembled around the car in front of the house.

Regardless of who had shot Aubrey Kilpatrick, James was the one on trial for murder. Although so much of the trial testimony had focused on who could have fired first in the exchange between Aubrey and the officers in the car, James's actions in the aftermath of this initial round of gunfire were ultimately what the jury had to consider. Had James acted in self-defense and defense of his home and family? Did he have a duty to retreat or to "stand his ground"? Did his alleged ignorance concerning the identities of the men in his yard allay the burden of guilt and justify his use of deadly force to repel men whom he believed to be dangerous invaders? Technically, James, as the defendant, did not have the burden of proving that he acted in self-defense, but once he entered such a plea, the state had the burden of proving beyond a reasonable doubt that the defendant did not act in self-defense. While all the prosecutors had whittled away at James's claim, Pilcher had succeeded at eroding the self-defense plea with simple yet irrefutable mathematical evidence: James had not been fired upon, and his retreat had been only to acquire a weapon with which he had returned to the immediate scene and shot four officers of the law who bore a legal warrant to arrest Aubrey Kilpatrick.

Closing arguments in a criminal trial offer both the prosecution and the defense one last persuasive entreaty before the jurors begin their deliberations. In a murder trial, the closing arguments embody all the passion, rage, and grief evoked by the prosecution, deflected by the defense, and felt by the families of both the victim and the accused. These speeches, full of high drama and oratorical flourishes, give a counterweight of pathos to the often-detached logos and ethos of the preceding testimony. In the closing arguments for James Kilpatrick's trial, Circuit Solicitor L. P. Waid presented the state's argument to the jury. Consistent with his demeanor throughout the trial, Waid was composed and dignified, emphasizing that Sheriff Boyles and the other officers were shot down responding to the call of duty:

Had he [Sheriff Boyles] not acted as he did, he would not have been worthy of the trust placed in him by the voters of Marshall County. This case has a meaning beyond the murder of a man. It will either proclaim Marshall County as a county that stands behind its peace officers, or brand this county as one that allows them to be shot down in cold blood and does nothing about it.

Boaz attorney John W. Brown, who had remained largely silent throughout the trial with the exception of questioning Justice of the Peace R. L. Turner, gave the closing argument for the defense. George Rogers could be as earnest and folksy as any good country lawyer, and even though he had earned his reputation in Birmingham, he had sprung from humble, civic-minded people in the small community of Morris in the northern, more rural part of Jefferson County. But Brown was a local lawyer with roots in Marshall County—he was one of them. To the jury filled with men he had known his entire life, Brown appealed to their deeply entrenched belief in family and manhood:

> James Kilpatrick didn't do any more than any red-blooded boy would have done in defense of his father. In some people's eyes Aubrey Kilpatrick may not have been all he should have been. But to James he was his father, a man that he looked up to and loved.

Waid and Brown sought to elicit similar emotions from the jury, relying on the men's cherished principles involving duty and loyalty. But Waid and Brown did not have the last word on James Kilpatrick or, for that matter, on Aubrey Kilpatrick.

In his rebuttal to the state's argument, George Rogers reiterated the conflicting testimony provided by Deputy James Lang and recalled earlier expert testimony that indicated the two shots fired by Aubrey Kilpatrick were not an opening volley but instead reactions to being fired upon first, due to the upward angle of each bullet's trajectory into the top of the Pontiac's windshield, suggesting that Aubrey had already begun to fall when he fired those two shots. Rogers clearly wanted to imprint on the jurors' minds the idea that the officers, Sheriff Boyles in particular, had been the aggressors in the incident, inciting a series of events that led James to the ineluctable action of defending himself, his mother, and his seven siblings. After this argument, Rogers asked for an acquittal on the grounds of self-defense, highlighting that the defendant had not brought on the difficulty that resulted in the encounter, had been in danger of bodily harm, and had not been required to retreat as he was at his own home. The two defense attorneys' closing remarks worked neatly in tandem. While Brown had presented an impassioned argument calling upon the jury's empathy, Rogers reminded the jury of the prosecution's high burden of proof and argued that there was, at a minimum, reasonable doubt as to the defendant's guilt. The state had no objections to Rogers's rebuttal. Special Prosecutor E. G. Pilcher rose to deliver his rebuttal against the defense.

For all his bluster and theatrics and chest thumping and thunderous objections during the testimony portion of the trial, George Rogers had been solemn and subdued once the defense had rested, deferring to John Brown's hometown touch for the closing argument. Pilcher, on the other hand, had been saving his fieriest condemnations for his rebuttal of the defense's closing argument. According to legal expert H. Patrick Furman, "Closing argument is the point at which trial lawyers' emotions are most likely to lead them astray into unprofessional and even unethical behavior." With bombastic ferocity, Pilcher exhorted the jurors to "bear down deeply in your minds and memories before you write the kind of verdict Mr. Rogers would have you write to whitewash his arch murdering client that stands before a jury of Marshall County." In reference to James Kilpatrick, Pilcher said to the jury, "Whitewash him. Turn him loose and let him shoot somebody else down like he did Zeke Boyles and the others." Of Elizabeth Kilpatrick, Pilcher remarked, "She knew what was going on. She knew what had gone on over there that evening that occasioned the warrant. She heard her husband say, in my judgment, just about like James said he heard his father say: 'Damn the law. I won't go with them.'" Even the late Aubrey Kilpatrick did not escape Pilcher's reproof: "He left his wife a widow and his children orphans and this defendant made of himself the bloodiest criminal that ever come into a courtroom, and before you whitewash him, write across the door of the courthouse of Marshall County: We are unworthy of the position we hold." Rogers became a virtual jack-in-the-box throughout Pilcher's rebuttal, objecting after almost every sentence and calling for a mistrial on five separate occasions. But Pilcher didn't stop, despite Judge Stone's admonition about "the heat of the argument."

With his customary antagonism, bordering on calumny, Pilcher asserted that James "had to tell some cock-and-bull story to keep from being lynched," which drew a resounding objection from Rogers: "We object and move the court to exclude that." Judge Stone agreed to the exclusion, but Rogers pressed on, asking for a mistrial "on account of the statement of the counsel. It is prejudicial and cannot be erased or eradicated by instruction from the Court." Pilcher was a gambler, both in and out of the courtroom, and he knew that his aggressive approach could have easily backfired. But the ace he held was his certainty that Judge Stone did not want another mistrial, especially not at the end of four days of testimony and the possibility of a conviction. Circuit court judges were elected officials, and the failure to secure a verdict in such a high-profile trial would have guaranteed that in the next election, the good citizens of Marshall County would have made their ire known at the polls. After five motions for a mistrial and five refusals from Judge Stone, Rogers could do nothing but stand by and listen as Pilcher wrapped up his rebuttal, piling inflammatory accusation after inflammatory accusation:

> [The defendant] hadn't been able to advise with his family and friends and before he had time to think, that man, whose heart is as black with murder as any man that ever came in a courthouse. . . . Gentlemen of the jury, that's what he did. Shot them down like the dirty murderer he is. . . . Gentlemen of the jury, they say, notwithstanding the law of the country because of his age you should whitewash him, turn him loose and let him send a .30 caliber through the heart, liver, and diaphragm of another citizen of Marshall County.

It must have seemed as if all the air had left the courtroom, the last pale strains of November sunlight fading outside the courthouse windows. The time for testimony and objections and examinations and cross-examinations was over. Now the jury would depart to decide James Kilpatrick's fate.

In a jury trial, once the prosecution and defense have rested their cases, the judge instructs the jury about what law to apply to the case and how to carry out its duties. Judge J. S. Stone took nearly an hour to instruct the jury, outlining each possible verdict with a thoroughness that would have made any law professor proud. He explained the entered plea of not guilty by reason of self-defense; then he instructed the jury regarding first-degree murder, second-degree murder, first-degree manslaughter, and second-degree manslaughter. The court adjourned, and the jury left to consider the charges and render a verdict. The foreman, E. O. Dickerson, and his eleven peers failed to reach a verdict by 10:00 p.m. that night, and after retiring to bed, they rose again the next morning to continue their deliberations. By 10:00 a.m. on the morning of Friday, November 16, 1951, they had their verdict: "We, the Jury, find the defendant guilty of murder in the second degree and fix his punishment at seventeen years, imprisonment in the Penitentiary." Under Alabama law, as described by Judge Stone, second-degree murder "is the unlawful killing of a human being with malice but done without any deliberation or premeditation . . . there must be malice and there must be intent to kill." When the verdict was read in the courtroom, Elizabeth Kilpatrick wailed in disbelief, collapsing into the arms of her sister. James stood between George Rogers and John Brown, staring stoically straight ahead, his already pale face blanched and immobile. Seventeen years—the same number of years he had been alive. Rogers immediately notified the court of his intent to appeal the verdict, and by November 30, the document had been filed with the Alabama Court of Criminal Appeals. James would spend Christmas of 1951 in the Marshall County jail in Guntersville, waiting once again for the legal system to continue its pursuit of justice.

∞

An old saying laments that the wheels of justice grind slowly, but in James Kilpatrick's case, especially when compared to twenty-first-century murder trials, the wheels of justice appeared to spin so rapidly that the axles must have seemed greased. By January 1952, a third trial was scheduled on the docket: on January 28 James would stand trial for the killing of Deputy Sheriff Washington Bennett. George Rogers had again filed a motion for bond at a circuit court hearing on January 11, but Judge Stone denied the motion. Rogers knew that he would have to go beyond the circuit court of Marshall County if his now-seventeen-year-old defendant would be allowed to leave the county jail and return to his family. As Rogers prepared his case for the Alabama Supreme Court, James remained in custody, still under Dr. Lavender's care for his unceasing stomach pains and sleeplessness, still waiting for each treasured letter from Ann Scott, who had started the second half of her junior year of high school when classes resumed after the holiday break.

In that same month, the Kilpatrick estate was out of probate, which allowed James's mother, Elizabeth, to sell property to pay the mounting legal bills. Not wishing to burden her son further with her personal and financial woes, Elizabeth tried to keep her visits to the jail positive and upbeat, but James could see the tremendous toll that the ongoing legal proceedings were taking upon his mother. The woman who had ridden so proudly on horseback alongside her husband and children throughout the Double Bridges community, who had taken such pride in being the best cook in the area, who had commandeered a household of eight rowdy, fiercely independent children, seemed broken. When an uncle informed him that his mother had begun working at the local chicken processing plant to keep food on the table and a roof over her family's heads, James covered his face with his hands and wept. The long, lonely Christmas season of 1951 was over, and the streets outside James's barred window bustled with new life as the people of Guntersville went about the business of 1952. More young men across America shipped out for the war in Korea, which had entered its fifth phase after armistice negotiations had stalled; the Korean War had, for the most part, fallen into a stalemate, costing men and material without changing the status or eventual outcome. James would not be one of those young men who would leave in 1952. He had his own battle to fight at home.

The trial that had been docketed to begin on Monday, January 28, had barely gotten started when a strange, startling occurrence abruptly ended the proceedings. The jury had been impaneled, and a day's worth of testimony had been heard, the witnesses taking the stand in almost the same order they had appeared in the previous trials. Then on Monday evening, after the court had adjourned for the day, George Rogers returned to the boardinghouse in Boaz to learn that his wife had called from their home in Birmingham with frightening news: someone had phoned the Rogers's home and asked for her, and, when informed by the maid that she was out, the caller (who was identified as male) issued a warning, saying that the Rogers home would be dynamited and that the attorney and his family were in grave danger. Roger was understandably alarmed, and he leapt into his car and sped up Alabama Highway 75 toward Birmingham. As he careened along the twisting roads outside Oneonta, a small town roughly halfway between Boaz and Birmingham, a 1,200-pound steer ambled into his car's path. Rogers struck the steer, smashed his car, and suffered a broken nose, fractured ribs, and a cracked kneecap. The hapless steer, as faithfully reported by Guntersville's *Advertiser-Gleam*, was killed.

The threat of one's home and family being blown up would certainly galvanize anyone into immediate action, but this specific threat eerily echoed a tragedy that had occurred earlier that month in Phenix City, Alabama. Businessman and civic activist Hugh Bentley, who had been working with State Senator Albert Patterson to rid Phenix City of gambling, drug trafficking, and prostitution, was returning on January 9 from a trip out of town when his house was dynamited, leaving the home in rubble, but his wife, son, and nephew miraculously escaped with only minor injuries. Bentley had made powerful enemies in his efforts to clean up Phenix City; likewise, George Rogers had made a few enemies of his own as one of the best-known defense attorneys in the state. The Rogers home was not dynamited, and the attorney opined that the threat had been made by "some crackpot." Despite his injuries, Rogers showed up for court in Albertville the next day, but the appearance of the bruised and bandaged lawyer, nattily dressed as always but looking like he had been worked over with a pipe, caused Judge Stone to declare a technical mistrial. Judge Stone, obviously displeased, told the court, "I hate very much to do this. It will cause the county considerable expense, besides delaying the completion of these cases. But under the circumstances I can't see that I have any choice." Thus ended the third trial of James Kilpatrick. A new trial date was set for the July circuit court term.

The accident and resulting mistrial did buy Rogers—and James—some breathing room in the meantime. Rogers could finish preparing his writ of habeas corpus for the Alabama Supreme Court, which would convene to hear his case in May. Although James would remain in the county jail, his days were not without some comforts—the daily letters from Ann Scott buoyed his spirits, and in April, just after Easter, a local musician, J. M. Connally, brought his two daughters, eleven-year-old Bettie and eight-year-old Mary, to the Marshall County jail to play the guitar and sing gospel songs for James. The visit made the small-town version of the society pages in two local newspapers, one notice carrying the heading "James Kilpatrick Entertained April 19," as if the jailhouse musicale had been performed for a visiting dignitary. Then, on May 15, the Alabama Supreme Court ruled that James could be released on bond from the Marshall County jail, and on May 18—a year and a day from the shooting—James was, if by no means exonerated, at least free to go home for eighteen months. The bonds were steep. For each of the indictments handed down by the grand jury that had convened in May 1951, the bond was set at $5,000: $5,000 for the death of Leonard Floyd, $5,000 for the death of Washington Bennett, and $5,000 for the assault on James Lang. Since a verdict of second-degree murder had been reached in the death of Ezekiel Boyles, the bond on that charge was $10,000. Twenty-five thousand dollars in 1951 would be approximately $293,000 in 2024, a staggering sum for any ordinary citizen, but between the proceeds Elizabeth Kilpatrick had received from the sale of almost everything the family owned and the contributions of close family friends Dures Thomas and Sam Bruce, James was able to post the bond. The home he would return to was not the same one he had left, both literally because the family had since moved into their new house, which had been under construction the night of the shooting, and emotionally because his father would not be there to greet him.

The release from jail and brief hiatus from the trials revived James for a while. The bloom of health returned to his face, and the many meals with Ann Scott and her parents helped put flesh on his skeletal frame. When he wasn't working odd jobs for his uncle, C. W. Cofield, he was a frequent visitor to the Scott home, where Ann's mother, Tiny, would slip him an extra piece of apple pie after he had eaten his fill at the supper table. He courted Ann with the old-fashioned gallantry of a bygone era, taking her to movies and restaurants and the occasional horse show in Boaz. Under the conditions of his release on bond, James could not leave Marshall County, but he had no intention of going anywhere else—he had everything he wanted within a twenty-mile radius of his home atop Sand Mountain. But the fleeting days of that summer seemed to magnify the precariousness of James's future. Going from the monotonous, dread-filled hours in the Marshall County jail to the dizzying illusion of normal life was more palliative than restorative. James had been allowed a glimpse of a life he feared he could never have, and as much as he reveled in his blossoming love for Ann and the joys of roughhousing with his siblings and helping his mother at home, he knew that another reckoning was looming on the horizon. As his trial date in July 1952 neared, James felt the old anxiety, lulled into uneasy dormancy, stirring within his gut. His smiles faded. His easy, joking manner, once so spontaneous and unaffected, seemed forced and artificial.

Even the outlandish antics of S. J. "Hot Dang" Otinger, with whom James drove cars to the local auto sale, failed to make him laugh. His appetite began to wane, despite Tiny Scott's ministrations of fried chicken, butter beans, and hot cornbread. By the July 4th holiday, James's weight had dwindled to 112 pounds, only a few pounds more than he had weighed the previous year when the jailors had withheld his meals and given him only hot water to drink. After a bout of blood-tinged vomiting and debilitating diarrhea throughout the weekend before his fourth trial, James visited Dr. Lavender, who went before the court to ask for a postponement of the trial slated to begin in mid-July. Judge Stone reluctantly agreed, and a new trial date of October 13 was entered into the docket. Time and tide wait for no man, as the ancient saying goes, but at least James Kilpatrick had a few more precious weeks to rest and recover in the light of Ann Scott's blue, blue eyes.

∞

"It's getting to be old news," announced the October 12 issue of the *Gadsden Times*, "but young James Kilpatrick will go on trial for murder for the fourth time at the Albertville courthouse on Monday." Decades before the introduction of twenty-four-hour cable news cycles and viral internet videos, the shelf life for even the most sensational and gruesome news accounts was relatively short, and in the seventeen months since the shootout at the Kilpatrick farm, most Alabamians had found other tales of murder and mayhem to occupy their attention. Hundreds of curious spectators had filled the Albertville courtroom for both trials in 1951 and the first day of testimony in the third (albeit abruptly terminated) January 1952 trial, packing the benches, standing along the walls, lining the hallway and foyer outside the courtroom, even clinging to the outer windowsills to witness what one local newspaper grandiosely pronounced "the trials of the century in Marshall County." In May 1952, as James Kilpatrick posted bond and left the Marshall County jail, most Alabamians had turned with morbid fascination to another trial, this one down in Wetumpka, a town about sixteen miles south of Montgomery, where a nurse named Earle Dennison faced first-degree murder charges in the poisoning deaths of her two little nieces.

Unlike the Kilpatrick case, which featured guns, violence, and bloodshed, the Dennison case revealed the quieter but equally deadly factors of stealth, betrayal, and greed. The seemingly ubiquitous Dr. C. J. Rehling, as state toxicologist, had conducted an autopsy on two-year-old Shirley Diann Weldon and determined that the child had been given a fatal dose of arsenic. The horrified Weldons, who had already lost their first child, three-year-old Polly Ann, in a manner similar to her younger sister, called for the exhumation of Polly Ann; Rehling also found arsenic in the older child's remains. The common factor linking both girls' deaths was their "devoted auntie," Earle Dennison, who had given each girl a sweet treat—in Shirley's case, an orange soda pop, and in Polly Ann's case, an ice cream cone—immediately prior to each child's torturous, convulsive death.

Dennison was arrested and eventually confessed to poisoning Shirley Diann, although she denied intentionally poisoning Polly Ann, claiming that she had "accidentally" left a saltshaker full of arsenic on the table where Polly and her brother Orvil were eating ice cream. (The arsenic was "to get rid of pests," Dennison later told investigators.) Detectives quickly discovered the motive: Dennison had taken out $5,000 life insurance policies on all three Weldon children, one of which she had collected after Polly Ann's death; just prior to her arrest, Dennison had submitted a claim on Shirley Diann's policy. The trial followed swiftly thereafter, and in August 1952 a jury took less than three hours to convict Dennison of first-degree murder. The state was abuzz when the sentence was announced: Earle Dennison would be the first white woman to die in Alabama's electric chair. While James Kilpatrick narrowly escaped meeting "Yellow Mama," Dennison was executed at Kilby Correctional Facility in September 1953.

By October 1952, a barely suppressed yawn seemed to lurk behind the newspaper accounts of James's fourth trial. "The drawn-out murder trials of James Kilpatrick apparently have lost their appeal to local residents," began an October 13 *Gadsden Times* article, published with the headline "Few Present as Kilpatrick Goes on Trial." The throngs had moved on to other concerns; only those personally invested in the outcome came to the courthouse in Albertville. A few members of Washington Bennett's family, including his widow and two children, sat on one side of the courtroom, while Elizabeth Kilpatrick and other family members sat behind James and his defense counsel. The participants in the proceedings—the judge, the lawyers, the witnesses, and certainly the defendant—must have felt caught up in a nightmarish cycle of déjà vu.

The prosecution team had undergone some changes: Ed Scruggs had resigned as county solicitor in January to spend more time developing his private practice, and he had been replaced by Clark Everette Johnson, a young attorney in Albertville and World War II veteran. When Scruggs had stepped down, his father, Claud, had also relinquished his role as special prosecutor in the Kilpatrick trials. Waid and Johnson now served as the official counsel for the state; Pilcher, funded by the deep-pocketed Alabama Sheriffs' and Peace Officers' Association, stayed on as a special prosecutor. Johnson's youth and political aspirations fueled his enthusiastic involvement in the October 1952 trial, but the timing seemed off. By that time, nearly a year had elapsed since the conviction for second-degree murder. James was out on bond, living what looked like the happy-go-lucky life of the average Sand Mountain teenage boy: working, courting his girl, taking in the entertainment around town. In short, those with no stake in the legal proceedings were tired of the whole affair and ready to move on. Tempers were short. Even George Rogers and E. G. Pilcher, who had jabbed so nimbly at each other in the first two trials, seemed alternately punch-drunk and volatile, two exhausted prizefighters pushing themselves off the ropes for one more swing.

This is not to say that the fourth trial was without its own fireworks. At least twice, the lawyers' exchanges erupted into more than the snarky testiness that had peppered the second trial. Early in the testimony, Fannie Whitehead, the mother of the young man who had obtained the warrant for Aubrey Kilpatrick's arrest, testified again that James had declared he would "kill all the sons of bitches." Rogers spat, "As a matter of fact, that's a figment of your imagination and thought up and got up after this thing." Pilcher objected, shouting, "Bullying somebody around! You try to run over everybody who comes into contact with you." Pilcher wasn't accusing Rogers of bullying Mrs. Whitehead—he was taking Rogers to task for attempting to bully *him*: "You are not going to run over me." Rogers retorted, "You are not going to run over *me*. You are not going to whip me. You can whip the solicitors around, but you are not going to whip me." Judge Stone snapped, "Take the jury out." After the jurors had filed out of the courtroom, Stone sternly admonished both attorneys: "When this gavel raps, that means quiet. I will let you pay $25.00 apiece, both of you, to the clerk. . . . When you have calmed down, the trial will resume." The two men grudgingly straightened their ties and apologized to the jury and the court once the jurors had returned to their seats, and the trial went on.

The only new witness in this trial was Fred Howard Burns, the boy who had been possum hunting with Billy Kilpatrick prior to the shooting and picked up by Sheriff Boyles and his men at the end of the drive leading to the Kilpatrick farm. Burns—who stayed with the Kilpatrick family much of the time because his mother, dying of terminal cancer, had been living with relatives and his father, who drove a night taxi in Boaz, could not take care of his son—was hardly the most reliable witness, even though he had been front and center for the gunplay that had occurred on the night of May 17, 1951. When he was four years old, Burns had been accidentally struck in the head with an ax and nearly killed. He recovered, but the traumatic head injury left him with blinding headaches, memory lapses, and recurring seizures during which he "lost time." Upon reaching the age of sixteen, Burns had advanced only as far as the fifth grade, so he dropped out of school and went to work for Aubrey Kilpatrick.

The night of the shooting, he had escaped from the sheriff's car and run into the Kilpatricks' house, where he hid under a bed for three hours, emerging only when the scores of law officers arrived and began investigating the scene. Illiterate and intellectually challenged, Burns answered most of L. P. Waid's questions with "I don't remember" and "I don't recall." When Waid, growing more frustrated with each of Burns's noncommittal responses, asked the boy if he remembered testifying before the grand jury in 1951, Burns replied, "No, sir." Waid produced the transcript from the grand jury proceedings and asked Burns to read his own words aloud to the court. Burns held the papers for a moment and then looked up at the prosecutor: "I don't know what that is. I can't read." Waid then seemed to realize that whatever this boy had witnessed, it would remain locked within the sealed compartments of his damaged brain—nothing would be gained by continuing to question a bewildered, frightened boy whose mental development had been impaired by an ax-blow to the head when he was a small child. Burns was dismissed from the witness stand. He grinned and gave a small wave to James as he exited the courtroom.

If the testimony in the fourth trial had ended as the second trial had, with James Kilpatrick fervently reiterating his claim of self-defense, the verdict might have been different. But James's words were not the last ones the jury would hear, and the final witness must have convinced the twelve men that the defendant, now a man of eighteen, should pay even more dearly for the crimes he had committed. The crowds were back, filling the formerly sparsely occupied courtroom. They knew this song by heart, but they wanted to be present for the new coda that would end the performance. The last witness to take the stand on Wednesday, October 15, was the Kilpatricks' neighbor, Robert Birdsong, known as "Rob" by the people in his community. Birdsong had not testified in the previous trials, and he was a last-minute addition to the witness list submitted by the prosecution. What he had to say undermined the most crucial points of James's testimony. James had claimed that just prior to the shooting, he and Fred Goble had been out guarding the barn in case the Whiteheads decided to retaliate for the altercation that had occurred earlier that day. Birdsong contradicted this claim, stating that Aubrey, James, and Fred had come to his house at 11:00 p.m. on May 17.

According to Birdsong, Aubrey had been agitated about the "trouble" that had occurred at the Whiteheads' house earlier that day but had boasted that he "had done some of the best fighting of his life." As the men stood talking in front of Birdsong's house, "a black car turned off the highway" and pulled alongside the car occupied by Billy Kilpatrick and Fred Burns. Birdsong testified that he then commented to Aubrey, "That looks like the law," and Aubrey had replied, in James's presence, "It is. They're after us." The last—and most damning—detail of Birdsong's testimony was his account of Aubrey's parting comment, also uttered in James's presence: "Rob, if they come after me, you will be in court as long as you live." Suddenly the word that George Rogers had fought so hard to suppress, that had been trumpeted in headlines across the country, that law enforcement throughout the state had promulgated from the night of the shooting forward, rose like a specter from the graves of Zeke Boyles, Leonard Floyd, and Washington Bennett: *ambush*.

It took the jury only three hours and twenty-five minutes to reach a verdict: "We, the jury, find the defendant guilty of manslaughter in the first degree and fix his punishment at ten years imprisonment in the Penitentiary." James showed little emotion after the verdict was read, but

Ann Scott, accompanied by two of her friends, burst into tears. She was not the only one—the *Birmingham News* reported that a "number of spectators wept openly in the courtroom." Washington Bennett's family wept out of relief, grateful that their lost loved one's death would not go unpunished. James was now facing not only the seventeen-year sentence for the second-degree murder conviction but also the additional ten-year sentence for first-degree manslaughter. In twenty-seven years, James would be forty-five years old, five years older than his father had been when he died. Members of the community speculated that the only reason the jury had not rendered another second-degree murder conviction was the questionable light that had been cast on Bennett's actions just as the shooting had begun. Had he, out of some protective, paternal instinct, grabbed Billy Kilpatrick as the boy jumped from the car to keep him from running headlong into a hail of bullets? Was he acting under the orders of his boss, Sheriff Boyles, who, according to one version of James's testimony, had shouted, "Grab that damn boy"? Or was his gesture more sinister—had he meant to use Billy as a human shield to protect himself in case Aubrey Kilpatrick turned that powerful .44 pistol in his direction? No one would ever know what had compelled Bennett to seize the boy's arm. His family and supporters must have taken great pride and comfort, at least, in his superhuman efforts to save James Lang and himself after both had been wounded—Lang, critically; Bennett, mortally. They could say that Washington Bennett had died a hero in the line of duty.

Rogers, stinging from yet another loss, promptly indicated that he would file an appeal of the conviction. The Alabama Court of Criminal Appeals would soon be considering two cases of *Kilpatrick v. State.* If both appeals were rejected, James would have to begin serving his two sentences immediately. The future he and Ann Scott had dared to imagine blew away like dandelion fluff in a tornado. What sixteen-year-old girl would or could wait twenty-seven years for her boyfriend to get out of prison? She knew girls who had vowed to their sweethearts that they would wait for them to come home from Korea, wearing promise rings on their fingers or on chains around their necks. But no war in American history had ever lasted twenty-seven years. Seventy years after the shooting and eleven years after James's death, Ann Scott Kilpatrick grew misty-eyed remembering October 1952: "We didn't know what to do. All I could do was pray."

CHAPTER 11

# The Penitent

Before he became a frontline chronicler of the nascent Civil Rights
Movement in Montgomery and a legend in Alabama journalism, Bob
Ingram was a young and ambitious reporter manning a desk at the *Gadsden
Times*. Only twenty-six years old but tempered by war, Robert Burrell
Ingram Jr. had returned from the Pacific front of World War II and gone
to college, graduating from Alabama Polytechnic Institute in 1949. He had
learned to love words and writing from his mother, the longtime librarian in
his hometown of Centre, a small town nestled in the Appalachian foothills
of north Alabama. After graduating from college, Ingram returned to
Centre and worked as a reporter for the *Cherokee County Herald*, and in 1951
he moved to Gadsden, where he served as the sportswriter and, later, as the
state reporter for the *Gadsden Times*. In early 1953 Ingram was considering
an offer he had received from the *Montgomery Advertiser*. He was reluctant
to uproot his new bride, Edith Faye Ragan, from the lovely, rolling hills of
north Alabama, but he had his sights on the rough-and-tumble world of
political journalism, and he wanted—he needed—to be in Montgomery, the
state's capital, to achieve his ambitions.

Throughout the 1950s and '60s, Bob Ingram covered the events that
shaped Alabama history: the Montgomery Bus Boycott, George Wallace's
"Segregation Forever" gubernatorial inauguration speech, and Wallace's
infamous "Stand in the Schoolhouse Door" at the University of Alabama.
After fourteen years with the *Montgomery Advertiser*, Ingram took on the
role of director of legislative affairs for the Medical Association of the
State of Alabama. Upon the death of Governor Lurleen Wallace, Governor
Albert Brewer appointed Ingram as state finance director. But journalism
was Ingram's first love, and he purchased *Alabama Magazine* in 1974; for the
rest of his career, Ingram was the state's most prominent and unflinching
political analyst, writing a weekly column for dozens of small newspapers

across Alabama. In 2003 he was inducted into the University of Alabama Communication and Information Sciences Hall of Fame, and Auburn University–Montgomery created a lecture series in his name. When he died in 2007 after a two-year battle with myelodysplasia, a rare form of blood cancer, newspapers all over the state mourned his death, with one tribute hailing Ingram as "a one-man fourth estate in Montgomery, placing Alabama's state capitol under a journalistic light that left no place to hide." But that lifetime of truth seeking and accolades lay before him as he sat at his desk in the bullpen of the *Gadsden Times* in April 1953, skimming a news story about a man named Oliver Brown from Kansas and pondering the implications that *Brown v. Board of Education of Topeka* would have for his native state. Another reporter strode through the bullpen and approached Ingram's desk. "Hey, Bob," the reporter told him, "you'll want this one. Jimmy Kilpatrick just accepted a plea deal."

☉

After spending a quiet Thanksgiving and Christmas with his family and friends, James Kilpatrick readied himself once again to stand trial in January 1953 for the death of Boaz police chief Leonard Floyd. James had already been tried for Floyd's death in July 1951, but the resulting mistrial had temporarily shelved the indictment in the case. The docket for the January circuit court term in Albertville was as full as a pretty debutante's dance card—James was scheduled to stand trial not only for Floyd's death but also for assault with intent to murder in the wounding of Deputy James Lang. Fred Goble and Tom Upton, the two sharecroppers on the Kilpatrick farm who had been arrested and taken into custody the night of the shooting, were also slated to stand trial for murder and assault. Yet after two completed trials, the evidence against Goble and Upton looked thin. Goble had been on the scene, huddling behind the Kilpatricks' house and holding a loaded shotgun as the shots rang out in the front yard, but he had never fired his weapon. Upton apparently hadn't even been on the scene at all until after the deputies had driven away. He had merely come to the house in the aftermath to find out what had happened and was caught up in the wholesale arrests of any male over the age of ten on the property. The local newspapers speculated that Goble and Upton would never see the inside of the courtroom, even though they remained under bonds of $10,000 apiece.

As it turns out, none of the three men saw the inside of the Albertville courtroom in January 1953. An influenza outbreak was plaguing many southern states, Alabama included. While not as deadly as the 1957 influenza pandemic, the 1952–53 epidemic sickened thousands of Americans, and the citizens of Sand Mountain, despite their relative isolation, were no exception. In Marshall County, the circuit court reporter, Mildred Bell Burdette, had been stricken with the flu and was therefore too sick to attend court. A replacement court reporter had been summoned from Birmingham, but she, too, fell ill. The absence of the swift-fingered and meticulous Burdette would have been reason enough to postpone the trial, but other factors contributed to the postponement as well. George Rogers had a case to argue before the Alabama Supreme Court, and the prosecution's most valuable expert witness, Dr. C. J. Rehling, had been subpoenaed to testify at another murder trial elsewhere in the state. Judge Stone, surely grinding his teeth in exasperation, announced that the Kilpatrick, Goble, and Upton trials would take place during a special session of the Marshall County Circuit Court set to begin on April 20, 1953. Then, at least for James Kilpatrick, a small miracle occurred.

Immediately after James's conviction for second-degree murder in November 1951, George Rogers had filed an appeal, a move regarded as standard practice after a murder conviction. After sixteen months, the Court of Appeals of Alabama had finally reached a decision on April 7, 1953. Justice Robert B. Harwood ruled that "the trial court erred in refusing defendant's requested charge to the jury that good character may, in connection with all evidence, generate a reasonable doubt and entitle defendant to acquittal, though without proof of good character jury would convict. Judgment reversed and cause remanded." The transcript of the decision faulted Judge Stone for "fail[ing] to instruct the jury or allude in any manner to the effect of proof of evidence of good character," even though the defense had offered more than fifteen character witnesses, among them two ministers, a Sunday school superintendent, and a highly respected teacher who had taught James in elementary school.

In his comments to the jury, Special Prosecutor Pilcher had described James Kilpatrick as "the bloodiest criminal that ever come into a courtroom" and "a dirty murderer" who would inevitably "send a .30 caliber through the heart, liver, and diaphragm of another citizen of Marshall County." These remarks, combined with Stone's negligence in instructing the jury as to the probative value of character witness testimony, had possibly prejudiced the jury in such a manner that a fair verdict could not be reached. Suddenly, seventeen years of the twenty-seven-year sentence James was facing were no longer a certainty. He could be tried again for Zeke Boyles's murder and again convicted (jeopardy does not apply in a retrial of a conviction that was reversed on appeal on procedural grounds), but on practically the eve of his fifth trial, this reversal must have seemed a gift from above.

Perhaps the prosecutors could see the handwriting on the wall—getting James Kilpatrick into prison was going to take a good deal longer and require significantly more of the county's funds than they had anticipated. Certainly the higher court's decision to overturn the second-degree murder conviction deflated the prosecution's elation over winning two trials in a row, and Circuit Solicitor L. P. Waid seethed privately to his close associates that Stone's carelessness and Pilcher's grandstanding had cost them a much-needed victory. On the morning of Monday, April 20, after the potential jurors had been assembled but none had been struck, Judge Stone called a recess at the request of both the prosecution and the defense. In the judge's quarters, the opposing sides argued over James's fate; the state pushed for a twenty-year term, then a fifteen-year term, then twelve, and finally ten. After consulting with James, Rogers agreed to withdraw the appeal for the ten-year sentence resulting from the first-degree manslaughter conviction. The state in turn agreed to drop all remaining charges against James as well as all charges against Fred Goble and Tom Upton. When the court reconvened at 1:00 p.m. after a lunch break, Judge Stone announced the agreement and declared that James would have fifteen days before starting his sentence.

To say the spectators in the courtroom reacted strongly to the announcement would be an understatement. James's friends and family crowded around him, shouting their congratulations, praising the Lord, slapping his back, shaking his hand, and hugging his neck. This time, tears of joy rather than sorrow streamed down the faces of his supporters, and James himself wept openly. Elizabeth Kilpatrick told a Guntersville reporter, "Right will win out. My son was not guilty of any crime. He's a good boy and has always been a good boy, but there were some folks up here who lied and did everything to get my boy's head. I can only hope that this prison sentence doesn't hurt Jimmy inside." When the jubilant celebration had subsided, James sat down to talk to *Gadsden Times* reporter Bob Ingram. Like many people in north Alabama, Ingram had followed the Kilpatrick trials closely, and although he maintained his consummate professionalism and journalistic objectivity, he was moved by the sight of the young man, who was literally shaking with relief. "How do you feel about this plea agreement, Jimmy?" Ingram asked. "I'm satisfied," James replied. "Mr. Rogers put it up to me, and I made my own decision. Now I know just where I stand, and it's a good feeling. This trial has caused enough trouble already to everybody, and I'm glad it's all over."

Of course, not everyone was thrilled with the plea deal. Marion Boyles Hodges, daughter of the slain sheriff, expressed her anger in no uncertain terms: "It was done without the consent of the families. We knew nothing about any plans for a settlement and feel that an injustice was done in making it without consulting us." Under Alabama law in 1953, the state had no obligation to inform victims' families before negotiating plea agreements, so several survivors were caught off guard when word reached them by word of mouth or newspaper articles. Former deputy James Lang, who had left law enforcement and was working at that time at a clothing store in Albertville, reacted indignantly: "Who reached any agreement? I sure didn't agree to it." He bore a ragged, star-shaped scar from being shot in the chest on May 17, 1951, and he had taken the stand on three separate occasions to relive that terrible night and to defend not only his own actions but also the actions of the three men who had lost their lives while serving a warrant. He must have felt that ten years was not long enough for James Kilpatrick to be imprisoned, paltry recompense for the lives of his fellow officers.

But it wasn't over, as it turns out. After the Alabama Court of Appeals overturned James's conviction for second-degree murder, the case didn't end there—instead, it was remanded to the lower court, which meant that the case would once again go before the Marshall County Circuit Court. In a last-ditch, Hail Mary effort, Waid and the other prosecutors requested the intervention of Alabama attorney general Si Garrett, who agreed to ask the court of appeals to review the decision. His request for a rehearing was denied, so Garrett issued a *certiorari* for the Alabama Supreme Court to review the appellate court's ruling.

Meanwhile, up on Sand Mountain, the verbal agreement reached by the opposing counsel was falling apart. Apparently, none of those seasoned lawyers had found it necessary to write down the details of the plea agreement, and as May rolled into June, with James's incarceration date well past due, the deal was declared null and void. Finally, on July 2, 1953, the Alabama Supreme Court refused to review the action of the appellate court in reversing James Kilpatrick's second-degree murder conviction. Since the deal was off, James would go on trial for killing Leonard Floyd and assaulting James Lang, and Goble and Upton were back on the hook for murder and assault. Bewildered and exhausted by the legal seesawing, the now nineteen-year-old defendant begged his attorney to try to renegotiate the plea agreement. James had had enough. George Rogers, however, urged James to stay the course. "I believe we can win," Rogers told James in September 1953. James looked into Rogers's broad, earnest face, seeking the reassurance he could not summon within himself, and nodded.

The stage was set for what everyone assumed would be the final performance, and all the players knew their lines, although the delivery lacked the potent urgency of earlier recitations. On Monday, October 12, 1953, a jury was selected, Judge Stone called the court to order, and James Kilpatrick's fifth trial began. There were no new witnesses, no surprise revelations, nothing of any substance to distinguish this iteration from the previous trials. In many ways, the trials had come full circle: James had been tried unsuccessfully for the death of Leonard Floyd in July 1951, only ten weeks after the shooting had occurred, when passions were high and hundreds of curious onlookers had flooded the Albertville courthouse and flowed around the building's grounds, hoping to catch a glimpse of the sixteen-year-old defendant or the grieving widows of both Leonard Floyd and Aubrey Kilpatrick. Now, in October 1953, far fewer came, and the foot traffic around the courthouse consisted of Albertville citizens going about their daily business, opting to find out about the verdict from the town gossips or the local newspaper rather than sitting among the spectators in the echoingly empty gallery. Leonard Floyd's widow, Opal Annie, attended the trial, but she was not among the witnesses who took the stand.

The trial proceeded at a rapid clip. By Tuesday, October 13, the state had completed its presentation of direct testimony, and by the next morning, after only two hours' deliberation, the jury returned a verdict: James Kilpatrick was sentenced to one year in the county jail and fined one dollar. For the former Boaz police chief's survivors, the verdict must have been a slap in the face. Stiffer punishments had been rendered for misdemeanors—for, say, running a still behind the barn or stealing a neighbor's cow. An article in the *Advertiser-Gleam*, Guntersville's weekly newspaper, wryly noted that "the sentences seem to be getting shorter and shorter, as feeling over the killing dies down. The first sentence was for seventeen years, the second for ten, and this week's was for one." Of all the victims from that tragic May night, Leonard Floyd was the one least involved in the conflict prior to the shooting, and his death was the saddest and most senseless. He had survived a near-fatal wound in World War II, regained his strength, and returned to Alabama to build his life anew. He had been a husband, a father to two children, a farmer, and a peace officer. He had not wanted to go with Zeke Boyles and his men so late at night to serve a warrant that could have waited until the next morning, but he had felt that he could act as a peacemaker to defuse a potentially volatile encounter. He had never drawn his gun. When the shooting was over, he lay face down in the dirt, one pants leg snarled in a coil of barbed wire, shot in the back, killed instantly. In the end, his life was deemed worth an evening for two at the picture show.

Fred Goble and Tom Upton, the two tenant farmers who had been so loyal to the Kilpatrick family, who had dined with them often, sharing jokes and playing with the children, now nervously awaited their trials after twenty-eight months of living under multiple indictments for murder and assault with intent to murder. Life had been hard for the two men—after Aubrey's death and the subsequent sale of almost all of the Kilpatricks' farmland, they had been without steady work. They had families to support, and Goble's wife was critically ill. Suspicion hung over them like a bad smell. They were uneducated and illiterate, which had not been an incapacitating liability when they were working on the Kilpatrick farm and benefitting from Aubrey's protection. But the staggering weight of paying the bonds ($10,000 for each man, the equivalent of over $100,000 in 2024), along with providing for their families and, in Goble's case, paying medical bills for his wife's care, had left both men destitute and desperate.

After their arrests, some of the financial support that had gushed onto the Kilpatrick family had trickled their way, but by late 1953, the outpouring had dried up almost completely. The plea deal back in April had offered Goble and Upton a glimmer of hope, only to be extinguished when the agreement fell apart in the months afterward. So much hinged upon the testimonies and outcomes of James's trials, the two men bound to the eldest Kilpatrick son's fate like twin carts hitched to a single, hard-pressed mule beset by a swarm of horseflies. George Rogers had managed to weave into James's defense the facts that Goble, although present at the house during the shooting, had never fired his shotgun, and Upton had not even been at the house at all until after the shooting was over. These facts, coupled with the state's readiness to put the whole matter to bed, seemed to be the most encouraging considerations in both tenant farmers' upcoming trials.

If hope is a thing with feathers, as Emily Dickinson wrote, then the plucked, bedraggled bird circling the five trials of James Kilpatrick came home to roost on Monday, October 19, 1953. An agreement was struck, and this time, it was in writing. The terms of the written agreement were identical to those of the previous, verbal one: James would accept the ten-year sentence for killing Washington Bennett, and he would withdraw his appeal on that conviction. The state also agreed to drop the eleven other indictments, including those against Goble and Upton. The two men were finally free and clear. James, however, was not. Under the terms of this final agreement, he was to voluntarily surrender and present himself within thirty days to the warden of Kilby Prison, located a few miles from Montgomery, Alabama. "Thus ended one of the worst homicide cases ever to be tried in a Marshall County Court," announced the *Albertville Herald* on October 22. Although the agreement had been signed by James, his attorney, and the prosecutors, and approved by the state attorney general, Elizabeth Kilpatrick refused to give up, canvassing the streets of Guntersville with a petition for the state parole board, even before James had arrived at Kilby. (The *Advertiser-Gleam* noted that she "didn't seem to be getting many signers.") The night before his surrender, James sat on Ann Scott's front porch, holding her hand, until her parents called her inside at midnight. The two young lovers embraced and kissed before Ann went reluctantly into her house. James walked down the Scotts' porch steps, into the darkness and whatever uncertain future lay before him.

Civilization gave rise not only to the civilized but to the criminalized as well. From Hammurabi's Code to Jeremy Bentham's panopticon, humans, once they learned to live together in complex societies, have pondered what to do with those who break the law. The earliest prisons, going back to the first millennia BCE, were primarily short-term detention centers where lawbreakers awaited punishment (often brutal, bloody, and public). Over the centuries, the objectives of locking a person away from society morphed from being predominantly punitive and retributive to ideals more humane and rehabilitative. In 1215 the Magna Carta introduced the right to trial by jury, a principle cherished and revived over five hundred years later when the architects of American independence penned the new nation's foundational documents. Shortly after the American Revolution, the Quakers were instrumental in changing the way imprisonment was viewed. Prior to the Quaker-led reforms, the singular purpose of prisons was to incarcerate criminals with virtually no regard for their physical or mental well-being. The Quakers believed that prisoners should be able to reflect on their crimes, to achieve penitence for their wrongdoings, and thus be rehabilitated and reintegrated more successfully back into society. The kinder, gentler word "penitentiary" came into common use in the early nineteenth century, although the modern, shortened reference of "going to the pen" conjures a place and experience that would set an eighteenth-century Quaker's wide-awake hat askew.

James Kilpatrick's sentence dictated that he would spend "ten years imprisonment in the Penitentiary." When he arrived at Kilby Correctional Facility in December 1953, he assumed that he would remain there for the duration of his sentence, but what was then known as the Alabama Department of Corrections and Institutions (DCI) had other plans for him. On December 15 James was transferred to Draper Prison, located in Elmore County, Alabama. Draper had been built in 1939 to replace the old Speigner Reformatory, and in 1941 Draper was reclassified by the DCI as a model prison for first-time offenders. Its mission, considered innovative at the time, was not merely to house prisoners but also to offer vocational classes whereby inmates could learn a trade that would aid their transition into postincarceration life. When James arrived at Draper, he was greeted by Warden B. R. "Burr" Reeves, a huge, hulking man who would have been right at home on the set of a 1950s prison B-movie. With a cigar stump protruding from his fleshy lips, Warden Reeves peered over his horn-rimmed glasses and told the scrawny nineteen-year-old, "I didn't send for you, and I can't do anything about it, so you'd better not mess up, or I'll send you to lockup." James meekly agreed, but that promise would be harder to keep than he knew.

While being a bootlegger's son had its downside in the free world, it had its advantages inside prison. Two of Aubrey Kilpatrick's former associates, Clayton Williams and Fred Wells, were already long-term guests at Draper, and they took James under their wing after his arrival. Having friends on the inside helped James get settled into this unfamiliar life. With no officially assigned cells or beds, the inmates at Draper took a more laissez-faire approach to where one bunked, typically relying on seniority, intimidation, or cold, hard cash to determine who slept where. Williams and Wells made sure that James had a bed and a relatively clean set of prison clothes, although James, with his twenty-five-inch waist, had difficulty finding pants that would stay up without a belt (an accessory that was, for obvious reasons, prohibited). He typically wore a size six shoe and had to stuff newspaper into the toes of the size ten prison-issue brogans he received. More important than a bed or clothing or shoes, however, was the protection afforded by the two older inmates. While not exactly hardened criminals, Williams and Wells were well versed in the transactional nature of prison life. Because of his youth and slight build, James soon became known as "Little Man" around Draper, but thanks in large part to the clout of his father's incarcerated friends, none of the inmates ever bothered him.

This is not to say that James's introduction to prison was without missteps and even horrors. The stomach problems that had bedeviled him throughout his trials flared up at the most inopportune times, including his first day at Draper. Guts cramping, James darted for the closest bathroom, unaware that only moments before, an inmate had been attacked and beaten to death in that same room. James had no choice but to relieve his aching bowels, even as blood and gray matter oozed down the tile wall. He may have been country-boy tough, but this was a whole new level of savagery. The guards at Draper, like the vindictive jailers back in Marshall County, saw James as a cop killer who had murdered not just one but three officers of the law. While James was never outright struck or openly abused by the guards, he was a frequent target of shakedowns, and the guards sent him to lockup for the slightest infraction. He saw men kill each other over a dice game. A lifelong animal lover, James was horrified when he witnessed an inmate working in the kitchen casually toss into a pot of boiling water a kitten that had wandered in through the back door; the cook then nonchalantly continued to add carrots and onions for a stew.

James learned about the ingenious yet dangerous (and disgusting) concoctions that prisoners would make to escape the alternating and unpredictable cycles of violence and tedium. Nasal spray could be disassembled and the paraffin core soaked in coffee and drunk to produce an amphetamine-like high. Sometimes, prisoners would take paregoric, an opium-based antidiarrheal medication available over the counter until 1970, and boil it down, strain it to remove the camphor, and then inject the remaining liquid—a makeshift version of heroin—directly into their veins. Toilet wine was a time-intensive but popular delicacy. Fortunately, the worst habits James picked up in prison, as he laughingly admitted forty-six years later, involved chewing on a cigar and "cussing."

Life at Draper was not always grim and brutal and dehumanizing. Some prison inmates played on stellar sports teams that competed against city and YMCA league teams. In 1950 twin inmates named Jimmy and Jack Kilpatrick (no relation to James) boxed in the Central Alabama Golden Gloves tournament representing Draper Prison; Jimmy captured the welterweight title after his twin conceded, refusing to pummel his own brother. Baseball teams from Draper dominated the Dixie Amateur League in Montgomery throughout the 1950s. Inmates with musical talent could join the Draper Prison Swing Band, which played at venues across much of central and south Alabama during the 1940s and '50s. According to Birmingham writer and radio host Burgin Mathews, the band was scheduled to perform at the

American Legion Hall in Troy for their annual Valentine's Day dance, but apparently the taste of simulated freedom was too tantalizing for some of the band members: "'I regret to inform you that our orchestra will not be able to fill your engagement,' Warden B. R. Reeves wrote to the Legion's dance chairman. 'Several members of the band escaped last Saturday night and have not, as yet, been recaptured.'"

Female inmates from the Julia Tutwiler Prison for Women, also located in Elmore County, were bussed to Draper once a year to put on a play for the men, an event that galvanized the male inmates into a frenzy of cleaning and tidying. Kathryn Tucker Windham, famous for her collections of southern ghost stories, recounts a visit to Tutwiler Prison in 1943. When she was a reporter for *Alabama Journal*, she accompanied E. P. Russell, the newly appointed director of the Department of Corrections and Institutions, to Tutwiler, where she sat with Russell as he listened to the inmates' concerns and requests. One inmate asked the director, "Couldn't we have a band come play so we could dance?" The next evening, the bus arrived from Draper, and the swing band performed for over an hour. It wasn't a country club cotillion, but it was a delightful suspension in time for all involved, a few moments to feel normal and free.

James, the perennial jokester, managed to gin up some fun of his own while in prison. His first work detail in Draper was in the prison laundry running the steam presser. Like every basic amenity in the prison, such as exchanging bed linens or getting deloused, having one's pants steam-pressed cost money. If the laundry workers did not collect the fees, the shortfall was deducted from their prison store accounts. To retaliate against those who refused to pay and deter future dereliction, James and his fellow launderers would take a contraband razor blade and slice through some of the seams, then steam and fold the pants. When the penurious pants owner next dressed, he found himself wearing what must have looked like a bizarre cross between a long loincloth and chaps.

Another prank James played became a brief tradition at Draper. Part welcome, part hazing ritual, the trick grew out of a harrowing experience in which James had decayed teeth pulled while three men held him down. When he saw the effect that his screams had on new inmates waiting to have their dentition examined, he conceived of a wicked jape: he would plant a capsule in his cheek that contained red dye and, after emitting convincingly agonized howls, stagger out of the prison dentist's office, holding his mouth while fake blood streamed down his chin. The waiting newbies shrank back and blanched in terror, until James began to grin and giggle. These episodes of juvenile humor helped pass the time, regardless of how much time inside each inmate faced.

Despite the moments of levity, there were dark, soul-crushing places in Draper Prison where no inmate wanted to go. In the general prison population, older inmates often preyed upon new arrivals who had no one to look out for them, pretending to offer protection and then exploiting the fledgling inmate's trust and dependency to procure money, labor, or sex. Sometimes older inmates who had established power and dominance within the prison pecking order simply took what they wanted by force. As dangerous as life among other prisoners could be, being apart from the general population could be worse. The two most feared physical spaces in Draper and Kilby Prisons were known as "lockup" and the "dog house." While "lockup" relied primarily on the mental torture of solitary confinement, the "dog house" offered a sadistic one-two punch: extreme physical beatings followed by solitary confinement. Suffocatingly hot in the summer and bitterly cold in the winter, lockup was a four-feet-by-four-feet cinderblock hut where a prisoner was cloistered for up to twenty-one days, typically for breaking a prison rule. The inmate went in completely naked (which would be far more advantageous in July than in December) and was removed at night to sleep in a tiny cell. An unwashed cotton sheath of varying proportions was lowered on a rope for the man inside to wear overnight, and before sunrise the next morning, a guard would escort the groggy inmate back to the concrete hold. The "dog house," on the other hand, was a torment reserved especially for those who refused to accept work details. After being tied to a fence and whipped with chains, the prisoner would then be confined in what was essentially a small crate for, again, up to twenty-one days, with stale bread and water for sustenance and only a five-gallon bucket for relieving himself. In a 1997 interview, James chuckled humorlessly when recounting the lengths that self-proclaimed "tough guys"—murderers, rapists, and thieves who professed to be inured to suffering—would go to avoid being sent to either hellhole.

Throughout his time at Draper, the weekend visits from Elizabeth Kilpatrick, Ann Scott, and other family members and friends sustained James and kept him from being drawn into the trouble and shady dealings that run like an underground current through all prisons. As long and difficult as the trip was, James's mother made the journey as often as she could, frequently inviting Ann to ride along with her. Boaz is roughly 150 miles from Elmore, and in 1954, without an interstate system completed in

Alabama, the only way to get from Marshall County to Elmore County was to follow a series of connecting two-lane highways (with the occasional, brief, four-lane wide spot close to larger towns). Elizabeth, who had adapted to her new circumstances by becoming increasingly independent, had finally taught herself to drive, although she had not bothered to get a license to operate a motor vehicle. She was nervous both about handling this large, unfamiliar conveyance and getting a ticket while driving without a license, so she refused to drive over twenty-five miles per hour, even if the speed limit was significantly higher. Ann Scott Kilpatrick gave a girlish titter as she recounted in a 2021 interview those slow, wending drives to Draper, with Elizabeth clutching the steering wheel as if the car might try to run away from her, her nose practically touching the windshield, and a line of frustrated, honking motorists stretching far behind her into the distance.

James was allowed to go home for two supervised visits during his incarceration, both on occasions when he feared he might not see his mother alive again. Elizabeth's health had deteriorated significantly since May 1951. She had endured the shock of witnessing her husband's death, the repeated stresses of her oldest son's multiple murder trials, the physical and emotional pain of delivering a stillborn child, the heartbreak of institutionalizing a differently abled child, and the incessant financial demands of paying legal bills and supporting the five children who lived at home (by this time, Billy had joined the army). These vicissitudes alone would have broken almost anyone, and when compounded by a genetic predisposition for heart disease and diabetes and a lifetime of nonexistent preventive care, Elizabeth was on the brink of utter, seemingly irrevocable collapse. On the first visit, James was allowed to spend two hours with his mother, and she seemed to gain strength from his presence. When James went home for the second visit, he asked the prison official who accompanied him if he might go in without handcuffs or leg shackles—it would do his mother a world of good, James pleaded to his handler, if she could see her boy, perhaps for the last time, unchained. The guard agreed. Elizabeth again recovered after the second visit, as if James was the elixir that could bring her back to life. Each time James visited her, she would give him what little money she could, often slipping a dollar into his shirt pocket before hugging him goodbye.

It was that dollar bill, given with love, that nearly kept James from getting paroled. In early December 1957 the Alabama Board of Pardons and Paroles ruled that James had been a model prisoner throughout his four years of incarceration. He had never been sent to lockup, and he had become a favorite among many of the guards at Draper. (Carrying on a practice he had begun at home with his family members, James gained the reputation in prison of being a skilled barber, and the guards lined up for him to cut their hair.) Although Elizabeth Kilpatrick's preemptive petition in November 1953 may not have acquired many signatures, a later petition on James's behalf, this one submitted in early 1957, had over one hundred signers. This petition, citing the need for James's release due to family hardship, must have made an impression on the board as they considered candidates for parole.

It was a common practice for the board to announce parolees in December as a gesture of holiday magnanimity, and James's name was among those slated for parole before Christmas 1957. During a cellblock shakedown prior to James's release, however, a guard—presumably one who did not find the young inmate as amicable as some of the other guards did—discovered the contraband dollar bill in James's shirt pocket. Inmates were expressly forbidden from possessing cash; such an offense meant the harsh punishment of lockup. Days before he was scheduled to leave Draper, James was transferred to lockup at Kilby Prison for a twenty-one-day stint.

James knew that no prisoner had ever been granted release while in lockup. The irony of his circumstances astounded him. Even as imprisoned gangsters from Phenix City hid pillowcases stuffed with money under their mattresses and circulated hundred-dollar bills among themselves, James had been caught with a one-dollar bill that might prove to be his undoing. More immediately concerning for James was the prospect of huddling naked inside a cinderblock cubbyhole in near-freezing temperatures. One of the guards who had befriended James, a man with the patriotic name of John Adams, sent him to the infirmary before he went to lockup and directed the prison doctor to give James vitamins and penicillin injections. It would have been especially cruel for James to have been granted parole and then die of pneumonia. After the temporary transfer to Kilby Prison, James spent eleven days in lockup, unsure of his parole status and fearful of its possible revocation. But on the twelfth day, guards opened the hatch, held him up as he wobbled on stiff legs, and put him on a bus back to Draper. There, he took a shower, shaved his peach fuzz, and got a haircut. The board was sticking by their decision to parole him, despite the last-minute punishment in lockup. James was going home.

On Monday, December 16, 1957, James Kilpatrick, dressed in a cheap blue suit and carrying a small cardboard suitcase containing his meager belongings, passed through the iron-barred gate that separated the inmate facilities from the front office of Draper Prison. For James, whose eyes had become accustomed to dimness while in the windowless cinderblock confines of lockup, the sunlight outside the prison was dazzlingly, blindingly bright, but he could make out two shapes in the parking lot—one, tall but stooped with care, the other, petite but on tiptoe with excitement. As his vision adjusted, he saw that the taller figure was his mother, Elizabeth. The smaller woman beside her was Ann Scott. James straightened his shoulders, tightened his grip on the suitcase handle, and walked out of the darkness, into the light.

# AFTERWORD

Robert Penn Warren opens his 1950 novel *World Enough and Time* with these lines:

> I can show you what is left. After the pride, passion, agony, and bemused aspiration, what is left is in our hands. . . . Here are the records of what happened in that courtroom, all the words taken down. . . . We have what is left, the lies and the half-lies and the truths and the half-truths.

I thought of these words a great deal while writing this book, as I pored over hundreds of pages of trial transcripts and hundreds of newspaper articles from the first half of the twentieth century, as I drove down the rutted path that took me to the former site of the Kilpatrick farm, now overgrown with weeds and trees. The road has been named Kilpatrick Circle, but no Kilpatricks live there now, and little is left of the old home place and outbuildings except for a decayed barn with a sloping, rusted tin roof. I rode in the cab of a giant Ford F-150 with eighty-six-year-old Sheril Thomas, now deceased, as he pointed out to me where the black Pontiac had turned off Highway 168 and made its way toward the Kilpatrick home close to midnight on Thursday, May 17, 1951; he also showed me the route that Washington Bennett had driven, blood pouring from the gunshot wound in his neck, from the farm to the police station in downtown Boaz. How long those three miles must have seemed to Bennett and his fellow deputy James Lang as they sped away from the carnage, both barely conscious and wracked with pain, the fallen left behind, far past saving.

I talked to dozens of people around the area, some of whom were children or teenagers when the shooting occurred, some the descendants of principal actors in the events surrounding that night. If I had a dollar for every story I listened to that began, "I heard tell," I would be able to retire early and comfortably. I became friends with a wonderfully garrulous group of men who, in their retirement, spend much of their time examining old documents and newspapers and discussing the history of Marshall County in the basement archival rooms across from the courthouse in Guntersville. One retired lawyer, whom I privately thought of as "The Contrarian," squinted at me and asked, skeptically, "Who's going to want to read about a bunch of Alabama farmers shooting it out with the law seventy years ago?" I replied, "Well, who would have thought that the murder of a farm family in Holcomb, Kansas, would have become a worldwide sensation and launched a true-crime craze that's still going on today? But Truman Capote made it work." The Contrarian barked a laugh and said, "So you think you're the next Truman Capote?" *No*, I thought. *I will never be that stylish.*

I ate a great deal of pie at diners and Huddle Houses. I brought lunch and snacks to interview sessions with Kilpatrick family members, including Ann Scott Kilpatrick, who resided in an assisted-living facility in Boaz until she passed away on December 23, 2023. She was still lovely, the same blue eyes that so captivated young James Kilpatrick often sparkling with merriment or tears as she described to me everything she remembered about her time with James, from meeting him for the first time in the Guntersville jail until their last hour together at his death in November 2009. I am grateful to have had that time with her. Her son and daughter-in-law told me that she had been experiencing some of the cognitive decline that sometimes comes with age—not so much "decline," really, but rather the insistent crowding of long-term memories jockeying for priority over increasingly capricious short-term recall. I hope she remembered the best times she and James shared, the heady though complicated days of their early courtship; the joy of reunion on that cold, bright December day in 1957 when James walked out of Draper Prison; the June wedding in 1958, both of them beaming beatifically in black-and-white photographs; the birth of their son, Marty, on the first day of 1961, Marshall County's official "New Year's Baby."

I met Zeke Boyles's grandson, Donnie Hodges, and listened as he described his grandfather's legendary status in Marshall County and the family's struggles after the sheriff's death. Hodges exclaimed, "I can remember exactly when he was killed. I was five, and I was outside playing." I didn't correct him—surely no five-year-old child, even in the relatively safer days of 1951 when folks left their doors unlocked day and night and children roamed freely through woods and towns, would have been outside playing at midnight on a Thursday. Perhaps that was his memory of being told his grandfather had been shot, when the grownups had decided it was time to initiate him into the grim and ineluctable lessons of loss.

I learned that a story can be like flypaper, or a pitcher of syrup, or a black wool coat—it picks up anything and everything that floats by. Many of the people I interviewed told me some variant of this disturbing story: they had heard that when Elizabeth Kilpatrick had rushed to the door as the first shots rang out, she was holding a baby, and the law had fired at her. That simply wasn't true. Nothing in any of the testimonies Elizabeth gave in court indicated that she had been holding any of her children or that anyone had shot in her direction. I wondered if those dramatic but false versions (would we call them "rural legends"?) had been the conflation of actual events with later news stories of a similar nature, perhaps that of Vicki Weaver, killed by an FBI sniper in 1992 as she stood in a cabin doorway holding her ten-month-old daughter during a standoff with the law. Most of the time, I just let people talk. I could sift through the hours of stories and pluck out the usable bits later.

When I began researching and writing this book, America was in its second year of the Covid-19 pandemic and the throes of a racial reckoning. I thought about how different James Kilpatrick's fate would have been if he had been a person of color, how, if James had been a young Black man instead of a white one, he would not have lived to see the sun rise. I thought about the current deplorable state of Alabama's penitentiaries, and how Fyodor Dostoevsky once claimed, "The degree of civilization in a society can be judged by entering its prisons." At nineteen, James Kilpatrick went into one of Alabama's most notoriously violent and dangerous prisons and emerged relatively unscathed (at least externally) at the age of twenty-three. Thousands of others who went into Draper were not so lucky. Although Draper Prison was closed as a correctional facility in 2016, it was reopened in April 2020 as a "quarantine dormitory" for Alabama inmates during the pandemic. So, the misery continued, just under a different guise.

James Kilpatrick left Draper a changed man, and he was one of the fortunate few who never returned to a life of crime or prison. He was enfolded into the warm embrace of his community and given a second chance. He found peace and salvation. Most people in Marshall County were willing to forgive him or, in many instances, had never believed him guilty in the first place. Public opinion is still divided, even now, over seventy years later. Contrary to Special Prosecutor E. G. Pilcher's courtroom predictions, James never shot another person in Marshall County or anywhere else.

Writing is a solitary business, often lonely, but I was never entirely alone, because the ghosts were with me. The oldest and the youngest of the Kilpatrick children have died—James, in 2009, and Danny, in 2006. Billy, Harold, and Jeretta, too, have passed on; three of Aubrey and Elizabeth Kilpatrick's children survive as of the writing of this book. The women widowed by the 1951 Sand Mountain shootout have died—Elizabeth Pankey Kilpatrick, Eva Etchison Boyles, Opal Coppett Floyd, and Jane Evans Bennett. Judge J. S. Stone died years ago, as did all the prosecutors and that indefatigable litigator George Rogers, gone on to other judgments. No one is alive who can say exactly what happened in front of the Kilpatrick house on May 17, 1951, although many purport to know, even though they weren't there or hadn't even been born yet. But that's fine, because they—whether through lineage, lore, or logic—are made of stories, too, just as I am.

Stories are mirrors. They are also spotlights and lenses, X-rays, kaleidoscopes, and prisms. Stories are both stars and telescopes, and we are simultaneously constellations and astronomers.

# ACKNOWLEDGMENTS

This book would not have been possible without the enthusiastic assistance of the inimitable Beecher Hyde of Boaz, Alabama, who introduced me to Ann Scott Kilpatrick, thus propelling the story from inside my head onto the page.

I would also like to thank Wayne Hunt of Boaz for helping me locate articles from the *Boaz Leader* concerning the shooting—Wayne put me in touch with several people who were alive in 1951 and remembered the shooting and subsequent trials, a precious and dwindling group. The city of Boaz is very fortunate to have such a loyal and passionate advocate and historian.

I would like to thank Fred Moore at the Gadsden Library's Genealogy and Reference Department for his patience and tireless efforts in not only providing invaluable newspaper articles from the *Gadsden Times* (and helping me with the microfilm machine) but also contacting sources and making crucial introductions.

The "Courthouse Gang" that meets weekly at the Marshall County Archives in Guntersville, Alabama, provided the best sounding board possible; Tyrus Dorman, Danny Maltbie, Larry Smith, and Pete Sparks patiently answered my questions about Marshall County history, located relevant newspaper articles from the *Advertiser-Gleam*, and occasionally took me to lunch at the cafeteria in the basement of the Marshall County Courthouse. I'm grateful to all of them.

Special thanks to George Barnett, Jimmy Carnes, and Eddy Cunningham, attorneys in Guntersville, Albertville, and Gadsden, respectively, who answered my legal questions and drew upon their own memories, expertise, and knowledge of local lore to help me reconstruct the past.

I'd also like to thank Anthony Campbell, general manager of the *Advertiser-Gleam* in Guntersville, for his help in digging through old photos and publishing an interview with me as I worked on the book.

I met author Robin Yocum at a crime-writing conference, and he was kind enough to read my manuscript with the eye of a seasoned journalist and an award-winning writer. I owe Robin an incredible debt of thanks for his time, expertise, advice, and encouragement.

My profound ignorance about guns did not deter Captain Kip Hart and Sergeant Tim Guy of the Tuscaloosa Police Department from teaching me about firearms and ballistics, and I appreciate immensely the time spent at the TPD gun range learning about the types of weapons described in the book.

My gratitude extends also to the many professional archivists, librarians, and museum directors who pointed me in the right direction: Meredith McDonough and Courtney Pinkard at the Alabama Department of Archives and History; Drew Green at the Cullman County Museum; Paul Prewitt at the University of Alabama Law Library; and Nancy Taylor at the Marshall County Archives.

Future attorneys Carter Ashcraft and Matt Hennington indexed the trial transcripts, poring through hundreds of pages and creating a key that enabled me to find individual testimonies instantly. Nic Noland's talent and vision helped me come up with a cover design. I anticipate great things from these brilliant young people.

Special thanks to my wonderfully supportive colleagues at the University of West Alabama, especially Kendrick Prewitt, Chris Haveman, Ashley Dumas, Debbie Davis, Rob Riser, Alan Brown, Joe Taylor, Rich Schellhammer, Eleanor Boudreau, Mark Davis, Sara Walker, Valerie Burnes, Amy Jones, Greg Jones, Jeff Gentsch, Danielle Hailey, Joy Cauthron, and Caleb Smith. These great folks played Wedding Guest to my Ancient Mariner, letting me ramble on about the minutiae of the shooting and trials, and I love them all for it.

John and Michelle McCall's Dog Street Café in Livingston, Alabama, is the closest thing to a literary salon I've ever known, and they graciously allowed me to publicly read a few bits and pieces as I worked on the manuscript. Thanks to them not only for encouraging my project but also for fostering the spirit of intellectual inquiry in Sumter County, Alabama.

Thanks to all my dear friends who have cheered me throughout this process—Gayle Hannah Hill, Maura Mandyck, Michelle Bennich, Charnita Knight Kirby, Robyn Abney, Kelly Burke Alcorn, Mark Boazman, Hugh Ruppersburg, Roman Shaul, Matthew and Stephanie Oliver, Todd Whinery and Jenni Miesse, and Vicki Crawford. To have one such friend is a boon; to have so many is an embarrassment of riches.

Nathaniel Holly, acquisitions editor at the University of Georgia Press, is surely destined for sainthood, as he is the soul of patience. His consummate professionalism, combined with his refreshing optimism and warmth, gave me peace and assurance as I sought a home for my story. I would also like to thank Daniel Simon, copy editor extraordinaire, for his wizardry in both smoothing and refining my writing.

I am especially grateful to the families who told me their stories, spending hours with me and supporting the project every step of the way: Ann Scott Kilpatrick, James Kilpatrick's widow; Marty and Rhonda Kilpatrick, James's son and daughter-in-law; Donnie Hodges, Zeke Boyles's grandson; Rob Bennett, Washington Bennett's great-nephew; and George Kilpatrick, Aubrey Kilpatrick's nephew.

I think the word that appears most often in these acknowledgments is "patience"—my mother, Gail Carnes, waited patiently for decades for me to write this book. I did not finish it before she died, but I know that she knows, somehow.

My father, Tom Carnes, was the first one to tell me the story of "the Kilpatrick shooting," one of the many, many stories Dad told me over the years. I hope he knows how proud I have always been to be one of his daughters.

My sister, Lynn Carnes Thrash, read every single word of the manuscript as I wrote, offering feedback infused with her remarkable insight into not only literature but also human nature. She is, and will always be, My Person. Her love and steadfast faith inspire me every day.

Understanding the mind of a sixteen-year-old boy might be achieved by reading books and conducting research, but I found the best resource of all was my son, Grayson. I loved every long car trip during which he was a captive audience to my obsession with this project. I doubt if he enjoyed these rides as much as I did, but he, as always, indulged me and contributed his own observations and insight. Thus the stories live on.

# NOTES

## Preface

xi    "It was through the presence of mind of Mrs. Miller": "Tornado Kills Two in Marshall County," *Southern Democrat*, March 9, 1944, 1.

xv    life of service and faith he led after getting out of prison: Dana Maria Hill's *Blazing Guns, Wild Horses, and the Grace of God* provides a moving and entertaining account of James Kilpatrick's life story. Hill watched videoed conversations between James and Billy Kilpatrick and crafted a first-person narrative from the details provided in the videos. Primarily concerned with Kilpatrick's conversion experience after his release from prison, Hill's book serves as a tribute to Kilpatrick's journey from idyllic childhood through tragedy to personal salvation.

## Chapter 1. The Bootlegger

1    "the finest white lightning in the South": Hill, *Blazing Guns, Wild Horses*, 1.

1    "the best peach syrup on the mountain": Hill, *Blazing Guns, Wild Horses*, 1.

2    to pay for their home and food for their families: Bindas, *Remembering the Great Depression*, 46. Bindas's book and William A. Link's *The Paradox of Southern Progressivism* are particularly illuminating concerning the impact of the Great Depression in the Deep South.

2    "Those were the good old days, but those good old days were pretty rough times": Bindas, *Remembering the Great Depression*, 47.

4    a "high-spirited and crazy" mare that only her master could ride: Hill, *Blazing Guns, Wild Horses*, 8.

5    "Imagine a small country boy like me breaking horses for a western hero": Hill, *Blazing Guns, Wild Horses*, 5.

7    "a widely known saddle horse trainer . . . known for his fiery temper and his willingness to fight on short notice": "Three Officers Killed in Ambush at Boaz," *Birmingham News*, May 18, 1951, 1.

7    "kept officers from searching his place for whiskey": "Grand Jury to Probe Deaths of Officers," *Guntersville (Ala.) Advertiser-Gleam*, May 23, 1951, 2.

7    "'We've had several complaints that you are too handy with a gun'": "Grand Jury to Probe Deaths of Officers."

Chapter 2. The Sheriff

9     forty-four times longer than the U.S. Constitution: Wayne Flynt's *Alabama in the Twentieth Century* was an invaluable source of information concerning the origin and effects of the Alabama state constitution.

9     "most if not all the state's formidable problems had their origins in the 1901 document": Flynt, *Alabama in the Twentieth Century*, 3.

9     "lack of concern about the state's negative national and international reputation": Flynt, *Alabama in the Twentieth Century*, 3.

10     "he shall be ineligible to such office as his own successor": Ala. Const. section 138.

10     "he shall be eligible to such office as his own successor": Ala. Const. amend. XXXV.

10     "Having made every effort possible to personally contact each voter": E. M. "Zeke" Boyles for Sheriff campaign ad, *Guntersville Advertiser and Democrat*, April 27, 1938, 4.

11     "starting things off at a lively speed": "Local and Personal," *Guntersville (Ala.) Advertiser-Gleam*, January 25, 1939, 3.

11     "a pair of mules, wagon, and thirty gallons of liquor": "Sheriff's Forces Raid Seven Stills Last Week," *Guntersville (Ala.) Advertiser-Gleam*, February 8, 1939, 1.

11     "a very unprofitable and unsatisfactory business in Marshall County": "Local and Personal," *Guntersville (Ala.) Advertiser-Gleam*, March 29, 1939, 5.

12     "Organs from Chandler's body were sent to Auburn for examination following his death": "Local and Personal," *Guntersville Advertiser and Democrat*, June 21, 1939, 5.

12     the sheriff and his family drove from Guntersville to Los Angeles to retrieve Carmen Burt: "Local and Personal," *Guntersville Advertiser and Democrat*, December 18, 1940, 5.

13     a performance that surely brought down the house: "Don't Miss the Womanless Wedding at the Palace Theatre," *Guntersville (Ala.) Advertiser-Gleam*, August 6, 1941, 3.

13     developed into a nationwide fad until World War II: Cynthia Graber and Nicola Twilley, "Inside the Bizarre Cow Trials of the 1920s," *Mother Jones*, March 2, 2015, www.motherjones.com/environment/2015/03/milk-bull-trials-gastropod.

14     Sheriff E. M. Boyles would preside as the arresting officer of this criminally inferior bull: "Scrubbiest Bull Will Go on Trial Tuesday," *Guntersville Gleam*, July 9, 1942, 1.

14     "Already a trickle of returning soldiers is appearing in our communities": "Did You Ever Stop to Think," *Guntersville Advertiser and Democrat*, September 12, 1945, 1.

16     "a relative of Sheriff Boyles" was arrested in a raid involving "stills, some whiskey and home brew": "Stills and Whiskey Caught; Six Arrested," *Guntersville Gleam*, May 24, 1946, 1.

19    "Ever since, the legend goes, defeated politicians are supposed to travel to Buck's Pocket": "Buck's Pocket Losing Allure for Defeated Politicians," *Gadsden Times,* June 10, 1986, B1.

20    "provided that the probate judge of any county, upon written petition of twenty-five percent of the qualified voters of the county at the last general election": Sellers, *The Prohibition Movement in Alabama,* 251.

22    "a tribe of swarthy complexioned people": "Indians (or Gypsies) Have Moved On," *Guntersville (Ala.) Advertiser-Gleam,* January 12, 1949, 1.

### Chapter 3. The Place

25    "How did a freedom-loving people decide to give up a private right": Okrent, *Last Call,* 3.

25    "awash in drink almost from the start": Okrent, *Last Call,* 7.

25    "[F]iguring per capita, multiply the amount Americans drink today by three and you'll have an idea of what much of the nineteenth century was like": Okrent, *Last Call,* 8.

26    "One of the most interesting of the regulations made by the Mississippi Territorial Assembly": Sellers, *The Prohibition Movement in Alabama,* 13.

26    "limit the sale of intoxicants to soldiers, to slaves, and especially to Indians": Sellers, *The Prohibition Movement in Alabama,* 13.

28    many of these settlers were well educated, and many had been government and civic leaders in their native states: Flynt, *Alabama in the Twentieth Century,* 4.

30    Auburn University historian Wayne Flynt sought to define this marginalized group that lacked clear margins: Flynt, *Poor but Proud,* ix.

31    Flynt mentions the prevalence of the alcohol-soaked "poor white trash" stereotype: Flynt, *Poor but Proud,* ix.

31    Conversely, the "poor but proud" whites "believed themselves more religious than the upper class": Flynt, *Poor but Proud,* 27.

31    "to live from hand to mouth; to get drunk, provided they can do so without having to trudge too far after their liquor": Daniel R. Hundley, qtd. in Flynt, *Poor but Proud,* 34.

32    "they regarded whiskey as a food and considered ardent spirits an important concomitant of hospitality": Sellers, *The Prohibition Movement in Alabama,* 25.

32    "unless anti-prohibitionists win, please give notice that Mobile is prepared to secede from the State of Alabama": Kirby, "'Boardwalk Empire' of the South."

### Chapter 4. The Fuse and the Fusillade

40    Tenant farming reached its peak during the Great Depression, with over 65 percent of all farmers working within the tenancy framework: Phillips, "Sharecropping and Tenant Farming in Alabama."

### Chapter 5. The Aftermath

47    "I learned more from working my way up in the newsroom than most students learn in journalism school": Katy Croft Likos, interviewed by author, Daphne, Alabama, July 2021.

48 "We were afraid feeling might flare up when the people learned what had happened": "Farmer's Sons, Two Tenants Held in Gadsden Jail," *Huntsville Times*, May 18, 1951, 1.

50 "You must be sure that you give coverage to other events which have occurred that day": Hayes, "How Can Newspapers Meet Competition?"

50 headlines across the front pages of Alabama newspapers: Numerous newspaper sources are included in this chapter—in all cases, the names of the newspapers and article titles are provided. These articles appeared from May 18, 1951, to May 24, 1951.

54 "I just can't understand how anybody would pull down on him deliberately": Bob Axelson, "Four Killings Stun Marshall County," *Huntsville Times*, May 18, 1951, 1.

56 "[g]reat crowds attended the last rites for each of the victims of the tragedy": "Four Persons Die as Officers Try to Make Arrest," *Albertville Herald*, May 24, 1951, 1.

56 "the biggest funeral ever held in Marshall County": Obituary of E. M. "Zeke" Boyles, *Guntersville (Ala.) Advertiser-Gleam*, May 23, 1951.

## Chapter 6. The Women

59 "the crowd was one of the biggest that ever came to a Marshall County trial": "Boy Shot Bennett, Lang Testifies," *Guntersville (Ala.) Advertiser-Gleam*, July 25, 1951, 1.

60 "We wanted to go see what everybody was talking about": Ann Scott Kilpatrick, interviewed by author, Boaz, Alabama, March 2021.

64 "smelling the fumes when he was pouring it into the bottles": Ann Scott Kilpatrick, interviewed by author, Boaz, Alabama, March 2021.

68 "anyone who had a momma who went eighteen years without a new dress": Bragg, *All Over but the Shoutin'*, xii.

69 The headline read, "Deaf and Dumb Makes Good Record at University": "Deaf and Dumb Makes Good Record at University," *Albertville Herald*, May 3, 1951, 7.

## Chapter 7. The First Trial

77 "tools attorneys use every day to perform their work are the very guts of good storytelling": Coscarelli, "Lawyers as Storytellers."

78 Such a defense carried its own complications and consequences: All statements made by and attributed to the prosecution, defense, and witnesses that appear in this chapter come from the trial transcript of *State of Alabama v. James Kilpatrick*, July 1951, case no. 2039.

78 "Insanity isn't an easy thing to prove, and it is often the defense of last resort": Cep, *Furious Hours*, 116.

79 he laid the groundwork for the modern insanity defense: Moriarty, *The History of Mental Illness*, 33.

## Chapter 8. The Scientists

92     "this is the first time in two years any such step-ins have ever been shown in any court of justice": Carter, *Scottsboro*, 204.

93     "scientific State agency with the specific duty of assisting law enforcement and the courts in the investigation and adjudication of criminal matters": Rehling and Rabren, *Alabama's Master Plan*, xliii.

93     "No funds, facilities, or remuneration were provided . . . for this purpose": Wheeler, "ADFS History."

96     "to uncover the truth, whether it tends to incriminate or clear any particular person in connection with a crime": Harold J. Fisher, "Work of State Toxicologist Nixon Has Dispelled Chair Shadow for Two," *Birmingham News*, April 4, 1937, 29.

96     "It is not our purpose to prove guilt or innocence": Paul Till, "These Crime-Fighters Rarely See the Scene," *Advertiser-Journal Alabama Sunday Magazine*, 4.

97     "At first blush, officers thought that it was just another sloppy job of murder": William McDonald, "Little Things Help to Solve Crime Puzzles," *Montgomery Advertiser*, November 21, 1948, 1B.

99     is considered the first textbook of forensic science: Sung Tz'u's *The Washing Away of Wrongs (Hsi yuan chi lu)*, printed in 1247, is the oldest extant book on forensic medicine in the world. Written as a guide for magistrates in conducting inquests, the book is a major source on early Chinese knowledge of pathology and morbid anatomy. The quotations from this text are from *The Washing Away of Wrongs*, 81, 111.

103     "since 1935, Alabama has not found it necessary to call on Chicago for a ballistics expert, nor on Washington for a handwriting expert": Irving Beiman, "Trained Investigator Will Aid in Prosecuting Criminal Cases," *Birmingham News*, July 29, 1943, 20.

107     "I am forced to declare the case ended in a mistrial": "Murder Trial Halted by a Technicality," *Guntersville (Ala.) Advertiser-Gleam*, July 27, 1951, 1.

## Chapter 9. The Second Trial

115     "a man's house is his castle": Light, *Stand Your Ground*, 20.

115     "The poorest man may in his cottage bid defiance to all the forces of the crown": William Pitt, qtd. in Ratcliffe, *Oxford Essential Quotations*, 147.

116     Henry Grady, proponent of the New South: H. Grady, "Against Centralization," 153.

116     "drove up into the yard of his [James Kilpatrick's] father's home": All statements made by and attributed to the prosecution, defense, and witnesses that appear in this chapter come from the trial transcript of *State of Alabama v. James Kilpatrick*, November 1951, case no. 2037.

## Chapter 10. The Reckoning

141     The hapless steer, as faithfully reported by Guntersville's *Advertiser-Gleam*, was killed: "Kilpatrick Case Ends in Mistrial," *Guntersville (Ala.) Advertiser-Gleam*, January 30, 1952, 1.

142    as if the jailhouse musicale had been performed for a visiting dignitary: "James Kilpatrick Entertained April 19," *Etowah News-Journal*, April 24, 1952, 1.

143    "It's getting to be old news": "Young James Kilpatrick Goes on Trial Monday," *Gadsden Times*, October 12, 1952, 10.

145    "have lost their appeal to local residents": "Few Present as Kilpatrick Goes on Trial," *Gadsden Times*, October 13, 1952, 1.

148    "number of spectators wept openly in the courtroom": "Kilpatrick Youth Gets Ten More Years in Mass Killing," *Birmingham News*, October 17, 1952, 10.

148    "All I could do was pray": Ann Scott Kilpatrick, interviewed by author, Boaz, Alabama, March 2021.

## Chapter 11. The Penitent

149    to be in Montgomery, the state's capital, to achieve his ambitions: "Centre Newsman Accepts Job with Montgomery Daily," *Cherokee County Herald*, August 12, 1953, 5.

150    "a one-man fourth estate in Montgomery": "Communication Leaders Inducted into UA's C&IS Hall of Fame," UA News Center, https://news.ua.edu/2003/10/communication-leaders-inducted-into-uas-cis-hall-of-fame (last modified October 3, 2003).

151    "the trial court erred in refusing defendant's requested charge to the jury": *Kilpatrick v. State of Alabama*, 59 So. 2d 61 (1952), 8 Div. 647, Supreme Court of Alabama, May 15, 1952.

152    "Right will win out. My son was not guilty of any crime": "Kilpatrick Cases Settled: Ten Years," *Guntersville (Ala.) Advertiser-Gleam*, April 24, 1953, 1.

152    moved by the sight of the young man: Bob Ingram, "Kilpatrick Gets Ten-Year Sentence in Boaz Slayings," *Gadsden Times*, April 21, 1953, 1.

153    "It was done without the consent of the families": "Kilpatrick Cases Settled," 1.

156    "Thus ended one of the worst homicide cases ever to be tried in a Marshall County Court": "All Cases Are Settled in Peace Officer Slaying," *Albertville Herald*, October 22, 1953, 1.

159    but apparently the taste of simulated freedom was too tantalizing for some of the band members: Burgin Mathews, "Alabama Prison Swing," Burgin Mathews (blog), October 15, 2020, https://burginmathews.com/2020/10/15/alabama-prison-swing.

159    "Couldn't we have a band come play so we could dance?": Kathryn Tucker, "Women's Prison Gets Music after Visit by Chief Russell," *Alabama Journal*, April 1, 1943, 3.

## Afterword

165    "the half-lies and the truths and the half-truths": Warren, *World Enough and Time*, 3.

167    a "quarantine dormitory" for Alabama inmates during the pandemic: "Three Alabama Inmates Positive for Coronavirus, One Dead," *Montgomery Advertiser*, April 20, 2020, A1.

# BIBLIOGRAPHY

In addition to the numerous newspaper articles and court documents cited in the notes, I relied on the following books and journal articles.

Agee, James, and Walker Evans. *Let Us Now Praise Famous Men*. Boston: Mariner Books, 2001.

Biles, Roger. *The South and the New Deal*. Lexington: University Press of Kentucky, 1994.

Bindas, Kenneth J. *Remembering the Great Depression in the Rural South*. Gainesville: University Press of Florida, 2007.

Blackmon, Douglas A. *Slavery by Another Name: The Re-Enslavement of Black Americans from the Civil War to World War II*. New York: Anchor Books, 2008.

Bragg, Rick. *All Over But the Shoutin'*. New York: Vintage Books, 1997.

Caldwell, Ernest. *God's Little Acre*. Athens: University of Georgia Press, 1995.

———. *Tobacco Road*. Athens: University of Georgia Press, 1994.

Capote, Truman. *In Cold Blood: A True Account of a Multiple Murder and Its Consequences*. New York: Vintage Books, 1994.

Carter, Dan T. *Scottsboro: A Tragedy of the American South*. Baton Rouge: Louisiana State University Press, 1969.

Cep, Casey. *Furious Hours: Murder, Fraud, and the Last Trial of Harper Lee*. New York: Knopf, 2019.

Coscarelli, Kate. "Lawyers as Storytellers: Strategies to Powerful Communications with the Public." *American Bar Association* (September/October 2018), www.americanbar .org/groups/gpsolo/publications/gp_solo/2018/september-october/lawyers -storytellers-strategies-powerful-communications-public.

Covington, Dennis. *Salvation on Sand Mountain: Snake Handling and Redemption in Southern Appalachia*. Reading, Mass.: Addison-Wesley, 1995.

Downs, Matthew L. *Transforming the South: Federal Development in the Tennessee Valley, 1915–1960*. Baton Rouge: Louisiana State University Press, 2014.

Faulkner, William. *Light in August*. New York: Vintage Books, 1991.

Feathers, Anne Herbert. "Catfights and Coffins: Stories of Alabama Courthouses." *Alabama Review* 61, no. 3 (July 2008): 163–89.

Flynt, Wayne. *Alabama in the Twentieth Century*. Tuscaloosa: University of Alabama Press, 2004.

———. *Poor but Proud: Alabama's Poor Whites*. Tuscaloosa: University of Alabama Press, 1989.

Graber, Cynthia, and Nicola Twilley. "Inside the Bizarre Cow Trials of the 1920s." *Mother Jones* (March 2, 2015), www.motherjones.com/environment/2015/03/milk-bull -trials-gastropod.

Grady, Alan. *When Good Men Do Nothing: The Assassination of Albert Patterson*. Tuscaloosa: University of Alabama Press, 2003.

Grady, Henry. "Against Centralization." In *The Complete Orations and Speeches of Henry W. Grady*, edited by Edwin Du Bois Shurter, 134–57. Whitefish, Mont.: Kessinger, 2007.

Hayes, John S. "How Can Newspapers Meet Competition of Radio and Television?" *Nieman Reports: 1951*, https://niemanreports.org/articles/1951-how-can-newspapers -meet-competition-of-radio-and-television.

Hill, Dana Maria. *Blazing Guns, Wild Horses, and the Grace of God: The James Kilpatrick Story*. Bloomington, Ind.: AuthorHouse, 2011.

Isenberg, Nancy. *White Trash: The 400-Year Untold History of Class in America*. New York: Penguin Books, 2016.

Kirby, Brendan. "'Boardwalk Empire' of the South: Prohibition Brought Violence, Corruption to Mobile." AL.com (June 23, 2013), www.al.com/live/2013/06 /boardwalk_empire_of_the_south.html.

Lee, Harper. *To Kill a Mockingbird*. New York: Warner Books, 1982.

Light, Caroline E. *Stand Your Ground: A History of America's Love Affair with Lethal Self-Defense*. Boston: Beacon Press, 2017.

Link, William A. *The Paradox of Southern Progressivism, 1880–1930*. Chapel Hill: University of North Carolina Press, 1992.

Moriarty, Jane Campbell, ed. *The History of Mental Illness in Criminal Cases: The English Tradition*. Vol. 1 of The Role of Mental Illness in Criminal Trials. New York: Routledge, Taylor, and Francis, 2001.

Okrent, Daniel. *Last Call: The Rise and Fall of Prohibition*. New York: Scribner, 2010.

Phillips, Kenneth E. "Sharecropping and Tenant Farming in Alabama." *Encyclopedia of Alabama*, http://encyclopediaofalabama.org/ARTICLE/h-1613.

Ratcliffe, Susan, ed. *Oxford Essential Quotations*. 4th ed. New York: Oxford University Press, 2016.

Rehling, C. J., and C. L. Rabren. *Alabama's Master Plan for a Crime Laboratory Delivery System*. United States Department of Justice, October 1973.

Rumore, Pat Boyd. *Lawyers in a New South City: A History of the Legal Profession in Birmingham*. Birmingham: Association Publishing, 2000.

Sellers, James Benson. *The Prohibition Movement in Alabama, 1702–1943*. Chapel Hill: University of North Carolina Press, 1943.

Snow, Whitney, and Barbara J. Snow. *Images of America: Lake Guntersville*. Mount Pleasant, S.C.: Arcadia, 2018.

Tz'u, Sung. *The Washing Away of Wrongs: Forensic Medicine in Thirteenth-Century China*. Translated by Brian E. McKnight. Ann Arbor: University of Michigan Center for Chinese Studies, 1981.

Vance, J. D. *Hillbilly Elegy: A Memoir of a Family and Culture in Crisis*. New York: HarperCollins, 2016.

Voss, Ralph F. *Truman Capote and the Legacy of "In Cold Blood."* Tuscaloosa: University of Alabama Press, 2011.

Warren, Robert Penn. "Wind and Gibbon." *In The Collected Poems of Robert Penn Warren*, edited by John Burt, 580. Baton Rouge: Louisiana State University Press, 1998.

———. *World Enough and Time: A Romantic Novel.* New York: Random House, 1950.

Wheeler, Brent. "ADFS History." Alabama Department of Forensic Sciences, www.adfs .alabama.gov/about/history.